D1083676

STUDIES IN
THE ITALIAN RENAISSANCE

LEO X WITH CARDINALS GIULIO DEI MEDICI AND DEI ROSSI
From the Painting by Raphael in the Pitti Palace, Florence

STUDIES IN THE
ITALIAN RENAISSANCE

BY

HERBERT M. VAUGHAN
M.A., F.S.A.

KENNIKAT PRESS, INC./PORT WASHINGTON, N. Y.

PREFACE

THE following Twelve Studies in the Italian Renaissance have been based on a series of lectures that were composed by me for the Oxford University Extension Delegacy. Most of these lectures have already been delivered in public at Hereford and elsewhere, and some have been given at the constituent colleges of the University of Wales, and at St. David's College, Lampeter.

They are intended to cover, roughly, the century and a quarter from 1430 to 1555, which may be taken as the hey-day of the Italian Renaissance. My earliest study describes the art and influence of Fra Angelico, who died in 1455 ; and the latest in date deals with the life and autobiography of Cellini in the sixteenth century. The all-pervading artistic influence of the Italian Renaissance is everywhere considered, especially in its relation to the political aims of the leading papal and princely families. In this respect the Medici popes and princes naturally stand out pre-eminent ; but I have likewise dealt with the Borgia, the Della Rovere, the Farnese, the Sforza, the Este, and other ruling Houses of the time, all of which were distinguished by their generous patronage of art, as well as by their political ambition. In my study of Savonarola both the political and religious questions of the day are touched upon ; whilst in that on Machiavelli I hope I have produced a just and lucid explanation of his unique genius and his lofty though premature patriotism, however incomplete my treatment may be deemed. My account of Caterina Sforza, the Lady of Forli, includes incidentally the story of the rise of the warlike Sforza and the upstart Della Rovere families.

As to the artists themselves, all of them closely attached

to the Medici and the other great families already mentioned, I have given a brief sketch of the career of that
elusive genius, Leonardo da Vinci, and also detailed accounts
of the work of Michelangelo and of Raphael at the Vatican
under Julius II and Leo X.   Fra Angelico may perhaps be
thought to stand somewhat outside the general scheme of
this volume ; but his place in the realm of art so closely
resembles that of Savonarola in the sphere of politics and
religion that I consider I am justified in including him.

H.M.V.

December 1929

CONTENTS

vii

LIST OF ILLUSTRATIONS

ix

STUDIES IN
THE ITALIAN RENAISSANCE

I

THE STORY OF THE MEDICI OF FLORENCE
(1434–1737)

IN dealing with the Medici of Florence, I shall try to recount in a short space the story of one of the most intellectual and interesting dynasties that Europe has yet produced. No other reigning House can present us with so well-sustained a record of natural gifts, allied with so much political wisdom and artistic intelligence. Nor is there any example, outside the Medici, of a royal family reigning in the direct male line for over three hundred years, almost without a break, and then vanishing, not by means of warfare or internal revolution, but simply owing to Nature's failure of progeny. For such is the record of the Medici, first as unofficial Princes of Florence, then Dukes of Florence, and lastly Grand Dukes of Tuscany. All this story lies between two clear-cut dates, the year 1434 when Cosimo dei Medici returned in triumph from exile as virtual tyrant of Florence by popular consent, and the year 1737 when Gian-Gastone dei Medici, seventh Grand Duke of Tuscany, died childless and without an heir, the last male descendant of the prolific stock of Giovanni di Bicci dei Medici, who was father of Cosimo, first tyrant of Florence. When we consider the prolonged association of this dynasty with learning, with statecraft, and with the arts, we feel that this House owns a unique position in European annals.

And when to-day we regard the city of Florence, with its marvellous mass of artistic treasures, that are the heritage of us all, and realize that all this wealth of human intellect and skill is very largely due to the judicious influence and patronage of the departed Medici over a space of three centuries, we must admit that the world of culture and learning owes a tribute of praise and gratitude to a family that is even to-day generally yet ignorantly reviled.

The family of Medici throughout the fourteenth century ranked as one of the many rich burgher families which directed the government of the Florentine Republic. The name appears frequently in these early civic annals, and members of the family at various times migrated and founded branches of the Medici at Milan, Naples, and elsewhere, some of which are still extant. Gradually their business, which was that of money-lending on security, or banking, began to surpass the ventures of their brother-merchants, till the Medici stood out prominently as the richest and most capable merchant-family in the city. The family coat of arms, the six red *palle*, or balls, on a golden shield, became a familiar sign throughout Italy. To wealth was now added personal ambition. The Medici started to intrigue with the unfranchised citizens of Florence against their own class, the plutocratic merchants. This attitude was clearly shown in 1387 in the so-called Tumult of the Ciompi (wooden shoes), when Salvestro dei Medici secretly encouraged this democratic movement of the voteless labourers against the ruling merchant class or *Ottimati*. This policy gave a peculiar if not very reliable popularity to the Medici, who spent their increasing gains freely on public works and public entertainment, and also, to their credit, in the patronage of the Florentine artists. At the beginning of the fifteenth century (the *Quattrocento*) we note the importance of Giovanni dei Medici, commonly called Giovanni di Bicci, the son of Averardo dei Medici and

grandson of Salvestro of the Ciompi, who was the leading
citizen of Florence at a time when the city was extending
its dominions far and wide.   But with the expansion of the
state the financial influence of this Giovanni dei Medici and
his two sons, Cosimo and Lorenzo, ever seemed to move
forward concurrently, so important and far-reaching had
become the financial credit of the Medici both at home and
abroad.   There is a portrait by Zanobi Strozzi of this
Giovanni di Bicci in the Uffizi Gallery at Florence, showing
us a shrewd, rugged old face.   His elder son was the celebrated founder of the earlier ruling branch of the Medici, of
whom I shall write presently; his second son, Lorenzo,
became the direct ancestor of the later line of Tuscan
grand dukes.

This Cosimo dei Medici, called in after years ' Pater
Patriae ', or ' Cosimo il Vecchio ', soon rose to a pre-eminent
position in the state.   He scattered his vast wealth truly
like a great prince, alike on noble and artisan; money to
him was but the means to a certain end, namely, political
power.   For he was no vulgar plutocrat; and his judicious
patronage of the great artists of his day has left us a noble
legacy.   He employed the great sculptor Michelozzo upon
the new Medici palace in Via Larga : he rebuilt on a splendid
scale the fine churches of San Lorenzo and Santo Spirito ; he
commissioned Fra Angelico to adorn the walls of his new
Dominican foundation of St. Mark's ; he was a sincere
admirer of the glorious pictures of Lippo Lippi. Cosimo dei
Medici, thanks to an insincere modesty, a genial manner, an
open-handed generosity, a discerning patronage of men of
genius, became the popular idol of the Florentines. His
character and attitude are very neatly summed up by the
old republican historian Varchi, who was no Medicean :
' By open and manifest virtues and by secret and non-
apparent ambitions, Cosimo made himself head and practically prince of a republic which still remained nominally free.'

And this contradiction of private ambition and scheming with public humility and largesse continued to be the hereditary key-note of the policy of his descendants.

Still, the Medici had their enemies. Some despised the Medicean money, and some did not need financial assistance from the Medicean bank, which was open to all. Many regarded this gradual whittling away of the powers of the republic to the wealthy Medici with alarm and indignation. Certain of the superseded aristocratic families were bitterly jealous of the wealth and increasing power of this pushful House, which, like themselves, had risen solely by its business capacity to influence in the state. A determined effort, led by Rinaldo degli Albizzi, was skilfully started to bring about the downfall of the great banker. The *Signoria*, or executive council of the republic, not daring to inflict the penalty of death, passed a decree of banishment upon Cosimo, whereupon the two Medici brothers with their many friends and satellites quietly retired from Florence into exile at Padua. But this bold action was by no means agreeable to the citizens as a whole. A large section of all classes in Florence were devoted adherents of the *Palle*, as the cause of the Medici was sometimes styled owing to their family coat of arms. Others, and especially the democratic element, missed their customary benevolences and entertainments ; the artists, who were in close touch with the people, bewailed the departure of their genial and generous patrons. Other Italian states too, that were largely dependent on the financial prosperity of the exiled Medici, protested vigorously. The powerful Pope Eugenius IV, who was then visiting Florence, worked actively for the recall of Cosimo. In any case, in the following year Cosimo dei Medici was invited back to Florence, and on his return to the city on October 6th, 1434, with his brother Lorenzo, he was received by the mass of the Florentines with frantic demonstrations of joy. From that day onward Cosimo's position as virtual head of the so-called Florentine Republic was secure. He became in very truth a sovereign, though a sovereign without a title, without official recognition, and without any civil list. Nominally and outwardly the government of the state was still carried on by means of the old republican institutions, whilst Cosimo himself continued to live, openly at least, as any other wealthy burgher of the city. But the real control of Florence, both in internal and in foreign affairs, was vested absolutely in this Medicean merchant, who manipulated all the existing machinery of state for his own ends.

This unusual but very real form of sovereignty, possessing all the power but none of the pomp of monarchy, now passed from father to son for four generations without a break. As tacitly admitted rulers of the Florentine State, however, the Medici were required to use their immense private wealth in the service of the republic ; and in his capacity of host Cosimo dei Medici was wont to entertain in his palace any passing king or illustrious visitor to Florence. For thirty years Cosimo's reign lasted, to the evident satisfaction of the city. Throughout this period he gave an immense impetus to learning, painting, architecture, and all the liberal arts, setting an example for his successors that was ever adhered to. Amongst the many fine paintings of this era, the reign of the first Medici prince, are to be seen portraits of himself, his son, his grandsons, and members of his court. Most noteworthy amongst these is the beautiful little family chapel in the Medici palace, now called Palazzo Riccardi, wherein Benozzo Gozzoli, the pupil of Fra Angelico, has shown us a wonderful glimpse of contemporary Florentine society, with the various members of the Medici family portrayed.

In 1464 died Cosimo dei Medici, rejoicing in the proud title of ' Pater Patriae ', which had been conferred on him by the grateful city. So fixed had Medicean rule become by this date that his son and heir, Piero dei Medici, at once stepped easily into his father's position. Yet Piero (Piero I, as he is sometimes styled) had inherited little of the genius of his father. His wife, the learned poetess, Lucrezia Tornabuoni, to some extent helped him in state affairs. But it might have fared ill with him had it not been for the exceptional abilities of his brilliant son and heir, Lorenzo, who, although only in his 'teens, was able to carry on the family traditions of jovial liberality and secret dissimulation. Life was fast and furious in those days for any public leader, and Lorenzo began his career young, and ended it when he was but little over forty, worn out with the cares of a political struggle that consumed all his time and energy. Piero rarely interfered in the affairs of state, spending his days in his beautiful villa of Careggi, a confirmed sufferer from the gout, whence he gained the nickname of 'Il Gottoso' amongst the unsympathetic Florentines. But Lorenzo, that precocious flower of the Italian Renaissance, undertook with marked success the duties and schemes that his invalid father avoided ; and when he died in 1469, Lorenzo was hailed with joy as the new ruler of Florence.

Lorenzo di Piero (otherwise Lorenzo I) may perhaps be reckoned the greatest of all the Medici, and he most certainly appears as the most remarkable figure of his age. He was eminent as statesman, diplomatist, financier, poet, scholar, and patron of art. He owned the inestimable gift of St. Paul of showing himself as all things to all men, whatever might be his underlying opinions and aims. Justly did he earn his name of 'Il Magnifico', whether that name be considered as his title of Prince of Florence, or as descriptive of his magnificence of outlook, behaviour, and mode of life. He was the ideal humanist of his age : deeply learned, yet a poet who loved to depict the pleasant country life of rural Tuscany ; a cunning politician, who could unbend on occasion, who could, as Machiavelli tells us, ' forget the dignity of his office in romping with his children ' ; a shrewd and mordant wit, yet full of affection and kindness to his friends ; above all, a man guarding his own secret ambition beneath an assumed mask of jollity and insouciance. Plain of face, like most of the Medici, and noticeable for a conspicuous underhung jaw, handicapped too by a rasping voice, yet he could prove soft and persuasive in an amazing degree when a difficult situation arose.

Nevertheless, Lorenzo had to take arms against a sea of trouble. The anomalous position of the Medici in Florence was regarded with deep misgiving by Pope Sixtus IV and by other Italian petty tyrants ; the old mercantile families of Florence were filled with envy and longed for vengeance. Out of this condition of affairs arose the famous Conspiracy of the Pazzi in 1478, an event which has been dramatized by the poet Alfieri. At the secret instigation of the Pope and Ferdinand, King of Naples, the family of the Pazzi and other malcontents in Florence were urged to assassinate Lorenzo and his brother Giuliano, and then to proclaim once more the Florentine Republic on the old plutocratic lines. The occasion chosen for the attempt was, of all times and places, the celebration of High Mass in the great cathedral of Florence on Easter Day 1478. During the service the Pazzi with their armed retainers rushed into the church and sought to slay the two Medici brothers. They succeeded in hacking Giuliano to death ; but Lorenzo, thanks to the courage and devotion of Politian and of his personal friends, escaped almost unhurt into the adjoining sacristy. The immediate result of this half-successful attempt proved the very opposite of what the conspirators hoped and expected to achieve. The whole Florentine population rallied round their rescued prince, and the rule of the Medici became more firmly established than before.

It was now that Lorenzo's marvellous talents of diplomacy were brought into active play. He was determined to put a stop to this unholy alliance between the Pope and the King of Naples. For this purpose he left the security of his brilliant court of scholars and artists at Florence, and all unarmed travelled to Naples to interview the treacherous old King Ferdinand in person. So great were Lorenzo's powers of persuasion and so weighty his arguments that Ferdinand was finally won over to his guest's views, and peace was concluded—a peace that brought content and prosperity to all Italy for some twelve years. A memento of this remarkable mission to the court of Naples exists to-day in Botticelli's fine allegorical picture of ' Pallas Athene Taming a Crouching Centaur ', to signalize the triumph of Medicean diplomacy over superior force.

Unlike his forefathers, Lorenzo sought a bride outside the circle of the old Florentine *bourgeoisie*, for he wedded Clarice Orsini, a daughter of the historic Roman feudal house. This marriage of itself caused no little offence to the Florentine burghers, and from their selfish standpoint they were right, for it was the first step taken by the Medici in social and political aggrandizement above the class from which they had sprung. Of this marriage there were born three sons : Piero, Giovanni, and Giuliano. As he watched their infant characters develop, Lorenzo was wont to declare that of his three boys Piero was *pazzo*, or headstrong ; Giovanni was *savio*, or discreet ; and Giuliano was *buono*, or virtuous. And in this surmise, as in most other matters under his observation, Lorenzo was proved in course of time to have judged correctly. Almost the last act of importance in his strenuous life was the obtaining for his second son, the discreet Giovanni, a cardinal's hat from Pope Innocent VIII, a family friend who had succeeded his old foe, the implacable Sixtus IV, on the papal throne. Giovanni was thus created a cardinal at sixteen, the first of a long succession of Medicean cardinals. In the ecclesiastical sphere, therefore, Lorenzo was also building up and strengthening the burgher House of Medici, so as to make it aspire to equal rank with the Italian reigning dynasties.

At this time—the spring of the year 1492—Lorenzo was sickening with his fatal illness. He was already in the clutches of the physicians, or rather quacks, at a date when medical science had sunk to its lowest ebb. What with his exhausted frame and the absurd nostrums of the doctors there was no hope left. He bade farewell to his favourite son Giovanni, as he dispatched the sixteen-year old cardinal to Rome, which city with more truth than politeness Lorenzo styled ' that sink of all iniquity '. He was weary of the turmoil of life ; his mind was uneasy as to many of his actions in the past. He summoned the new prior of St. Mark's, Girolamo Savonarola, to his sick-bed, but to that pathetic interview I mean to refer in my special study of Savonarola. Finally on April 8th, 1492, in the forty-second year of his age, Lorenzo il Magnifico expired at the family villa of Careggi outside the walls of Florence.

The judgement of posterity has, in my opinion, been unduly harsh on Lorenzo dei Medici. He was undoubtedly a mixture of good and evil, but I consider that in his case the good outweighed the evil. And in the right scale certainly lay the intense love that he bore both to Florence and her people. He had given the city peace at imminent risk of his own life ; he had enriched and beautified her churches and palaces ; in his own person he had added yet another illustrious name to that long list of great Florentine citizens which has always been her boast.

Lorenzo had died at a most critical juncture in the world's history. The year 1492, that *annus mirabilis*, saw Europe pass through a series of rapid changes in every phase of life. In Italy, that year was marked by the deaths of Lorenzo himself and of Pope Innocent VIII, and by the election of the Borgia Pope, Alexander VI. Piero dei Medici (Piero II), was wholly unable to deal with the altered conditions. He owned, moreover, most of the failings, but very few of the virtues, of his late parent. The three Medici brothers (for Giovanni the cardinal had retired from Rome on the election of Alexander VI) did what they could to stem the tide of unpopularity that had now set in against the Medicean rule ; but the general feeling of unrest and discontent, and especially the influence of Savonarola, were heavily directed against them. The tottering dynasty after sixty years of popular support finally fell during the invasion of Italy by Charles VIII of France in the autumn of 1494. Piero weakly ceded certain Florentine fortresses to the invader, and the whole city rose in angry commotion. Piero and Giuliano fled in terror, the family palace was sacked by the mob, and the Cardinal Giovanni alone tried to rouse the populace with the old cry of ' *Palle! Palle!* ' that had once been received with shouts of devotion. It was all in vain. At last Giovanni himself had to flee for safety, disguised as a friar, and joined his two brothers in exile at Bologna.

The exile of the reigning Medici lasted for nearly eighteen years, during which period the Florentine Republic was once more in active being. Of the theocracy set up by Savonarola, and of that reformer's evil fate, I do not intend to write here. Suffice it to say that during those eighteen years, in spite of many tentatives, the three sons of Lorenzo il Magnifico were successfully excluded from their native city, their estates were confiscated, and a price was even put on their heads. With them in their poverty and exile was the young Giulio dei Medici, the natural son of the murdered Giuliano, a handsome dark boy, who had been adopted and brought up with his children by his uncle Lorenzo il Magnifico. After a time the brothers separated, Giovanni, with Giulio for his companion, travelling afield over Europe ; whilst Piero fought under various leaders, always on the losing side, and was finally drowned in the river Liris in the kingdom of Naples. This unlucky and incompetent Medici had married a cousin, Alfonsina Orsini, an ambitious woman, who had borne him two children—Lorenzo, the future Lorenzo II of Florence, and Clarice, afterwards the wife of Filippo Strozzi, the builder of the famous Strozzi palace in Florence. As to Giuliano—*Giuliano il buono*—he haunted the courts of Mantua and Urbino, where his charming manners and his love of learning made him a welcome guest. He figures in that popular treatise *Il Cortegiano* of Baldassare Castiglione, wherein he is evidently regarded as the ideal courtier and scholar of his age.

With the death of the terrible Alexander VI in 1503, Cardinal Giovanni could venture once more to Rome. With him came his obsequious cousin, the bastard Giulio. Under the new pope, Julius II, the Medici cardinal became at once a personage of importance in Rome, a position to which his geniune ability fully entitled him. But I shall deal more fully with Giovanni when I come to write of his career as Pope Leo X. In the summer of 1512 Giovanni, Giuliano, Giulio, and the young Lorenzo were with the papal army near Bologna. The recent retreat of the French from Italy had left the city of Florence more or less open to attack, and Pope Julius deemed this a grand opportunity to attempt a political restoration of the Medici. At that time the Florentine Republic was being governed by an elected president for life, or perpetual Gonfaloniere, Piero Soderini, and he had for Secretary of State Niccolò Machiavelli. By advice of Machiavelli hasty preparations for defence were made and a militia put in training. But these Florentine forces made a very poor show indeed against the Spanish veterans of the papal army led by Cardona, with the Cardinal Giovanni in nominal command, before the walls of the little town of Prato, a few miles to the north of Florence. Prato was taken by assault, the raw Florentine levies broke up in confusion, and Florence lay at the mercy of Cardona's army. A revolution now took place in the city, Soderini fled, and the Medici were invited to return on the old footing of untitled princes. The cardinal, accompanied by his nephew Lorenzo, and his cousin Giulio and his brother Giuliano, now entered Florence in triumph, and Medicean rule was restored.

This ' rebound to power ' (as Cardinal Giovanni called it) of the Medici in Florence did not complete the revived fortunes of their House. A few months later Julius died, and in March 1513 Cardinal Giovanni dei Medici was elected Pope under the title of Leo X, at the age of thirty-six. Apart from the spiritual claims, this event gave an immense impetus to the political influence of the Medici. Leo was now master both of Florence and of Rome, and had thereby become one of the most important rulers in Italy. In addition to this, one of his first acts as Pope was an expedition against that unruly vassal of the Church, Francesco della Rovere, Duke of Urbino. The papal and Florentine armies seized Urbino, and Leo placed his nephew, the young Lorenzo, on the vacant ducal throne. The increasing power of the Medici awoke further thoughts of ambition in the breast of Leo. Using his diplomatic skill, he next arranged royal marriages for his brother and nephew, the former with Filiberta of Savoy, and the young Lorenzo with the Princess Madeleine of France. This pretty evident bid for a royal status and royal alliances at once aroused fierce protests from the enemies of the upstart Medici both in Italy and abroad : ' Now that the Duke of Urbino has been dispossessed,' writes a bitter German critic of Leo's policy, ' a similar fate awaits the Duke of Ferrara. When both these dukes are exiled, we may be called on to salute that Florentine merchant, Lorenzo dei Medici, as King of Tuscany. And now he must needs espouse some French princess. Long, aye, too long, have we remained mere apothecaries (*medici*), cry these upstarts, now is our chance to make of ourselves kings and princes ! '

On the other hand, this rapid accretion of power and prestige by the Medici aroused keen hopes in the mastermind of Machiavelli. He foresaw in the Medici a powerful native Italian family who might unite all Italy in a national campaign to expel the alien invaders, both French and Spanish. With a Medici to lead a patriotic Italian army, he looked forward to a victory over the foreigner and the establishment of a United Italy under one Italian sovereign. With these lofty but premature views, Machiavelli now composed his famous work, *The Prince*, which he dedicated to the young Lorenzo, calling upon him to form Italy into a nation. Such a vision of Italian unity and independence seemed feasible at this moment and possibly it might have been turned from a vision into a reality, but for a sudden and wholly unforeseen occurrence. Early in 1517 there died the gentle and beloved Giuliano, Leo's brother, leaving no legitimate issue ; and still more disastrous, in the spring of 1519, Lorenzo, Duke of Urbino, expired, leaving only a baby daughter, Catherine, afterwards Catherine de Médicis, Queen of France. When the little infant in her swaddling-clothes was brought to her great-uncle, the Pope, in the Vatican, he regarded this frail atom of humanity with his spyglass, and observed whimsically with a sigh, ' She brings with her all the misfortunes of Greece ! ' For Catherine was now the sole heiress of her house, and all Leo's schemes of family aggrandizement and Machiavelli's dreams of a Medicean monarchy for Italy had been rendered useless and vain.

There were now left of the male descendants of Cosimo il Vecchio only the Pope himself, and the three bastards of the family, namely, the Cardinal Giulio, and two boys, Ippolito, the natural son of the late Giuliano, and Alessandro, a mysterious personage, who is generally described as a natural son of the late Lorenzo, Duke of Urbino, and therefore half-brother to the infant Catherine de Médicis, but who was with far more probability the natural son of the Cardinal Giulio himself by a Turkish slave-woman. Of this pair, Ippolito was handsome and attractive, as we can see him portrayed in one of Raphael's frescoes in the Vatican; whilst Alessandro was ugly, swarthy, and malicious. Yet Leo could never make up his mind how to deal with the question of the reversion or succession of Florence, and in this matter his wishes had never been expressed at the time of his sudden death at Rome in December, 1521, at the age of forty-six.

On Leo's death the Cardinal Giulio retired to Florence, where he carried on the Medicean traditions of clemency, entertainment, and patronage with fair success. Under his care were the little Catherine and her two boy cousins, Ippolito and Alessandro. Giulio had failed to secure his election to the papacy after Leo X, but during the brief and ill-starred reign of Adrian VI he was commonly regarded as the most influential of the cardinals. Within two years of Leo's death he was chosen pope as successor to Adrian with the title of Clement VII in the conclave of November 1523. His reign proved the most disastrous in the whole annals of the papacy. With the capture and sack of Rome in May 1527, the dominion of the Medici was also overthrown in Florence, where for the second time the republic was set up. The two Medici boys were expelled with ignominy from the city, the proud and arrogant Clarice Strozzi, sister of the late Lorenzo, Duke of Urbino, being loudest of all in her denunciation of her bastard relatives, not excluding Clement himself. Together with the Florentine magnates did Clarice, the granddaughter of the wise Lorenzo il Magnifico, enter the old family palace of the Medici and pour forth her scorn upon the two terrified youths. ' You show plainly,' she cried, ' what is already known, that you are not of the blood of the Medici ; and not only you, but also Pope Clement, wrongfully made pope and now most righteously a prisoner.'

But this second break in the long period of Medicean rule was destined to prove of short duration—in fact, only three years. In spite of much enthusiasm and self-sacrifice, with a noble leader like Ferruccio and with the skill of Michelangelo to assist him, the city was beleagured by the joint army of the angry Pope Clement and the Emperor Charles V. There was little hope of success against such a combination, and after a twelve-months' siege Florence capitulated in August 1530, and the *Signoria* and the old executive privileges and offices of the former republic, all of which had been, nominally at least, respected by Cosimo and his successors, were swept away. Florence was erected into a duchy, and its first-appointed duke was the unprepossessing bastard, now about twenty years of age, Alessandro dei Medici. Alessandro had always been the favourite of Pope Clement (who was probably his real father), whilst the attractive Ippolito had been kept in the background by the Pope, who had com-pelled him much against his will to become a cardinal. For forcing on him this highly improper arrangement, Clement owned two reasons. First, he wished to remove him as a rival from the path of Alessandro's fortunes ; and second, he feared the result of a boyish attachment between Ippolito and his little cousin, Catherine, of whom he was fond. This early devotion to her handsome cousin, Ippolito, is perhaps the only romance to be found in the career of Queen Catherine of France, and one cannot wonder at her liking for Ippolito, when we regard his noble portrait by Titian that hangs in the Pitti Palace. Like all these early Medici, Ippolito died young, being only in his twenty-fifth year when he fell a victim to fever at Itri in the kingdom of Naples, on his way to make an appeal to the Emperor Charles V, after Pope Clement's death in the autumn of 1534, that he might be made Duke of Florence instead of his unpopular cousin Alessandro.

Meantime Alessandro reigned in Florence, the creature of

the Pope and Emperor. The latter had bestowed on him for wife his own natural daughter, Margaret of Austria, but the marriage proved childless. Although dissolute and cruel, this young tyrant was not without ability, and he well understood how to make himself feared as well as hated. His reign ended with appalling suddenness early in 1537, when he too was only twenty-four. His kinsman, the eccentric Lorenzino dei Medici (a descendant of that Lorenzo dei Medici who was younger brother of Cosimo il Vecchio) had made a mental vow to rid the city of this base monster. With infinite pains and with characteristic Medicean craft, Lorenzino overcame Alessandro's suspicions, and with the aid of a hired assassin, called Scoroconcolo, suddenly attacked the duke in bed one night in the Medici palace and murdered him after a fearful struggle. In Alessandro expired the last male descendant of Cosimo il Vecchio, and the lordship, now dukedom, of Florence, became once more vacant.

With the extinction of the males of the senior line, it was clear that if the Medici were still to rule in Florence the new duke must be a member of the junior line, of which I have already spoken. Of this branch the nearest heir was the very Lorenzino who had so lately slain his cousin Alessandro, the nominee of the emperor, who would scarcely place an assassin in the room of the murdered duke, who was, moreover, his own son-in-law. Now, there was a promising lad who also belonged to this junior line of the Medici on whom hopes were fixed by all adherents of Medicean rule. This was Cosimo, only son of Giovanni dei Medici, surnamed ' John of the Black Bands ', who had married Donna Maria Salviati, her mother, Lucrezia dei Medici, having been a daughter of Lorenzo il Magnifico and sister of Leo X. Cosimo was therefore on the distaff side very nearly related to the Medici of the senior branch, and this fact undoubtedly weighed heavily in his favour. His father, Giovanni delle

Bande Nere, was the only military commander of ability that the mercantile family of Medici ever produced, and he had done his utmost to serve Pope Clement. Indeed, but for his early death at the age of twenty-seven (how appallingly brief were the careers of these great men of the Renaissance!) he might have been able to avert the sack of Rome and rescue the Pope, his kinsman. He was a rough and ready soldier, but skilful and brave. When wounded at the battle of the Mincio in the early part of 1527, John of the Black Bands had himself held the torch that enabled the clumsy surgeon to amputate the injured limb. Not that he gained much from this prolonged torture, for he died a few days later of gangrene.

With a patriotic warrior for his father, and with an able and ambitious mother, the niece of Leo X, the young Cosimo's claim to succeed the late Alessandro was certainly a strong one. True, he was only seventeen, but youth was deemed an advantage rather than a drawback in those days, when most men looked for a short life and an active one. He was duly invested with the dukedom of Florence in 1537, and he reigned for nearly forty years. Under him the Medici family achieved their main ambition, that of a recognized royal status, a title, and a crown. It was Cosimo I, ' the Great ', who consolidated and enlarged the Tuscan State, acquiring first the lordship of the free city of Siena, and later, in 1569, obtaining the title of Grand Duke of Tuscany from Pope Pius V. At the opening of his reign, Cosimo, who may perhaps be called the last of the great Florentines, showed himself cautious, firm, calculating, and industrious beyond his years. Rather than a Florentine lady, he married a princess, Eleanora of Toledo, who presented him with ten children. Florence owes much to Cosimo's patronage and taste. It was he who removed the ducal residence from the old Medici palace in Via Larga, first to the Palazzo Vecchio, and thence later to the vast

Pitti Palace across the Arno. He built the immense range of public buildings known to-day as the Uffizi; he laid out the superb gardens of the Boboli behind the ducal palace. On all sides the streets and buildings of Florence bear ample witness to his tastes, his energies, and his ambition. He kept up the old Medicean tradition of patronage of the arts, and if the artists whom he employed were inferior to those who flourished in the far-off days of Lorenzo il Magnifico and his grandfather, that was the fault of the age and not of the first Tuscan grand duke. He improved the port of Leghorn; he built a fleet to keep the Turkish pirates from harrying the Tuscan coasts; he founded the knightly Order of San Stefano with its head-quarters in the old neglected town of Pisa. To have built up single-handed one of the chief realms in Italy, and the equivalent of a second-class European power within a half century, is no mean achievement for any ruler. For Cosimo started his reign with little else than the city of Florence for his realm, and he left to his successor a spacious and prosperous grand duchy.

The reign of Cosimo I has always been selected by writers of the past as the period most prolific in family murders, crimes, and horrors generally. There is scarcely a vice or a villainy that has not been attributed to Cosimo and his numerous progeny. And yet, in the light of recent research, it would seem that there is little if any ground for all these alleged scandals and abominations. The fact seems to be that these libels on the first Grand Duke of Tuscany and on his wife, his children, and his court, took their rise from the propaganda (as we should term it now) issued by the many Florentine exiles, fierce enemies of the usurping Medici, scattered throughout Italy; people who thought, not without reason, that if they flung sufficient mud at the object of their hatred, some at least would stick. And the mud thus thrown has stuck very effectually, and it is only now that it is being removed by modern historians, who have found no valid documentary basis for these repeated assertions of unscrupulous foes. A life of Cosimo I has lately been published by Miss Boothby, which ought to impress on the reader that not only was Cosimo a really great man, but also that he was innocent of most of the vile charges that have been passed on without comment and without any serious attempt at verification from one generation to another.

Cosimo died in 1575, and was succeeded by his son Francesco I as second Grand Duke of Tuscany. Here, perhaps it may be urged, the account of the Medici of the Renaissance ought to cease ; but I am anxious to carry out my brief sketch of the family till its final exit, in order that the story of the Medici may be better understood and appreciated as a whole. Francis, whose first wife was the Archduchess Joanna of Austria, was not a worthy son of his father. Yet he too carried on the Medicean tradition of learning and culture. He was not popular, largely owing to his infatuation for the beautiful Venetian adventuress, Bianca Capello, whom, after being for some years his mistress, he finally married amid public festivities as a recognized ' daughter of the State of Venice ', not a little to the concern and scandal of the more thoughtful of his subjects. Henceforward Francis and Bianca led a private existence of selfish indulgence, and general relief was expressed when both the grand duke and his chosen grand duchess died rather suddenly at the villa of Poggio a Cajano in the autumn of 1587. Francis I was probably the least reputable of the Grand Dukes of Tuscany, yet he ought to be remembered gratefully as the founder of the *pietra dura* industry, or inlaying of coloured marbles, which is still to-day a flourishing source of wealth to the citizens of Florence. His elder daughter, Maria dei Medici, was married to King Henry IV of France—another instance of a notable Medicean match—and became the mother of Louis XIII and of our Queen Henrietta Maria, consort of Charles I.

Leaving no son, Francis was succeeded on the throne of Tuscany by his brother, the Cardinal Ferdinando. Ferdinand I now divested himself of his ecclesiastical character, and married the Princess Christina of Lorraine, who bore him nine children. He proved himself an able and enlightened ruler, and, like all the Medici, he was a warm supporter of the liberal arts. To him Florence owes the great mausoleum of the Medici at San Lorenzo, an imposing structure lined internally with most precious marbles. His heir, Cosimo II, who succeeded in 1609, also did much for the material improvement of his hereditary realm. He was especially lavish of his favours to the growing port of Leghorn ; he was the friend and protector of his famous countryman, Galileo ; he sheltered that strange English exile, Sir Robert Dudley, Duke of Northumberland. Cosimo II died in 1620, and by his early death Tuscany had the misfortune to fall for some years under the regency of two well-meaning but incapable women, namely, the Grand Duchesses Maria-Maddalena of Austria and Christina, the mother and grandmother of the infant Grand Duke, Ferdinand II. These two women did no little mischief by their injudicious patronage of the monastic orders, on which they bestowed money and privileges in profusion. Meanwhile, the formation of the famous picture galleries in the Pitti and the Uffizi was proceeding apace. Started originally by Francis I, each of his successors had added to these noble collections, which form no small part of the world's treasure-house. By his marriage with Vittoria della Rovere, heiress of the last Duke of Urbino, Ferdinand II was able to enrich these galleries by many splendid heirlooms from the castle of Urbino ; whilst his brothers, the two cardinals, Leopoldo and Gian-Carlo dei Medici, assisted in the work of adding and selecting. If we recognize our debt to the artistic taste and generosity of the earlier Medici of the senior branch, at least we should feel grateful to these later Medici, not only for their actual gathering-in of these works of art, but also for the generosity wherewith they vested the owner-ship of these priceless objects in the city of Florence, whose property they remain to-day.

Ferdinand II died in 1670, and was succeeded by his son Cosimo III. This, the sixth grand duke, proved of a bigoted and gloomy cast of mind, and as such he suffered his mother, the Grand Duchess Vittoria, to interfere overmuch in the affairs of state. As a youth Cosimo had travelled widely, and there exists an interesting account of his visit to England soon after the restoration of Charles II, which was printed with many illustrations in the following century. Cosimo's long inglorious reign of over fifty years ended under circum-stances of great sadness, for it had now become evident that the historic dynasty of Medici, once so prolific in sons and daughters, was drawing to its close for lack of heirs. Cosimo's elder son Ferdinando had died without issue in 1713; his other son, Gian-Gastone, was also heirless; his only daughter, the Electress Palatine Anna-Maria, was a childless widow. In 1723, on the death of his father, Gian-Gastone, a dissolute and decadent but mild and cultured prince, succeeded as seventh grand duke. He resided in the Pitti Palace, together with his more ambitious but quite incapable sister, the widowed electress, taking little interest in his realm, whose political future had already been settled by the great powers of Europe in the event of his death. He died, the last male descendant of Giovanni di Bicci dei Medici, in 1737, and the Grand Duchy of Tuscany under the terms of the Treaty of Vienna now lapsed to the reigning House of Lorraine. The old electress survived her brother for a few years, keeping up regal state in the Pitti Palace to the last, and expired in 1743.

Such, very rapidly sketched, is the story of the Medici

family from the days of Salvestro dei Medici in the fourteenth century to its final extinction in the middle of the eighteenth. Unlike most dynasties, the House of the Medici shows a gradual yet well-marked ascent from a plain bourgeois family to a recognized reigning European House. The process is unusual, and, taken in its entirety, the rise of the Medici offers many interesting points of study. But apart from this aspect, no family in any sphere of life has exhibited such a continuous and well-balanced average of intellectual powers as were shown in the descendants of the Florentine merchant Giovanni di Bicci dei Medici, over a space of three centuries and a half. Other families have produced a notable figure here and there, but in no instance has there yet appeared so marked a succession of hereditary ability combined with intellectual tradition as was held by all the Medici from Cosimo ' Pater Patriae ' even down to the languid and .ete Gian-Gastone, in whom the family tree of the Medici finally withered and disappeared.

II

THE TWO MEDICI POPES

LEO X (1513–1521). CLEMENT VII (1523–1534)

IN my brief account of the rise and decline of the Medici family I omitted, so far as was practicable, all reference to two of the most eminent of the Medici. These were, of course, Giovanni dei Medici, Pope Leo X, and Giulio dei Medici, Pope Clement VII. Their careers lie beyond mere family history, seeing that these two Medici for nearly twenty-two years (with one short interval) occupied the papal throne, and were therefore closely connected with the course of events in Western Christendom at a most critical period of flux and reform. Their importance is certainly due, however, in part to the fact that they were hereditary princes of the great city of Florence as well as Popes of Rome, and this circumstance gives a special character to their policy both in Italy and in Europe. Both Leo and Clement were, moreover, largely swayed, perhaps unconsciously, by the master-mind of the greatest political thinker of their own, or indeed of any, age, Niccolò Machiavelli, whose tempting but alarming invitation to the Medici to possess themselves of the complete sovereignty of a United Italy often gives us the key to the tortuous and obscure policy of both these famous pontiffs. In addition to their political attitude, we have in Leo's reign the first warnings of the coming religious storm of the Reformation, and under Clement we see it bursting upon Western Europe. Besides these political and religious aspects, we have, moreover, in these two Medici popes the enormous interest of the artistic and literary activity of the so-called Leonine Age, which covers the years 1513–1527.

Giovanni dei Medici, the future Pope Leo X, was born in Florence on December 11th, 1475. He was, as I have already shown, the second son of Lorenzo il Magnifico, by his Roman wife, Clarice Orsini. At his birth Giovanni was destined by his father for the Church, and it would seem that even as a boy he owned ecclesiastical tastes and leanings. ' Together with his mother's milk,' writes his tutor, the famous humanist Politian, with a flattery that was not wholly insincere, ' did he suck in piety and religion, preparing himself even from his cradle for the holy offices.' His father, with his usual perspicuity, adjudged him *savio*, or discreet, and that single quality then sufficed for a churchman's career, though no doubt piety and religion might be found useful adjuncts. He was a singularly plain child, with a pronounced squint, and he grew into a stout, unwieldy man. This was against his prospects of success, yet he owned many mental gifts to compensate for his physical deficiencies. He had a real love of learning, a ready wit, a quick brain, a powerful will, and an unusual gift of dissimulation, which he frequently turned to use in his political dealings. He owned a charming voice, and showed manners of unfailing courtesy even to those he hated or despised. We see him perfectly portrayed in Raphael's superb picture in the gallery of the Pitti Palace in Florence. The portrait is so lifelike, so full of insight and character, that the artist seems to usher us into the very presence of the Pope. Without stooping to flattery, Raphael has managed to invest the fleshy, sensual face with dignity ; he shows us the white, well-moulded hands that were the pride of their owner ; the spyglass in his fingers proclaims his feeble vision ; the jewelled bell and manuscript before him announce his true inherited Medicean taste for art and learning. We feel after gazing on this picture what manner of man he really was, who openly said he meant to enjoy the papacy ; the man who was defied by Martin Luther ;

the man who bestowed the title of ' Fidei Defensor ' on our Henry VIII ; the man to whom Machiavelli looked vainly for support in his grandiose scheme of Italy's regeneration ; in short, that Leo X in whom the secular popedom achieved at once its highest and its lowest note.

In the same picture there stands in obsequious pose behind Leo's chair Cardinal Giulio dei Medici, afterwards Clement VII, the most unlucky of all popes. And still more in the background appears another cousin of Leo's, the Cardinal dei Rossi. Both these standing figures act as admirable foils to the resplendent figure of Leo X, which dominates all else.

Close to Leo's portrait hangs Raphael's equally famous likeness of the Medici's predecessor, Julius II (of which we own a fine replica in our National Gallery). Here again the artist has invested the rough, violent old man with an atmosphere of dignity, to which is added a hint of power in suspense. ' A sleeping volcano ' has been one metaphor applied to this portrait of Julius, sunk wearily in his velvet chair and in a state of momentary repose. What contrasts and what reflections do these two portraits suggest to us !

But Leo was already past forty when Raphael painted him thus, and I must hark back to his childhood in the Medicean palace of Florence—' So large a house for so small a family,' as the wise old Cosimo dei Medici, its builder, had once declared with affected humility. Whilst still in the nursery the little Giovanni was at seven years of age declared capable of ecclesiastical preferment, and was accordingly loaded with canonries and abbeys. He became, in fact, an infant pluralist, all very shocking to our modern sense, but deemed neither shocking nor unusual in that period. ' Heavens, what a mass of benefices concentrated in one fortunate child ! ' commented the pious Fabroni, Leo's first serious biographer. Yet it is hard to deny the satirical comment of a later biographer, the Liverpool Unitarian,

William Roscoe, who dryly observes : ' What difference
can it make if benefices be bestowed on an infant who
cannot, or upon an adult who will not, perform their requisite
duties ? '

At this early period an addition was made to the Medicean
nursery in the old Florentine palace of a small dark-eyed,
dark-haired little boy, called Giulio, the bastard son of the
Giuliano dei Medici, Lorenzo's younger brother, who was
murdered by the Pazzi conspirators in the cathedral of
Florence in 1478.   This adopted sprig of the Medici tree was
some two years younger than the little Giovanni, and the
two boys became firm friends, and continued so throughout
life.   In fact, through good and ill fortune Giulio never
quitted Giovanni, whom he served with unswerving fidelity
and whose confidence he alone fully shared.   To his elder
cousin Giulio certainly owed everything from the very
beginning ; his whole career is commensurate with, and
subordinate to, that of Leo, and must be taken in conjunction with it.

When Lorenzo had laid down an ecclesiastical career for
his second, and as time went on his favourite, son, it was
with the open intention of his pushing the interests and
aggrandizement of the House of Medici in the Church.   He
was to become the first cardinal in this newly-sprung
family that was burgher by birth but royal in practical
power.   Lorenzo was an intimate friend of Pope
Innocent VIII, and had therefore little difficulty in obtaining the red hat for Giovanni, though Innocent, to his credit
be it said, refused to bestow this high dignity upon the
boy till he was sixteen, which was reckoned the age of
discretion in that era of human precocity.

Giovanni received in public the red hat at the abbey of
Fiesole outside Florence, but his father was too ill to attend
the ceremony.   In a few days the young cardinal set out
for Rome to take his part in the fierce battle of politics and

intrigue. After his departure, Lorenzo, from his sick-bed, whence he never rose again, sent him an admirable letter of advice, in which, as one may well suppose, the exhortation to lead a virtuous life was subtly blended with astute Medicean counsel as to worldly success. Above all, in this letter, his parent impressed on him the paramount duty of serving his family : ' You should be the link to bind the city of Florence closer to the Church, and our family with the city.' In many respects this letter still stands as a memorable piece of wisdom to any young cleric at the outset of his career, and Lorenzo seems therein to have neglected no helpful detail from the smallest to the highest. He especially warned the young cardinal against the dangers which awaited him in Rome, ' *che è sentina di tutti i mali* '— ' the sink of all iniquity '. He cautions his son too to guard his health, for Giovanni was always of a full habit, and had already shown signs of the infirmities that beset him early in life and prematurely ended it : ' Rise early in the morning ', was one special item of counsel, and this sound maxim, I regret to say, Giovanni did not follow, for he was lazy and unpunctual all his life. So Giovanni departed to Rome with the paternal blessing to take his due place as the youngest of the cardinals of the corrupt court of Innocent VIII.

Scarcely had Giovanni settled in Rome than the news reached him of Lorenzo's death, and only three months later occurred the death of Pope Innocent, and thus was this youth of sixteen plunged almost at once into the scandals and intrigues of a papal election. In August 1492 there was chosen Pope, largely as the result of judicious bribery, the Spanish cardinal, Rodrigo Borgia, under the title of Alexander VI. Rome was now rendered neither a safe nor a respectable place for a young cardinal, and Giovanni prudently returned to Florence, where he assisted his elder brother Piero in his rule. The fickle Florentines were by this time tired of the Medici; the whole city was running after Savonarola, the popular idol of the hour; the dynasty was tottering to its fall. In the autumn of 1494 there broke out the almost inevitable revolution, and the three Medici brothers, Piero, Giovanni, Giuliano, and their cousin Giulio were all expelled from the city. For the next nine years Giovanni continued poor and insignificant, a wanderer in exile, for he had lost his domestic home in Florence, and he dared not venture to Rome under Alexander. With his cousin Giulio he now travelled, more or less incognito, over Europe, visiting and noting the various conditions of foreign life. At length Alexander died in 1503, and his son, Caesar Borgia, fled from Italy. Giovanni was now able to return to Rome, together with another brother-cardinal who lived in dread of Borgian vengeance, namely, Giulio della Rovere.

Giovanni now participated in two conclaves, or papal elections. At the first of these Pius III (Cardinal Piccolomini) was elected, an admirable choice, but he died within a few weeks of his election. At the second conclave, della Rovere was chosen Pope under the title of Julius II, the famous warrior-pope, who has ever been regarded as the true founder of the temporal power of the papacy.

The Cardinal Giovanni dei Medici was now about twenty-eight, and the practical head of his House, for his brother had died in the previous year. Julius treated him with deference, and Medici was only too anxious to retain his favour. Never were two men more unlike in every possible aspect than Julius and the young Medici. The Pope old, coarse, garrulous, ignorant, plebeian in his birth and tastes: the Medici a young prince, suave, courteous, learned, refined, a perfect master of his tongue and of himself; the Pope, fond of wars and campaigns, with a soldier's violence and sympathies; the cardinal hating strife and fatigue in every form. Yet Medici endured all things to improve and strengthen his position under Julius. Though of feeble health and so blind that he had always to use a spyglass, he followed his master with dogged zeal through his many Italian campaigns of aggression. He made himself indispensable to Julius both on the field and at the council board. As papal legate, Giovanni took an active part in the famous battle of Ravenna in April 1512, where the papal troops were routed by the French and where Giovanni was himself taken prisoner.

After some months of an honourable but very irksome captivity, Giovanni managed to escape and rejoin the papal army of Spanish mercenaries under command of Cardona. The cardinal now enjoyed the full confidence of Julius to such an extent that the Pope deemed it advisable at this crisis to strike at the city of Florence and to restore the exiled dynasty of the Medici. Using the papal army, the Cardinal Medici now advanced towards Florence. The forces collected and trained by the energetic Machiavelli, then holding the post of Secretary of the Florentine Republic, were easily routed. The little town of Prato was taken by assault and sacked, a chance incident of war that certain historians have never ceased from casting in the teeth of the Medici. In August 1512 the Medici family, consisting of the Cardinal Giovanni, his nephew Lorenzo (only son of the late Piero), his brother Giuliano, and his cousin, the faithful Giulio, re-entered Florence as conquerors, after an enforced absence of nearly eighteen years. Their enemies had fled from the city ; the greatest genius of his age, Machiavelli, was anxious to transfer his services to the returning dynasty ; their restoration was on the whole welcome to the Florentines of all classes. How rapidly had the wheel of fortune revolved in favour of the Cardinal Medici! Five months before he had been a prisoner in the hands of the French ; now he was ruler of Florence and also the most important and revered member of the whole College of Cardinals. And he was still only thirty-five.

Early in the following year, 1513, Julius II died, and at the ensuing conclave in March Medici was elected Pope. He assumed the title of Leo X. His election was hailed with delight both in Italy and abroad, for men were weary of the restless aggression of the rough and warlike Julius. The poets, scholars, and artists of the day acclaimed the new pontiff with genuine delight, and not without reason. The court of the Vatican now became the haunt of all that was intellectual, artistic and original in Italy, and even in Europe. 'In my opinion,' wrote the Imperial envoy to his master, ' the new Pope will be gentle [*mitis*] as a lamb rather than fierce as a lion [*leo*]. He will certainly be no friend to the French, yet on the other hand he will not continue their implacable foe, like Julius. He dreams of honour and glory. He will patronize men of letters; at least, *improvvisatori*, poets and musicians. He will perform the sacred offices with care and dignity. He will not rush into any war. But' (he adds prudently enough) ' men change from hour to hour, and the Divine power often plays tricks with our human calculations.'

Although this general estimate of character and this forecast of Leo's policy sounded fairly accurate at the date of his election, the writer was not sufficiently aware of the new Pope's overweening but carefully concealed family ambition, which was little suspected by those who had chosen him. As the son of Lorenzo il Magnifico, he had from his boyhood been the willing recipient of his father's subtle statecraft. During the years of poverty and exile under Alexander VI, and of hard, uncongenial service under Julius II, the Medici had been digesting the paternal advice and principles of his youth. Throughout this waiting period of nearly twenty years Leo had found ample opportunity for the cultivation of those arts of dissimulation

whereof his father Lorenzo had shown himself a past-
master. Just as Lorenzo had ever masked the machinery
of his tyranny and ambition by genial manners and a wise
rejection of outward pomp, so had Leo learned to hide his
most cherished schemes in the event of future success under
a cloak of careless gaiety and even of idleness. And now
the expected hour for putting into practice the theories
privately formulated in past years had verily arrived. He
was now master of Florence and also Supreme Pontiff.

Soon after the ceremonies of his coronation, which were
conducted on a scale of unsurpassed splendour and extravagance, so that the savings of the frugal Julius in the
papal coffers were swallowed up in a few days, Leo took the
first step towards an extension of Medicean sovereignty.
On the pretext of punishing the Duke of Urbino for his past
failure as a vassal of the Church to serve the papal cause,
he started an expedition against that duchy with papal and
Florentine troops. Francesco della Rovere was forcibly
ejected from his capital, and the Pope's nephew, the young
Lorenzo, was installed as Duke of Urbino. This act of
aggression came as a disagreeable surprise to the cardinals,
but it was an accomplished fact, and there the matter
ended.

It was at this juncture that Machiavelli came forward
with suggestions and proposals, of course in secret, and also
indirectly, for the Medici family to unite the whole people
of Italy under their banner, and to set up a national kingdom
of Italy with a Medici for king. I shall refer more fully to
this important matter when I come to deal with Machiavelli himself. No doubt Leo, who considered himself a
patriotic Italian, was taken with this grandiose idea,
although, in the unkind words of an English critic, it
divided his attention with manuscripts and sauces, painters
and falcons. But the grand conception, though hidden to
many observers, was certainly existent. ' It was this great

though mutable ambition of Leo's that continually deceived Machiavelli,' comments Professor Villari. ' It was thus that Machiavelli had been inspired to compose *The Prince* in order to fan the flame of patriotism. But whenever seeming to burn most brightly, the fire always expired on a sudden without leaving a spark behind it.'

Early in his reign Leo found himself beset with political difficulties that arose first from the Italian invasion of Francis I of France, and a year or two later from the accession of the youthful Emperor Charles V. Caught between the two rival powers of France and the Empire, Leo found abundant scope for that particular species of statecraft which he had inherited from his father and had carefully studied. Just as Lorenzo had once essayed to become ' the beam of the Italian scales ', so did Leo now seek to play off the French king against the Emperor. It was dangerous and delicate diplomacy, but it must be admitted that Leo showed himself an adept in this political game —the old Medicean game of meeting superior force with superior cunning. He held the balance pretty well throughout his reign ; it was left to his cousin, Giulio, his successor on the papal throne, to play the same game with inferior skill and to lose it badly.

In exalting his family Leo used less caution and subterfuge, pushing his aims openly. To the anger and disgust of his cardinals, he now bestowed a red hat on the bastard Giulio, whose base birth made him actually ineligible for so exalted an office. He negotiated royal marriages for his brother and nephew. Yet this latter scheme, as I have already explained, eventually came to naught, owing to the unkindly operation of Nature, which in a few months' time deprived him both of Giuliano and Lorenzo, and left only the baby girl Catherine to inherit the fruits of all his intrigue and ambition. The Pope was now a lonely man, constantly ailing, yet none the less keen to snatch all the fleeting joys of an uncertain life. With the total collapse of his family schemes for future sovereignty, he took a less active interest in politics, and threw his energies more and more into the pursuit of pleasure and luxury. He also surrendered still further to the influence and judgement of the Cardinal Giulio dei Medici, who is probably more responsible than Leo himself for the later policy of his reign. It was in all likelihood as much the action of Giulio dei Medici as of the Pope that the famous bull of excommunication was launched against the troublesome German monk, Martin Luther, in 1520, which started the great movement of the Reformation. ' Since God has given us the papacy, my Giuliano, let us enjoy it,' had been Leo's words to his favourite brother at the time of his election ; and amongst his notions of this enjoyment was a constant refusal to be worried by religious troubles and factions. So Leo, careless of the morrow, had preferred to shut his eyes to the storm brewing in Germany and enjoy the papacy according to his own fashion amid the pleasures and amusements of his court.

I now come to deal with the court of Leo X. His reign has been called ' the Leonine Age ', and it may be described as lasting from his election in 1513 to the siege and sack of Rome in 1527 under his cousin Clement VII, who carried on the traditions and manners of Leo's pontificate. And certain it is that the court of Leo X constituted the most brilliant, the most cultured, and withal the most extravagant and corrupt court that Europe had beheld since the times of Imperial Rome. It was, in the language of the day, ' the Light and the Stage of the World ' ; it was the chosen seat of learning and of fashion, the home of the courtier no less than the haunt of the poet. It is easy to conjure up a picture of the Rome of Leo X from contemporary writings and witnesses ; it is not so easy to realize that this was the head-quarters of the Vicar of Christ. For not only were splendour and culture and luxury

to be found therein, but also a strange seasoning of buf-
foonery, scandal, and license.   Raphael would be hastily
summoned from work at his superb frescoes in the Vatican
to paint the drop-scene for some indecent comedy such as
Cardinal Bibbiena's *Calandria*, which is full of the coarsest
Tuscan humour and ' little more than a farce stuffed with
obscene jests '.   If Machiavelli composed *The Prince* for
Leo's political enlightenment, knowing the seamy side of
his character, he also wrote the *Mandragola*, a witty but
revolting play, which especially delighted the Pope.   The
foreign ambassadors, even of the Italian courts, were
shocked at the vulgar and licentious entertainments in
the Vatican, which included bull-fights, masked balls, and
battles of oranges.   At the banquets hobnobbed cardinals
and dwarfs, princes and jesters, bishops and buffoons.
Practical joking of a most brutal type was very prevalent
at the papal table ; on one occasion a courtier bolted forty
eggs at a sitting, and the feat won a smile of approval and a
gift from His Holiness.   At night there was fast and furious
gambling, whereat the Pope was often seen playing for
hours at a stretch, paying his losses but flinging his winnings
over his shoulder to a scrambling crowd of parasites.   Nor
was this wild exhibition of fun and extravagance confined to
Rome itself.   Amongst his many passions, even greater
than his genuine love of literature, music, and the fine arts,
was Leo's craze for hunting-parties.   For a pope to hunt
at all was not only traditionally improper but actually
against the canon law.   Not that this objection stopped
Leo from his favourite amusement.   After one brief period
of scruple, the Medici flung himself with increased zest into
the pastime of hunting in the Campagna, or plain that
surrounds Rome.   Accompanied by his cardinals, his poets,
his buffoons, his pages, and his sycophants, Leo took part
in great drives of game, which was specially preserved for
his pleasure.   He loved to give the final spear-thrust to the

dying boar or stag ; he loved to watch with his spyglass the careers in mid-air of his falcons, on which he had squandered hundreds of golden ducats. I only wish I could continue and give some more picturesque details of the pleasures and pursuits of the Leonine Age ; they must be read in the literature of the period. But no wonder the papal treasury was depleted and the local bankers in tears of despair. 'The Pope can no more save a thousand ducats than a stone fly up into the sky,' comments the Venetian ambassador. And the normal expenses of the domestic life of Leo's court were immeasurably swollen by the huge sums spent on objects so varied as the decoration of the Vatican by Raphael and his pupils ; the rebuilding of St. Peter's, that fatal legacy of the grandiose but careful Julius ; the buying of ancient manuscripts ; the endless stream of charities to the old, the poor, and the sick ; the innumerable commissions to artists and jewellers ; the doles to poets, to musicians, and indeed to anybody who could interest or amuse His Holiness. The court of Versailles under Louis XV and the Pompadour must have been sedate and economical compared with that of Leo X in Rome.

From these growing financial and political and religious embarrassments Leo was released by his sudden death towards the close of 1521, after a reign of nearly nine years. To the last he kept a close secret of his policy—perhaps he did not really know his own mind—though a few months before his death he had made a formal treaty with the Emperor and had openly rejoiced in the defeat of Francis I before Milan. But Leo feared and hated the Spanish element in Italy fully as much as the French, and his policy was ever one of vacillation between the two powers, whom he dreaded equally. He expired in Rome after a very brief illness at the age of forty-six. The usual rumour was at once started that the Pope had been poisoned, but it seems

certain that Leo, who was in wretched health, fell a victim
to the effects of Roman malaria or a feverish chill. His
one and only confidant, the Cardinal Giulio dei Medici, was
absent at the time, for he was acting regent in Florence for
his cousin ; but a sister, Lucrezia Salviati, grandmother of
Cosimo, the future first Grand Duke of Tuscany, was in Rome
when Leo died. Leo was deeply bewailed by the poets and
painters and scholars and other less reputable hangers-on
at the Vatican. His body was buried in the church of Santa
Maria Minerva, where in after years his nephew, the Cardinal
Ippolito dei Medici, Giuliano's bastard son, who had received
many kindnesses from Leo in his boyhood, raised a large but
unlovely monument to his memory. I have only space here
to quote the pith of Guicciardini's verdict upon Leo as ' a
prince who greatly deceived the high expectations formed
of him at his election to the papacy, since he therein displayed more cunning and less goodness than the world had
imagined of him '—a very mild and cautious meed of
criticism.

On Leo's death the Cardinal Giulio dei Medici, despite
his bastardy and his false position in the Church, became
the acting head of that family. I have described his early
history and his unbroken connexion with his cousin and
his fortunes, and to Leo he owed every success in life.
Giulio now aspired to be chosen Pope, and hurried to Rome
for the conclave. In this hope he was disappointed, for a
humble and pious Flemish cardinal, Adrian of Tortosa, was
elected as Adrian VI. But the expected honour of the
tiara was only postponed for two years in Medici's case.
During the short reign of Adrian, the Medici cardinal
contrived to increase both his popularity and his power
in Rome to such an extent that he was able to reach the
height of his ambition after Adrian's death in 1523, when
he was elected Pope under the title of Clement VII.

In appearance the new Pope was wholly unlike his obese,

plain, jovial cousin, Leo X. For Clement was tall, thin, dark, handsome, with well-marked features. In character and deportment too he was the very opposite of Leo, for he was grave, quiet, serious, and somewhat cold in his manner. In his case too that puzzling frivolity, which was so marked a feature in both Lorenzo il Magnifico and his son, was wholly absent ; Clement never unbent, and disliked the grosser and sillier of the pleasures that had marred Leo's tenure of the papacy. Guicciardini applauds the choice of Medici and describes him as ' a person of the greatest power and capacity '. Like his cousin Leo, however, Clement was a true Medici in his love and patronage of the arts, though showing himself more judicious and frugal than Leo. He had likewise absorbed and digested his late cousin's political theories and schemes, and he even carried Leo's secretive tendencies to excess. Nobody at first knew the new Pope's mind on current events, so that both the Imperial and the French factions in Rome were bidding for his support. As it happened, Clement held precisely the same views and intentions as Leo, namely, to play off the French party against the Imperial party and vice versa, in the manner that would best redound to the advantage of the Holy See and the House of Medici.

Once more the interrupted course of the Leonine Age (though in fairness to Clement, it should be added, with more regard for decorum) was resumed at the Vatican after the dismal interval of the pious and ascetic Adrian's brief reign. Once more were Giulio Romano and his fellow-artists working on the apostolic palace and on St. Peter's ; once more the humanists and scholars were hurrying back to the papal court. In Florence, Michelangelo was promptly set to work upon the Laurentian library and the famous new sacristy of San Lorenzo, with its superb effigies of departed Medici. In short, many of the noblest works of the Renaissance in sculpture, painting, and architecture are due to the fine taste and liberality of Clement VII, and for this at least he merits the gratitude of posterity.

Although Clement largely owed his late election to the Imperial influence, yet he very soon resorted to the old Medicean policy of keeping the balance of power, to the intended advantage of the papacy. Thus early in his reign he began to lean more and more to the side of King Francis, much to the indignation of the Emperor. He was already deeply committed with Francis and his aims when in 1525 the famous battle of Pavia was fought. In this decisive action the French king was taken prisoner, the flower of the French nobility was slain or captured, and the French cause in Italy was lost. Under these circumstances the only sensible policy for the Pope would seem to have been one of immediate reconciliation with the victorious Charles V. But Clement, that clumsy disciple of Machiavelli, whose works he deeply studied in secret, could not bring himself wholly to abandon the traditional policy of the Medici. He certainly professed devotion to Charles, but at the same time kept up a constant intrigue with the defeated Francis. He even contrived to form a holy alliance between the reigning Italian princes, the French king, and Henry VIII of England, who was far too remote to be of any practical help in Italian affairs. Charles was deeply angered by this duplicity, and vengeance was vowed at the Imperial court against the cunning but inept pontiff. Meanwhile Clement raised an army, mostly of Italian troops, with his distant kinsman, young Giovanni dei Medici, ' of the Black Bands ', for its general. A better or more devoted leader Clement could not have selected for the post in this critical time. But, alas ! the Medici warrior-prince fell in a skirmish near Mantua in the early spring of 1527. The command of the papal army was now given to Francesco della Rovere, Duke of Urbino, who was either incompetent or treacherous, and not improbably was both. The Duke had, moreover, no love for the House of Medici, since Leo X had some twelve years before ejected him from his duchy, which he had since recovered.

Meantime the Imperial forces were preparing to descend from the Lombard plains towards Rome. This army consisted very largely of Spanish veterans and Lutheran adventurers, or *landsknechts*, under Frundsberg. Their nominal commander was the French renegade prince, the Constable of Bourbon. Against the Imperial forces was arrayed the Duke of Urbino with his army, which carefully kept out of the way of the southern advance of the Imperialists. Slowly and with great effort these undisciplined forces under the Constable of Bourbon proceeded southward, till they reached the neighbourhood of Rome where they were joined by a number of Italian troops of the powerful Colonna family, bitter foes of the Medici. The united army then of Spaniards, Germans, and Italians took up a position close to the walls of Rome near the Vatican. So far Clement had done nothing to prepare the city of Rome for defence. He seems to have hoped against hope that the laggard army of the Duke of Urbino would arrive at Rome, which it never did, and probably was never meant to. The attack on Rome was begun in a misty morning on May 6th, 1527. At the outset the Constable de Bourbon was killed by a stray bullet, and the command was passed on to the young Prince of Orange. The Roman force of defence made a most feeble resistance, and within a few hours the whole city was in the hands of the fierce, unruly soldiery of the Imperial army. Only the great papal castle of Sant' Angelo, the former mausoleum of Hadrian, which was connected by a gallery with the Vatican, remained uncaptured. To its shelter fled the cardinals and nobles and other citizens of Rome. Clement himself was only just in time to save his life. Paolo Giovio, the historian of this period, implored the unhappy Pope to leave the Vatican and hurry with all speed along the secret corridor into the fortress castle of Sant' Angelo. With Paolo Giovio holding his robes of state so as to assist his master, Clement had to run as fast as he could and make an undignified entrance into the beleaguered castle, which was already crammed with fugitives.

The encroaching troops failed to capture the castle and hang the Pope, as they openly boasted was their intention ; but they wreaked their vengeance and their unholy passions on the wretched citizens of Rome. A foul and blasphemous orgy, such as had never yet been equalled, now took place. The details of the sack of Rome by the Imperial army are even to-day almost too terrible to read. Needless to say, the German mercenaries distinguished themselves not only by their cruelty, lust, and greed, but also by their drunkenness and their profanation of the churches and nunneries. They respected neither age, nor sex, nor altar, nor cradle. The holy relics of St. Peter's were trodden underfoot, and the famous basilicas were purposely polluted.

For nearly a month the Pope and the refugees held out in their impregnable fortress amid sights, sounds, and stenches that brought continuous horror and alarm. Finally, at the end of the month Clement capitulated to the Emperor. Charles, however, refused to allow the wretched Pope to leave the castle of Sant' Angelo, and at last after several months of captivity Clement escaped in disguise to Orvieto. Here the English envoys Gardiner and Foxe, charged with a commission from Henry VIII to obtain his divorce from Queen Catherine of Aragon, found the Pontiff in a ruined palace and living in poverty and dejection. Such was the ignominious end of the brilliant Leonine Age—all its splendour and culture and gaiety turned into massacre, plague, and humiliation.

Meantime the Republican party in Florence, profiting by Clement's disasters, had expelled the two young Medici bastards, Ippolito and Alessandro, and had once more re-established the republic. Clement was filled with intense anger and bitterness at this destruction of his political schemes, and with the object of regaining Florence for the Medici he humbled himself more than ever before his master, the Emperor. A compact was now arranged between the Emperor, the Pope, and the French king, whereby, amongst other matters, Charles promised his aid for the recovery of Florence, and preparations were made for a solemn meeting of reconciliation between Charles and Clement at Bologna. In the autumn of 1529 appeared the allied Imperial and Papal army under the Prince of Orange (who had sacked Rome two years before) outside the walls of Florence, and the last long siege of that city began in earnest. I have spoken already of the siege of Florence, which ended in August 1530, with the surrender of the city, the destruction of its old republican constitution, and the appointment of the young Alessandro dei Medici as first Duke of Florence. Whilst the siege of Florence was proceeding, Pope and Emperor effected their projected meeting at Bologna, and here amid great scenes of pageantry Charles was crowned with the Imperial Iron Crown by the Pope, and a concordat, or religious treaty, was made between the two great secular and spiritual potentates. Henceforth Clement was bound to support the ecclesiastical policy of the Emperor, and thus a certain direction was given to the course of the Reformation in Germany and in the countries of Northern Europe. The chief weapon of fear that Charles ever held over Clement's head was the threat to summon a General Council of the Church. And the very first act of such a council, as the unhappy pontiff realized only too clearly, would be his own deposition on account of his base birth and his detested policy.

Clement had therefore to walk very warily. He could not afford to quarrel with Charles again ; yet he never ceased intriguing on the sly with Francis when he dared. He had obtained from Charles what he especially wanted, the re-annexation of Florence and the dukedom conferred on the odious Alessandro dei Medici, who was probably the Pope's own natural son. He had got the inconvenient Ippolito out of the way by forcing him to become a cardinal. There still remained, however, the little Catherine dei Medici, heiress of the House and titular Duchess of Urbino. She formed Clement's chief political asset at this moment, and he was casting about to find the most influential match for the child, who was still only thirteen. By a clever ruse Clement obtained from the unsuspecting Charles his per- mission for Catherine to be married to a son of the King of France. The Emperor contemptuously assented, supposing that King Francis would never give any son of his in marriage to ' one who was little more than a private gentlewoman of a Florentine burgher house '. Yet the wily Pope brought off the match in due course, and himself attended the ceremony of the marriage of his ward Catherine dei Medici and Prince Henry of Orleans, second son of Francis, at Marseilles in the autumn of 1533. Thus did the House of Medici become closely allied with the great reigning dynasty of Valois, and in due time Catherine became Queen of France and the mother of the three last Valois kings.

Such was the secular policy of Clement, a policy that made him hated throughout Italy and despised and dis- trusted in Europe. In Florence, where once the Medici had been so popular, Clement never dared show his face after setting up the bastard Alessandro as duke, and his name is execrated to this day by his countrymen. His spiteful cruelty to many of the leaders of the late Florentine Republic too was very marked, even in that age of violence. Thus by his express orders the unfortunate friar, Benedetto da Foiano, was starved to death in a dungeon of the castle

of Sant' Angelo in Rome, as reward for his part in the
Florentine rising of 1527. Yet he had the grace to pardon
Michelangelo for his prominent help given in the defence
of Florence during the siege. The great sculptor had fled
and hid himself in a church tower in Florence ; but Clement,
ignoring his late lapse of loyalty to the Medici, insisted on
his returning to his work at San Lorenzo, whither Michelangelo now repaired with a heavy heart, ' moved thereto
more by fear of the Pope than by love for the Medici ',
so records naïvely his biographer Condivi. It must at least
be reckoned to Clement's credit that, amongst a host of
crimes and failings, he did possess a very real love and
understanding of art, and especially the art of Michelangelo.
In truth, Clement's treatment of that genius after the siege
of Florence offers a striking instance of the peculiar regard
and privileges which surrounded and protected the great
artists of the Renaissance.

I have said little as yet of Clement's attitude towards
the reformation in the Church. The distant rumbling of
rebellion beyond the Alps that had alarmed the indolent
Leo so little had now grown into a veritable storm that
threatened to overthrow the whole existing fabric of the
Church. Clement was powerless to act save with the permission and at the suggestion of the Emperor, who ever dangled
the threat of a General Council before the eyes of the luckless
Pope. It was owing more or less directly to the Imperial
policy that England was lost to the Holy See. The question
of the attitude of the powerful Henry VIII towards the
papacy turned almost wholly on the matter of that King's
desired divorce from his queen-consort, Catherine of Aragon,
who was the aunt of Charles V. No doubt Clement would
have been only too willing to grant the King's plea but for
the Emperor's hostile attitude. At the best, under the
circumstances the Pope could only shuffle and promise and
lie and delay, trying the old Medicean tricks of diplomacy

on the English King and his envoys, till their patience was exhausted. Finally the English King broke with the Holy See, and Clement saw England disown the claims of the papacy and the Protestant party triumphant at court and in the country.

Clement died within a year after his return from Catherine's marriage at Marseilles. During the last months of his life he grew more and more unpopular at Rome, which had only ten years before so warmly welcomed his election. He felt bitterly the loss of England, but still more did he fear the wrath and vengeance of the Emperor, who was indignant at being tricked by the cringing Pope over the recent French marriage. There was trouble brewing in Florence, which groaned under the tyranny of his odious relative, Alessandro dei Medici. Harassed thus on all sides by domestic quarrelling and political difficulties, yet scheming and shuffling and lying to the last, the exhausted Clement fell ill with a slow fever, and finally expired in the Vatican on September 25th, 1534, in the fifty-seventh year of his age and the eleventh year of his reign, the most humiliating and disastrous in the whole annals of the papacy. ' The joy at Rome is twofold (writes the envoy, Gregory of Casale, to the Duke of Norfolk) ; the election of the new Pope Paul III (Farnese) and the death of the old one being alike causes of jubilation.' So Clement sank loathed, despised, and dishonoured into the grave. Attempts were now made to pollute his tomb, and even to drag his corpse with a hook through the streets of Rome, and it was only by Cardinal Ippolito's bodyguard being placed for protection of the Pope's coffin that outrages were prevented. Nor can we wonder at this outburst of pent-up indignation, for it is hard to palliate or excuse either the conduct or the character of Clement, beyond quoting Ranke's expressive phrase that he was ' the very sport of misfortune, without doubt the most ill-fated pope that ever sate on the papal throne,' this weak and clumsy disciple of the principles inculcated in Machiavelli's *Prince*.

Clement was buried near his cousin Leo X, in the choir of Santa Maria sopra Minerva in Rome. In later years Cosimo dei Medici, first Grand Duke of Tuscany, who had a mania for erecting memorials to all the famous personages of the House of Medici, no matter how remote the relationship to himself, caused a monument to be raised to Clement's memory. It is by that inferior artist Bandinelli, of whom Cellini has left us so unpleasing an account. Clement's handsome bearded face—he was the first pope of modern times to wear a beard, for he ceased to shave in token of grief after the sack of Rome—makes a strong contrast with the dull, flabby countenance of Leo X. Here, then, the two Medici pontiffs stand in effigy side by side, the fortunate and frivolous Leo and the unfortunate and serious Clement, ' the two reverses of the coin of life '. Both monuments, with their heavy classical features, combine ill with the painted windows and gothic architecture of the church. Yet it is as well that Leo X and Clement VII, who grew up together and studied the same school of politics, who were both fine patrons and connoisseurs, and were both typical Medici, should be undivided in their final resting-place.

III

THE HOUSE OF BORGIA

RODRIGO BORGIA, POPE ALEXANDER VI (1431–1503)

CESARE BORGIA, DUKE OF THE ROMAGNA (1476–1507)

LUCRETIA BORGIA, DUCHESS OF FERRARA (1480–1519)

IT was once wittily said that the worst of *white*washing any historical bad character was that so many other people had to be *black*washed in the process. But I am not going to whitewash the Borgias ; still less am I out to blackwash others. Yet I do think we should try to obtain a true perspective of this famous family, whose name for eleven years was perhaps the most renowned and feared throughout Christendom, and that during a critical period in the world's history ; for the name of Borgia will always be associated with the discovery of America and the papal award of the Americas to Spain and Portugal. I admit at once that the Borgias were bad—even in their own day they were deemed evil ; but it was left to a later generation, after the family had fallen from power, to find out that they were such unmitigated monsters of iniquity that the world had never seen their like ; that Pope Alexander VI for a fact had sold his soul to the devil ; that people had seen the Prince of Darkness in Rome at the date of the Pope's death, and indeed some fortunate eavesdropper had overheard a very interesting conversation between the Pontiff and his Satanic Majesty. You know how this sort of tradition grows from mouth to mouth, till it culminates in a legend which is sometimes accepted and sometimes rejected by historians. And in the case of the Borgias the absurd legend was taken over entire and even embellished, nor were particular and interested reasons lacking for this attitude, as I shall show presently. But we can afford to be fair and unprejudiced, even to the maligned Borgias, and we should be found ready to admit that their evil was at least tempered with greatness.

The founder of the fortunes of the Borja, or Borgia, family in Italy, was Alfonso Borgia, a member of a noble Spanish House and Bishop of Valencia. Coming to Italy in the earlier half of the fifteenth century, Alfonso Borgia made a name for himself as a diplomatist and a scholar, and was finally created a cardinal by Pope Eugenius IV in 1444, when he was already sixty-six. On the death of the great humanist Pope, Nicholas V, in 1455, the conclave, as was too often the case, failed to agree as to a successor. A compromise was the result, and old Cardinal Borgia of Valencia was chosen pope, not because he seemed the most eligible candidate but because he was deemed somewhat insignificant and was also seventy-seven years of age, and therefore likely to expire at no distant date. Such an election would at least afford breathing time. This was the stroke of luck that secured the Borgia family its foothold in Italy and made the name of Borgia conspicuous in its annals for nearly fifty years. The new Pope, though reckoned a nonentity and indeed chosen as such, proved himself not altogether unworthy of his election. He was capable, blameless, and a scholar. He was, moreover, very eager to undertake a crusade against the Turks, who only two years before had destroyed the Eastern Empire by the capture of Constantinople. The new Pope assumed the title of Calixtus III, and under this name called loudly on Christendom to unite in an expedition that would drive the Moslem from Europe. This is all to his credit ; unfortunately, he had little taste for art or letters, and at once the grand schemes of Nicholas V were dropped for the warlike policy of a Turkish campaign.

But this ardour for a crusade was not the sole characteristic of Pope Calixtus's policy. Although, or perhaps because, he probably had but a short reign before him, he at once made arrangements for enriching and helping his nephews. It was not a new policy, and the cardinals could hardly complain with sincerity or surprise, though complain they did as a matter of course. Two young men, sisters' sons, both aged about twenty-five, were promptly created cardinals by their august uncle ; these were Louis de Mila and Rodrigo Lançol, who assumed their mothers' name of Borgia forthwith. Another nephew, the son of a brother, Don Pedro Borgia, was named captain-general of the Church, and a little later the Pope made him Papal Vicar or Duke of Benevento in the kingdom of Naples. This was not a little ominous. It seemed probable that the aged Pope was scheming to found a Borgia dynasty in Italy itself ; but, if so, in this effort Calixtus failed owing to his advanced age, for after a reign of three years and three months he expired rather suddenly. There was a strong feeling in Rome against these Spanish adventurers, or ' Catalans ', as they were nicknamed, and Don Pedro Borgia was lucky to escape with his life from Rome on the very day of his uncle's demise. But though Don Pedro Borgia's schemes for a dynasty in Italy were definitely over, the two cardinal-nephews, Louis and Rodrigo Borgia, remained in Rome, and took up their position there as wealthy and influential princes of the Church. This brief pontificate, then, was the foundation of the importance of the House of Borgia, which a generation and more later was destined to affect Italy, and indeed Europe, so powefully.

After the death of Calixtus III his nephew Rodrigo became in time a prominent member of the papal court. His wealth, his capacity, and his charm of manner gained him many friends and supporters. ' He is handsome (writes a contemporary), with a genial face and a honeyed tongue ; he owns the art of making ladies love him, and he draws them to him in a marvellous manner, as a magnet attracts iron.' His gifts were acknowledged by the famous humanist Pope, Pius II (Piccolomini of Siena), who had succeeded Calixtus, and he often made use of Borgia's diplomatic powers. Yet at the same time Pope Pius, who was by no means strait-laced, was scandalized by Cardinal Borgia's amours, and in 1460 wrote him a strong letter of reprimand on this score. No doubt Borgia did not stand alone among the cardinals in his feats of gallantry ; still, his reputation was notorious, even in these early days. We hear of two children of his, a son and a daughter, who were living in Rome, and were grown up about 1480. The name of their mother is unknown. Later, Cardinal Borgia became attached to a certain Roman lady, Vannozza dei Catanei, who was openly regarded as his mistress. Vannozza was a woman of some character, and she even passed as pious in that age of laxity. Although Borgia's mistress, Vannozza was twice, if not thrice, married, her last husband being one Canale, a scholar, for whom Borgia obtained some literary post at the Vatican. Four children of Vannozza's and of Borgia's grew up to maturity. These were Giovanni, for whom his father bought the dukedom of Gandia in Spain ; Cesare, or Caesar, who was born in April 1476 ; Gioffrè, afterwards Prince of Squillace ; and Lucretia, born in April 1480. The position of these children was peculiar. Of course they were illegitimate, but their mother was a married woman, was respected and lived in a palace, and their father, who adored them all, was one of the leading personages at the Roman court. Rodrigo Borgia delighted in his children, and he seems to have owned a real regard for Vannozza dei Catanei, whom, of course, he was unable to marry, for Vannozza never took advantage of her chances, but led a retired life and is never once mentioned even by the ubiquitous gossips of her day as haunting the Vatican or meddling in political matters, even after her lover became pope. In a letter to her daughter Lucretia in after years Vannozza signs herself ' Your Happy and Unhappy Mother ', for she was proud of her children's fame but wretched over the evil fate of Giovanni and Cesare.

Rodrigo Borgia continued a cardinal for thirty-six years, and as such voted in four conclaves. Undoubtedly he learned much statecraft during this long spell of waiting at the papal court. He watched the complete effacement of the old ideals of the papacy after the election of Cardinal della Rovere as Sixtus IV in 1471. Borgia was just forty at this important date. He took the lesson to heart and digested it, as he observed with what ease the whole atmosphere of the Vatican was changed from that of a spiritual to a secular court under the efforts of Sixtus IV and his vulgar pushing nephews, the Riarios and the della Roveres. Borgia was not in the least disturbed or shocked ; he merely realized the enormous opportunity that awaited himself if only he could obtain the tiara, and by this means seize principalities and wealth and influence for the beloved children of Vannozza and himself. At least the Borgia were preferable to the plebeian grasping Roveres and Riarios : the Borgia were noble and knew how to rule ; whereas the nephews of Sixtus IV were naught but greedy peasants, intent on filling their pockets and aping the vices of their social superiors. When Sixtus's inglorious reign came to an end in 1484, Borgia, who was then over fifty, made a bid for election ; but he soon recognized that his chances were hopeless. So he supported the claim of Cardinal Cibò, a feeble, unworthy candidate, who became pope with the title of Innocent VIII. For the next eight years Borgia was consolidating his forces in order to obtain the papacy at the next election, for Innocent's life was a precarious one. It was Borgia's only chance, for he was rapidly approaching sixty, reckoned an immense age at that period ; indeed, on the actual date of Innocent's demise, in July 1492, Rodrigo Borgia was already in his sixty-second year.

It has generally been held that Cardinal Rodrigo Borgia secured his election in the summer of 1492 by shameless bribery ; in other words, that he was the highest bidder for the highest and holiest office in Christendom. This is true enough both of Borgia and of his predecessor Sixtus IV ; yet, on the other hand, we must remember that Borgia was one of the most powerful members of the conclave : he was wealthy, he had immense experience behind him, he was popular. Altogether, apart from the question of bribery, Borgia stood a very fair chance of election. To make his choice secure, he had won over the Cardinals Ascanio Sforza of Milan, Raffaelle Riario, and Orsini by promises of future honours and posts. I do not suppose there was *exceptional* bribery in the case of Borgia's election ; the corruption of the Church, or rather of the College of Cardinals, was complete a generation before the event of 1492. His moral reputation was bad, certainly ; but then, he was over sixty, so presumably had sown his wild oats. ' I am Pope and Vicar of Christ ! ' he shouted joyfully when he was assured of his election. There followed the usual insincère gush and nauseous cant amongst the cardinals of the Borgia's choice being directly inspired by the Holy Spirit. The first shock the Sacred College received was on hearing the official name chosen by the new Pope. It was presumed Rodrigo Borgia would assume the title Calixtus IV, in memory of the uncle who had laid the foundations of his successful career. Not so. ' We desire the name of the invincible Alexander ! ' This answer, to use a vulgarism, made the expectant cardinals ' sit up '. Young Medici, only sixteen but discreet and discerning beyond his years, as befitted the favourite son of Lorenzo il Magnifico, on hearing these ominous words, whispered into the ear of young Cardinal Cibò, his neighbour in the conclave : ' We are in the jaws of a rapacious wolf ; if we do not flee, he will devour us.' Altogether, the election of Alexander the Sixth produced very mixed feelings in the conclave.

Yet outside the conclave the choice of Borgia was hailed with joy. Though a Spaniard by birth, he was thoroughly Italian by long residence and training, and it was hoped that his connexion with Spain might be of value in the cause of peace. At once he began to restore order and decency in Rome, where, under the feeble Innocent, lawlessness had lately prevailed to a disgraceful extent. The cut-throats and thieves were hunted down and hanged ; justice untempered by mercy was administered ; it became safe once more to walk the streets of Rome in daylight. The citizens of Rome were grateful to the new Pope for these measures. ' *Vive diu Bos !* ' (' Long live the Ox ! ') they cried, in allusion to the Borgia coat of arms, which contains an ox feeding in a meadow (and is not, as a modern novelist of some repute recently informed us in a book about the Borgias, ' a golden bull's head on a red ground '.) Why will not people either learn something about heraldry or else leave alone what they obviously don't appreciate ? For heraldry was a living science, and a popular science, in the days of the Renaissance, when every citizen knew the armorial bearings of popes and princes, and spoke of them and discussed them in clear terms of understanding.

The year of Borgia's elevation, 1492, is one of the most important dates in history. It marks with some clarity the transition from the medieval to the modern world. The change was an abrupt one, and in Italy the new order of things was felt early. The death of Lorenzo dei Medici in Florence, the election of the Borgia pope, the accession of the ambitious Charles VIII to the throne of France, the rise of Savonarola, the anxiety felt by Ludovico Sforza (' Il Moro ') at Milan and King Ferdinand of Naples—all tended to create an atmosphere of political unrest throughout

Italy. Yet there was no common patriotism, no mutual
bond of defence. ' Each for his own ' was the motto of the
day. In this crisis the papacy, had it remained true to its
proper ideal as the central force of Christendom, might have
acted with power and profit to Italy and to mankind. But,
thanks largely to the late policy of Sixtus IV, the papacy
had now fallen merely into the position of any other Italian
secular state ; and the reigning Pope, though he did not
scruple to make use of his spiritual powers when it suited
his private policy, had developed into an Italian despot of
the usual selfish and short-sighted type. Such was the
state of affairs in Italy when, two years after the election
of Alexander VI, there came the famous invasion of Italy
by Charles VIII of France, which opened out a new era of
aggression in the history of Europe and heralded a number
of fundamental changes.

I have not the space here to describe that invasion nor to
dwell upon its causes and effects. Charles of France was
bent on seizing the crown of Naples—that was his main
objective ; and this aim he actually achieved in the early
months of 1495. Yet Italy failed at first to appreciate the
momentous and novel character of this invasion. Indeed,
more ·than one of the Italian princes and cardinals had
been instrumental in calling in the French. Others wholly
misinterpreted the event. Savonarola had welcomed the
French King, whom he announced as the destined saviour
and purger of the corrupt Church. Charles's march from
the French frontier to Naples had been one triumphal
progress. Every city opened its gates as to a conqueror.
Alexander, who had a pungent wit, declared that ' the
French came into Italy with wooden spurs, carrying in
their hands chalk to mark their billets '. Charles had been
received with frantic delight at Pisa ; he had entered
Florence unopposed, and a few weeks later his vast army
approached Rome. Alexander has been charged with

indecision and cowardly conduct on this occasion ; but in reality the Pope was helpless. As it fell, he gained by cunning diplomacy what he certainly would never have achieved by force, had he defied the victorious French forces. The silly conceited Charles was no match for the smooth-spoken clever Alexander, who made good use of his spiritual attributes on this occasion to impress, and finally to overawe, the French King.

Four months later Charles and his army had to return homeward from Naples, where Charles had been crowned king of a kingdom that he was forced to abandon in a few days' time. By this date there was general alarm throughout Italy, and a patriotic League against the so-called ' Barbarians ' had been formed amongst the various Italian States, with the Pope at its head. Charles had to force his way northward against the army of the League, narrowly escaping a severe defeat at Fornovo. Before the end of the year all the French had recrossed the Alps, and the whole incident of the late invasion must have appeared like some evil dream that was past and gone for ever, though in reality it was but the first step to an alien domination of Italy that has lasted till well into our own days.

With the departure of King Charles the Pope was able to breathe freely again, and to turn once more to the main object of his policy, which was the aggrandizement of his family. He had now, as I have said, three sons aged between twenty and thirty—Giovanni, Duke of Gandia, Cesare ; and Gioffrè. The eldest was already provided with wealth and a dukedom ; the second son, Cesare, generally called Caesar Borgia, was nominated a cardinal by his father when he was only eighteen and given the rich bishopric of Valencia and innumerable benefices in the Church ; the youngest, Gioffrè, who seems to have been of a mild and retiring disposition, was already married to Donna Sancia, of the royal House of Naples, and was now Prince of

Squillace in that kingdom. But besides these three sons there was also a daughter, the ever-famous Lucretia Borgia, who was now of marriageable age. All four were the children of the Pope and Vannozza dei Catanei. Whilst Alexander was still a cardinal and Lucretia only ten or eleven years old, two betrothals had been arranged for her by her father; but first one and then the other of these early matrimonial schemes had been thrown over by Alexander when he became Pope, as not being of sufficient importance to the Borgia family. Finally, Lucretia, who seems to have been content to behave as a mere pawn in her father's diplomatic game, was given in marriage to Giovanni Sforza, Lord of Pesaro in the Romagna, and vassal of the Church. In addition to his sons and daughter there were other members of the Borgia family whom the Pope enriched and supported. There was the Cardinal Giovanni Borgia, a nephew, son of the Pope's brother; and a somewhat mysterious youth, of doubtful parentage, also called Giovanni Borgia, who was possibly the Pope's grandson. Of all these various Borgias, however, only one possessed undoubted ability, and that was Caesar, the young Cardinal of Valencia, of whose career I shall write presently. Neither Giovanni, Duke of Gandia, nor Gioffrè, Prince of Squillace, seems to have owned any special gifts of mind; the elder was licentious, selfish, and violent; the younger agreeable and modest, but both were equally without political talent. The Cardinal Giovanni and his younger namesake were likewise of no great promise. The cardinal died young of fever in 1500; and the latter faded into obscurity after the fall of his House. As to the famous Lucretia, whose name is so well known from the drama of Victor Hugo and the opera of Donizetti, whose beauty and alleged crimes have long been made the theme of numerous writers, it is only left to state that Lucretia was in plain fact something of a nonentity. That she was amazingly beautiful in her youth is proved by Pintucrichio's picture of her in the Vatican, where she appears as a graceful fair girl, with lovely golden hair. The artist has depicted her in the character of St. Catherine, dressed as a royal princess with diadem and robe, and talking theology with Prince Djem, the brother of the reigning Sultan and a hostage in the hands of the Pope. But beyond her undeniable beauty and the circumstance that she was Pope Alexander's daughter, there is absolutely no corroboration of any of the scandalous legends about poor Lucretia Borgia. She was cultured and amiable, but she was not brilliant, any more than she was criminal. Her one and only misfortune (which tradition and slander have converted into crime) was the mere fact of her birth— she was the daughter of Pope Alexander and the sister of Caesar Borgia. True, she was, as I have said, a pawn, perhaps an all-too-willing pawn, in the Borgia political game, but there her impiety ends. Even her critics—I am speaking of serious historians and not of credulous novelists—have to admit that the last seventeen years of her life, as Duchess of Ferrara, are completely without blame or scandal. There needs no apology for destroying an ugly and slanderous legend, and I shall only add that the Lucretia Borgia of fiction and the Lucretia of history are totally distinct personalities.

Now, the main aim of Alexander was to found a dynasty, and for his all-absorbing purpose this was the material at hand. His eldest son, Giovanni Borgia, Duke of Gandia, was too indolent and dissipated to rise properly to the occasion ; Gioffrè of Squillace lacked both ambition and ability ; but Caesar, the Cardinal of Valencia, owned both qualities in an unusual degree. Caesar hated and despised the clerical tie which bound him to the Church, although it provided him with an immense income. He was eager to become a layman, and be a prince and a leader of men. It is on this side of his secular ambition that Caesar has been credited, not without some show of reason, with a strange and foul murder, which has remained a mystery even to the present day. One night in the summer of 1497 Caesar Borgia and his elder brother, the Duke of Gandia, supped at the house of their mother, then Vannozza Canale. The two brothers left the house together, separated, and then went their several ways homeward. Next day the Duke of Gandia was missed. Search was made, and eventually his body, riddled with wounds but clothed and with a full purse, was found floating in the Tiber by some boatmen. Who slew the Pope's heir was never discovered; but in after years the guilt was fixed in popular belief on Caesar Borgia. No doubt the reasoning ran on these logical lines : 'Caesar was desperately ambitious; his elder brother, the Duke of Gandia, stood in his path to success; therefore he had him assassinated.' We know that Caesar was utterly unscrupulous; it certainly was to his advantage that he should supplant the Duke of Gandia; yet it is hard to believe that Caesar was a fratricide on these simple grounds alone. It is far more likely, as Dr. Creighton suggests, that the Duke of Gandia fell a victim to some revengeful citizen or baron whose wife or lover he had seduced, for the duke's amours were notorious. Having slain the Borgia duke, the assassin in his fear of discovery had the body flung into the Tiber, where, as the Roman boatmen naïvely declared, it was a common occurrence any night to hear a splash and find a murdered corpse in the water. Yet the fact remains that Caesar Borgia *did* gain by his eldest brother's death. He was now the Pope's heir and confidant, and was therefore able to obtain more attention and more practical aid in his deep-laid schemes for a kingdom in Italy. His father's efforts had hitherto been wasted on a frivolous fop such as Gandia; henceforth he, Caesar, would be able to turn the Pope's immense sources of power to better account. For, as Machiavelli had noticed shrewdly, 'Pope Alexander was the first who showed how much a pope, with money and forces, could make his power prevail'. And again, he, Caesar Borgia, was the sole and fitting instrument for that purpose, and not an incompetent idler, like the late Duke of Gandia.

It is therefore not unreasonable to suppose Caesar instigated or contrived this murder, even though it were fratricide. Albeit we must always remember there does not exist a tittle of evidence in proof thereof ; it is purely a question of probability. On the other hand, as time went on, the name of the Pope himself, as well as of Caesar, began to be coupled with the story of Gandia's murder. Now, this supposition rests on nothing beyond the Pope's personal reputation. Alexander was known to be devoted to his eldest son, the duke ; why on earth, then, should he have had him foully slain ? It is a fact that the news of Gandia's assassination overwhelmed Alexander with grief and remorse—grief for his own child, and remorse for the evil deeds of his past life. He openly declared that he regarded the duke's murder as a judgement on himself for his many sins of the past. He shut himself up in his chamber ; he refused to eat or drink ; he would accept no comfort. For days he remained thus, a prey to sorrow and repentance. In this condition Alexander openly bewailed his misdeeds, and promised reform of the Church. Altogether, he was struck with a deep sense of sin and with a momentary but sincere desire to make reparation. This does not look like the attitude of a guilty man. Nobody for one moment suspected the sorrowing Pope of so awful a deed ; letters of condolence poured into the Vatican, including even a letter from Savonarola, who certainly did not believe in the Pope's crime, but did believe in his grief and in his genuine desire for amendment and reform. Yet this implication of Alexander in his eldest son's mysterious fate, though it is a posthumous libel, has never died out, but continues to be repeated in nearly every book that deals with this period of history. In conclusion, it is *doubtful* whether Caesar Borgia was concerned in this murder ; it is *certain* the Pope was wholly innocent in the matter.

With Caesar now the heir and the mainstay of the family, Alexander began to plan and act in collusion with his able and precocious son. At the time of his elder brother's death Caesar was but twenty-one ; indeed, for precocity and genius combined he can only be compared with Lorenzo dei Medici, who had to take up the reins of government almost in his teens. It is a curious instance of youth and age in close combination, though a very effective instance. Alexander was now approaching seventy, and time was precious, for with the Pope gone Caesar would have to stand alone ; and at the present moment nothing had been accomplished of that hereditary secular state which the Borgias intended to build up in Italy by means of the papacy. A few months later Caesar Borgia divested himself with evident relief of his ecclesiastical orders, and became a layman. In the following year he was sent to France as papal ambassador to greet the new King, Louis XII, formerly Duke of Orléans, who had lately succeeded his cousin, the miserable Charles VIII. Caesar made an ostentatious appearance at the French court, where he was well received by Louis. He was promptly created Duke of Valentinois by the French King, and by that title Caesar is often named by writers. In addition to this, the King found him a princess for wife in the person of the beautiful Charlotte d'Albret, his own niece and the sister of the King of Navarre. Indeed, Caesar Borgia carried out a most successful mission to the French court.

By the end of the century the Borgia scheme of a secular state was ready to be put in practice. With France for his ally, with a body of captains and mercenaries, well paid out of the papal coffers, Caesar started on his task of subduing the Romagna, whilst Alexander remained at the Vatican, guiding diplomatic events, sending supplies, and keeping Caesar well informed by messengers. The Romagna is that part of Italy which lies between the Apennines and the Adriatic, to the south of the Po. It is situated between the territory of the Venetian Republic, the Florentine Republic, and the Kingdom of Naples. It is a fertile, thickly-populated country, full of towns and castles, and with ports on the Adriatic. The Romagna had for centuries formed at least nominally part of the States of the Church ; but for many generations all local authority had been usurped by a number of petty princely Houses, who held their princi-palities as vicars of the Pope, and paid him tribute. Although recognized fiefs of the Holy See, the cities of the Romagna were at this date practically independent. Various popes had in the past tried to recover this long-lost territory for the Church, but always without success. Cesena, of all its towns, alone remained in papal keeping. It was now the Pope's and Caesar's united aim to form a principality out of this Romagna, not for the benefit of the Church, but to make of Caesar Borgia a great secular ruler. In firm anticipation of this result the Pope created his son Duke of the Romagna.

The first of the princelings of the Romagna to feel the heavy hand of the Borgias was Caterina Riario-Sforza, the Lady of Forli. In vain did this plucky virago call for aid. Her kinsfolk at Milan were themselves on the verge of final collapse ; the French refused to listen to her arguments ; none of the Italian states would send her help. With a mistaken courage Caterina Sforza held out in the castle of Forli against Caesar for three weeks, until the fortress was taken by assault and she found herself a prisoner at Rome. The fate of Forli became the fate of every castle that resisted. Most of the local tyrants fled ; those who did not, such as the young Astorre Manfredi of Faenza, were captured and sent as prisoners to Rome, where their ultimate end was usually tragical. In a year or two Caesar had laid the foundation of a powerful and well-governed state, for he built up as well as destroyed. He favoured the merchant, the peasant, the quiet citizen, who found in the new Duke of the Romagna a very different type of overlord from their late masters. ' I am not here,' said Caesar haughtily to the Florentine envoys, ' to play the tyrant, but to extinguish tyrants.' That was the key-note to this new Borgia policy, and at least it commended itself strongly to one who was the greatest thinker of his age, Niccolò Machiavelli, who could write thus of Caesar Borgia on a personal acquaintance :

' This lord is splendid and magnificent, and is so bold there is no enterprise so great that it does not seem to him small. To gain glory and win a realm he robs himself of repose, and knows neither fatigue nor danger. He makes himself popular amongst his soldiers, and has chosen the best men in Italy. These things make him victorious and formidable, with the aid of perpetual good fortune.'

Nor was this Machiavelli's only appreciation of the Duke Valentino, as he sometimes calls Caesar Borgia. Several pages of his famous treatise, *The Prince*, are devoted to an account of Caesar's campaigns and policy, and on almost every point Machiavelli expresses his warm approval. In short, the great Florentine writer extols Caesar Borgia as a model for the true Prince who is to arise and deliver Italy from the invading foreigner—the Prince of his imagination that never appeared, and whose non-appearance was the direct cause of the servitude of Italy from Machiavelli's day almost to our own. We must not neglect this side of Caesar Borgia's career. He is not a mere blood-thirsty if picturesque adventurer, running amok across the pages of Italian history. He is a serious and important figure, a statesman who understood the political canker of his times and tried to cure it with drastic but wholesome remedies.

The very want of scruple that modern critics lament in
Caesar Borgia made a very different sort of appeal to the
mind of the patriotic Machiavelli. He praises, for example,
Caesar's master-stroke of treachery at Sinigaglia, when,
imitating the cunning of his treacherous captains, he decoyed
them with honeyed words (surely a gift he had inherited
from his father !) into the castle of Sinigaglia and had them
all arrested and executed there and then. Dr. Creighton
is of opinion that one reason why the Borgias have been so
execrated by posterity is that they always acted without
hypocrisy ; in other words, that they showed themselves
so markedly un-Italian. They knew their own minds ;
they went straight to their goal ; they never left any means
untried till they got there. That was the Borgia method
of enforcing the Borgia policy. This famous coup of
Sinigaglia took place on the last day of 1502. But the
term of the Borgia power was rapidly drawing to an end,
and Caesar was trying feverishly to consolidate his new
duchy so as to stand in a secure position in the imminent
event of the sudden demise of his septuagenarian father.
He himself confessed in after days to Machiavelli that he
had made every arrangement in case of the Pope's death,
or even of his own illness ; the one combination he did not
foresee and did not guard against was the dual chance of
the Pope dying and of himself—the strong, youthful,
indefatigable Caesar Borgia—stretched helpless on a sick-
bed. Yet so it fell ; and by this double mischance there
fell likewise the Borgian realm in Italy.

' I can find no fault with him (says Machiavelli) ; nothing
but the shortness of his father's life and his own illness prevented the success of his designs.' And, remember, Caesar
Borgia at the date of the Pope's death was but twenty-seven.

In writing thus of the campaigns and policy of Caesar
I am wandering somewhat from my general theme. The
political side of the Borgias has been treated in all the papal

histories, notably and fairly in that of Dr. Creighton, who does justice to the grander side of their ambition, prompted though it was by purely selfish ends. I come once more to a closer consideration of the Borgias as a family, and as to why their name and fame have descended to posterity with such evil repute clinging to them, although the House of Borgia, be it remarked parenthetically, has given canonized saints as well as execrated sinners to the world. This evil reputation is exaggerated ; yet it is not undeserved, although two members of the family only are implicated in the charge, namely, Pope Alexander VI and Caesar Borgia, Duke of the Romagna and Duc de Valentinois. Assassination and poisoning, the dagger and the drug, are, and probably always will be, associated with the very name *Borgia*. I shall take the charge of poisoning first. It has no historical corroboration whatsoever. The Borgias were not expert poisoners. In the first place, from a medical point of view, the standard of knowledge at the time was very low indeed ; and where medicine is at a low ebb the science of drugs and subtle poisons must also be correspondingly low. People did poison, or try to poison, in that age ; but it was a clumsy affair, and very little understood by those who practised it. There is no reason to suppose the Pope and Caesar owned any exceptional skill or insight in this direction. At that time the death of any and every public personage was vulgarly attributed to poison. There were no doctors in our sense of the word, only ignorant and grasping quacks with bizarre or repulsive nostrums that often hastened but never averted death. Read any contemporary book (say, for example, Cellini's *Memoirs*) and you will realize the depth and degradation to which the noble art of healing had fallen at the time of the Renaissance. I think we may dismiss the Borgian stories of subtle poisonings as pure moonshine, the inventions of a later age, whose only foundation is some back-stairs gossip of Venetian envoys. Very possibly the Borgias, like many of their contemporaries, may have employed poison ; but with their miserable modicum of knowledge they were necessarily quite innocent of the poison-rings, and poisoned feather-beds, and poisoned wine and bread which figure so largely in what I may venture to call Borgian fiction. The story of the death of the aged Pope himself is typical of this class of scandal. For generations it was accepted as a positive fact that Alexander obtained his mortal illness from partaking by mistake of the wine he had already loaded with poison for Cardinal Adrian of Corneto. As a plain matter of fact, the Pope and Caesar Borgia did sup with the Cardinal Adrian in his garden above the Tiber on a sultry evening in August, 1503, at a time when the malarial fever was raging in Rome. That both host and guests were taken ill with ague and fever after this supper is surely an instance of natural cause and effect. Until fifty years ago anybody supping late at night on the banks of the Tiber in a hot, unhealthy August might have incurred the .illness that carried off Alexander and very possibly have suffered the same fate.

With regard to assassination, the charge stands on a much surer footing. I have already shown that possibly Caesar Borgia caused the Duke of Gandia's murder in 1497, though there is nothing definite to prove his guilt. On the other hand, it is pretty clear that Caesar was directly responsible for the murder of his brother-in-law, the Duke of Biseglia, the second husband of Lucretia Borgia, whose first marriage with Giovanni Sforza of Pesaro had been annulled. There was much bitterness between the two young men, and each seems at odd moments to have tried to assassinate the other ; but Caesar was the superior at this game, and one day he sent his servants to the house of the Duke of Biseglia and had him strangled before the eyes of his wife. Lucretia, who was really attached to her husband, was distraught with grief, and appealed to the Pope, her father. Alexander was

very awkwardly placed. Finally, he sent away the sorrowing Lucretia from Rome to act as his deputy at Spoleto, and
did all that was possible to hush-up and minimize this family
tragedy ; indeed, it is hard to see how else he could have
acted under the circumstances. It was commonly said that
Alexander feared as well as adored his son Caesar. It is
probably true. Outside persons noticed the different
natures of the pair : the old Pope garrulous and affable,
full of compliments and jests ; Caesar, young and handsome
certainly, but sinister, silent, mysterious, always dressed
in black, rarely seen by day, a creature of the night. A
peculiar dread was evidently inspired by this strangely
contrasting pair, who worked together in such perfect
harmony, yet used such diverse methods to attain the same
end. The success of their joint policy was fully as amazing
as it was disquieting ; every uncanny or evil incident of
the day came in time to be attributed somehow to the
Borgia father and son. And perhaps some of the murders
and disappearances of well-known people in Rome during
these few years *were* contrived by the Borgias. The castle
of Sant' Angelo was filled with their prisoners, and many a
corpse was found in the Tiber. Dead men tell no tales ; no
doubt Caesar was fully aware of the sound policy contained
in this cynical aphorism.

Yet many of the crimes long ascribed to the Borgias seem
quite pointless, and of such at least they may be fairly
acquitted by a more critical posterity. After all, the dagger
of the bravo was one of the recognized means employed in
that day ; everybody made use of the hired assassin, and
nobody was particularly shocked at the procedure. Very
likely, however, the Borgias were less sparing of this secret
mode of riddance of their foes than other princes of the
time, for Caesar was no coward, and was rather given to
making a public example of the fate of an enemy. It will
be objected, then, why have the Borgias been branded with

this special mark of villainy, which has been related and upheld for centuries ? I think the answer is to be found in the genuine terror that the Pope and Caesar Borgia inspired in their contemporaries, who perceived not only wickedness but also strength and method in their policy. For sheer ability and definite will to power these two Borgias surpassed easily all their neighbours in Italy. And, in addition to this, it must be remembered that a couple of generations later, when the era of the unscrupulous secular popes had come to an end, men began to look back with an intense sense of shame upon the manifest corruption of the papacy that had lasted with hardly a break from the election of Sixtus IV in 1471 to the death of Paul III in 1549, a stretch of nearly eighty years. Out of this series of worldly and wicked popes it was not unnatural to select a scapegoat ; and what more obvious scapegoat to be found than the foreigner, the Spanish Pope, Rodrigo Borgia of Valencia, Alexander VI ? By holding up, then, the Spanish Borgia to execration the misdeeds of the various Italian pontiffs were to some extent palliated in the eyes of the uncritical. There was started a notion that this papal corruption was of Spanish rather than of Italian origin and complexion. Of course such a notion is false, but it was an attractive notion to the Italian mind, and to some extent it answered its purpose. Of these pontiffs Alexander VI was no more cruel, no more corrupt, no more treacherous, no more blood-thirsty than, say, Sixtus IV, Julius II, Leo X, or Paul III. We must look facts—historical facts—in the face, and deal with them fairly and squarely. And if we do so in this case we shall come to the conclusion that the Borgias were no worse from a moral point of view than their contemporaries.

Alexander died very suddenly in August 1503 of a virulent attack of Roman malaria. That is a fact. Caesar Borgia was prostrated by the same malady from the same cause, namely, his imprudence in supping in a Roman garden during a period of feverish epidemic. Men were at that time extraordinarily imprudent as to their health ; perhaps they were all at heart fatalists as to health or ill-health in an age that was wholly without doctors or remedies or any system of hygiene. With his father lying dead in the Vatican and himself helpless and racked with fever on a sick-bed, Caesar saw, or rather heard, the whole fabric of Borgian greatness collapse like a house of playing cards. True, Caesar still owned some influence through the Spanish cardinals wherewith the Pope had lately packed the Sacred College, and he had forces in his pay ; but without health or power to move freely these advantages could avail him little for any length of time. With the election of the worst foe of the Borgia House, Cardinal della Rovere, as Pope Julius II, Caesar's chances were definitely and for ever destroyed. He fled to Naples, and after a spell of imprisonment there was released and sailed to Spain, once more a needy adventurer, a duke without a duchy, a leader without money and without men. In Spain he was again clapped into prison, and languished there for two years. Again he escaped, in November 1506, and this time made his way to the court of his brother-in-law, the King of Navarre, who gave the wanderer a command in his army. Fighting for Jean d'Albret, King of Navarre, in some mean revolt, the famous Caesar Borgia, Duke of the Romagna, was slain at the castle of Viana on March 12th, 1507. He was only thirty. He will always live in the pages of Machiavelli's *Prince*.

Lucretia Borgia survived her brother Caesar for over twelve years, yet she was only thirty-nine at the date of her death. Her early life, as I have said already, is closely bound up with the career of her father, both as pope and cardinal. Twice, when she was a slip of a girl, not even in her teens, did Alexander, then Cardinal Borgia, affiance

his beautiful child to Spanish noblemen ; but on his election
as Pope, Alexander at once sought to make political capital
of his daughter, of whose beauty he was proud and of whom
he was genuinely fond. Her first marriage to Giovanni
Sforza, Lord of Pesaro, which at the time aroused hopes
at the Vatican, was dissolved a few years later, apparently
without opposition from Lucretia, who bore this first spouse
of her father's choice no love whatsoever. It was a purely
political match, and with her rather phlegmatic nature
Lucretia bore its rupture with philosophic resignation,
perhaps with relief. Alexander next suggested his emanci-
pated daughter to the Lady of Forli as a suitable bride for
her eldest son, Ottaviano Sforza-Riario, an offer that was
haughtily but perhaps not wisely declined by Caterina
Sforza. This matrimonial scheme having failed, Lucretia
was next proposed as wife to a young Neapolitan prince,
Alfonso, Duke of Biseglia, natural son of King Alfonso II.
For her second husband Lucretia seems to have owned a
real affection, and the pair lived happily for a couple of
years in Rome, until a quarrel, arising from some unknown
cause, broke out between Caesar and the Duke of Biseglia,
which ended in Alfonso's assassination on August 18th, 1500.
For many months Lucretia was prostrated with grief and
horror, and her tears and reproaches were found highly
inconvenient by her hard-hearted brother. Caesar finally
persuaded the Pope to send off the grief-stricken Duchess
of Biseglia to Spoleto, there to administer the place as
her father's deputy, though the appointment of a female
governor in the States of the Church was in truth a startling
novelty. From Spoleto she retired to Nepi, whence she
wrote some letters which are extant. The letters themselves are of no special interest, except for Lucretia's
ominous signature, which is given as ' La Infelicissima '
(' the most unhappy or unfortunate woman ').

But she was very young, and time softened the shock.

Before the end of the year the widowed Duchess of Biseglia, with her one son Rodrigo, seems to have resigned herself once more to her former position of a pawn in the political game that was being played by her father and brother. This time the Pope and Caesar looked to making a higher alliance for Lucretia. Finally, they decided to offer her hand, with an immense dowry, to the hereditary Prince of Ferrara, Alfonso d'Este, who was a young widower of twenty-four, Lucretia herself being but twenty. Ferrara was the most powerful of the fiefs of the Church, and indeed a leading state in Italy, whilst the Este family was one of the most ancient and haughty of Italian reigning Houses. The Pope's suggestion was distasteful to the pride of the Duke of Ferrara, Ercole I, and abhorrent to his son and heir Alfonso. Yet the Borgias were set upon the match, opposition or no opposition. There is no better example of Borgian policy and determination than this scheme of forcing Lucretia as a bride upon a family that was anything but pleased to receive her. But the union of the papacy with the increasing power of Caesar, now Duke of the Romagna, was not to be withstood, even by the Este, and at last the old Duke of Ferrara consented to the match upon certain conditions. The surrender of the Este family was hailed with joy at the Vatican, where the formal betrothal of the Pope's daughter to the heir of Ferrara was celebrated with much pomp. On January 6th, 1502, the bride-to-be set out with a brilliant train from Rome towards Ferrara, which she reached on February 2nd. It was a long and tedious journey, half across Italy, and one of her halts was made at Pesaro, the city of her first husband, Giovanni Sforza, but now a possession of her brother Caesar by right of recent conquest. This short sojourn at Pesaro must have given the bride some food for reflection, and one is not surprised to learn that during her stay in Pesaro Lucretia did not appear in public.

On her arrival at Ferrara it is evident that Lucretia quickly made a most favourable impression on both prince and people, which she maintained throughout the seventeen years she lived there, first as crown princess and later as reigning duchess. Alfonso d'Este soon laid aside his not unnatural prejudice against the bride chosen for him against his will. For Lucretia made him an excellent and helpful wife. She bore him three sons, and was generally held a pattern of all the domestic virtues. She was extolled by the poet Ariosto in his famous work, and was the generous patron of artists and men of letters at the court of Ferrara. But no doubt the strongest proof of Lucretia Borgia's virtues and popularity at Ferrara, alike with her husband and the people, is to be found in the plain fact that after the death of Pope Alexander and the rapid downfall of Caesar Borgia, which occurred within two years of her arrival at Ferrara, there never was any question of her repudiation by the House of Este, although such a step was quite feasible on the utter collapse of that very Borgian power which had imposed her as a bride on the once unwilling Alfonso d'Este, who ascended the throne of Ferrara as Alfonso I in 1505. Lucretia died on June 24th, 1519, to the grief of Duke Alfonso and of the city of Ferrara. Almost her last act was to write a pathetic letter to Pope Leo X asking for his blessing, as she felt herself on the point of death after having just given birth to a stillborn infant. (Her mother, Vannozza, had died in Rome the preceding year.) Of her children, the eldest, Alfonso II, succeeded his father as Duke of Ferrara and Modena in 1534, and with his son, Lucretia's grandson, Alfonso III, the legitimate line of the Este family came to an end, and Ferrara was annexed as a vacant fief to the States of the Church in 1597. The beautiful Eleonora d'Este, the adored mistress of the great poet Torquato Tasso, was Lucretia's granddaughter.

Such is a very brief sketch of the House of Borgia in

those days when it played a prominent part in Italian and even in European history. Whatever we may think of Alexander VI and of Caesar Borgia, we cannot think evil of Lucretia, if only we examine the true facts of her life and strive to forget the scandalous twaddle that has somehow become associated with her name and her career.

IV

GIROLAMO SAVONAROLA

(1452–1498)

IN our passing phase of unrest and uncertainty and gross materialism, it is at least some consolation to learn that certain great minds of the distant past have of late won fresh admiration and reverence among thoughtful men and women. The influence of the Middle Ages is far from being extinct to-day; I need only mention the continued and increasing popularity of that wonderful book *The Imitation of Christ* to testify to this. The pure motives and sincere piety of that era of our human progress still bear lovingly—nay, pressingly—on the problems and special requirements of our present age. And amongst such noble souls may confidently be included the name of Girolamo Savonarola, Prior of St. Mark's in Florence, who may perhaps be styled the ' last of the great Medievals ', for he suffered on the scaffold so late as the year 1498. In his life-story, with its high ideals, its fearless reforms, and its final tragedy, we can all of us find a lesson and an example for our daily conduct of life, both public and personal, in the twentieth century.

Although the honoured name of Girolamo Savonarola is so closely associated in the popular mind with Florence, and with Florence only, yet he was not a Florentine by birth, nor did he spend more than a third of his life in that city. He was born on September 21st, 1452, the third of the seven children of Niccolò Savonarola. It was at Ferrara that his earliest years were spent. Tradition must report truly when we read that Savonarola was always a serious youth ; for who could ever associate gaiety with that

72

stern, determined face that is tolerably familiar to all of us from numerous prints and photographs ?

And at this point it may be useful to describe Savonarola's personal appearance, although his profile framed in the black cowl of a Dominican friar is familiar to most of us. Few historical portraits own a deeper interest or a more human significance than the likeness by his disciple, the Dominican painter and friar, Fra Bartolommeo, which hangs in the prior's cell of St. Mark's convent in Florence. From its countless reproductions it is the best known of all Savonarola's many portraits. Besides the artists, however, contemporary writers have also left us their impressions of him. He was of medium height, spare and sinewy. He had a dark, swarthy complexion, with red cheeks, a Jewish-looking nose, and heavy prominent features, together with a wide mouth and remarkably thick lips. The chin is square, the forehead sloping, the eyes grey and piercing, and with a trick of emitting flashes of fiery light under stress of anger or excitement. In spite of the dominant harshness of tint and feature, however, all his intimates agree in admitting a certain air of nobility in the rough-hewn face, and at times they even speak of a strange sweetness in that usually dour and forbidding countenance.

Ferrara, under the Este dynasty, held a high place amongst the leading cities of Italy, though this fact is hard to realize in the sad, silent town with grass-grown streets and mouldering palaces that survives to-day. It was therefore in an atmosphere of Ferrarese culture, pageants, and intrigue that the boy Girolamo was educated, though we know few details of his early years. Strangely enough, in a somewhat belated discovery amongst obscure archives the story of his first and only love-affair has come to light. In·certain natures love is like the whooping-cough : one sharp attack will leave the patient immune for life ; and this was undoubtedly the case with Savonarola. The object of his youthful adoration was a certain Laodamia Strozzi ; and it is evident that the episode was brief, passionate, and ill-starred, owing to the determined opposition of the Strozzi family to the match. The young man, then aged about twenty, no doubt suffered severely during the course of this romance, but its collapse must have left him heart-free. With the elimination of passion, the path was now cleared of every obstacle to that rigid life of cloistered rule which seems to have been his natural bent as well as his preordained fate.

At the age, therefore, of twenty-two this grave youth, to the bitter sorrow of his parents, decided to embrace the monastic life in all its asceticism and self-denial. In his own words, he was minded ' not merely to change from an Aristotle in the world to an Aristotle in the cloister ', but to become a true friar in the genuine spirit of the founder of his chosen Order, the great St. Dominic. Secretly, then, in April 1475, he stole away from his home to Bologna, to seek admission as a novice in the historic convent of San Domenico, wherein St. Dominic himself had died and which contains the saint's splendid tomb, one of Niccolò Pisano's masterpieces. Here the young enthusiast was gladly admitted, and here he spent some years in a life of contemplation, drudgery, and pious exercises, till he became so emaciated as almost to resemble a spectre, and his superiors had to curb his austerities out of fear for his life. Whilst acting thus, he was ever pondering in his heart the particular theory of coming disaster to the Church and to Italy, which he had already described in his treatise called the *Contempt of the World*. This early composition was written some months before his entering the monastery at Bologna, and it gives us the key-note of Savonarola's subsequent writings and conduct. One passage from it will suffice to show that this youth of twenty-two was then holding views from which he never wavered throughout the whole of his career.

' Not one, not a single righteous man is left ' (so writes the young citizen of Ferrara) ; ' it behoves us to learn from babes and women of low estate, for in these only does there linger any shadow of innocence. The good are oppressed and the people of Italy become like unto the Egyptians who held God's people in bondage. But already famine, flood, pestilence, and many other signs betoken future ills, and herald the wrath of God. Divide, O Lord, divide once again the waters of the Red Sea, and let the impious perish in the flood of Thy wrath ! '

This is already both in the style and spirit of Savonarola's later and more famous sermons and tracts during the hey-day of his power and authority in Florence. Already he was reading the signs of the times in the light of his own inner vision. It is therefore certain that there was stealing upon him within that quiet retreat in Bologna the close conviction that he himself was doomed to become the agent and the mouthpiece of the offended Deity ; that he was not only destined to warn Italy but to regulate her measure of punishment.

In the Bolognese convent, then, Savonarola continued to work, to study, and to mortify himself. Ere long his remarkable personality brought him to the favourable notice of his superiors, so that he was nominated first instructor, and later preacher, within the convent. In 1481 he was sent to preach at his native Ferrara, and later in the year he was dispatched to Florence, crossing the Apennines on foot, and finally reaching the monastery of San Marco, which was henceforth to be for ever closely associated with his name.

The convent of St. Mark at Florence is to-day reckoned one of the most interesting buildings in all Italy, and each year brings thousands of reverent pilgrims to this spot, as to a shrine both of art and history. Yet at the first glance it does not seem a striking or beautiful structure, for its church has been largely altered in rococo style. Yet the original monastery itself remains to-day in much the same state as when Savonarola entered it that autumn day in 1481, finally to quit it for a martyr's death some seventeen years later. Externally, one sees only blank whitewashed walls pierced by small round-headed windows, the whole structure being only two stories high. Within is a small square cloister with a garden in its centre that is filled with damask rose-bushes, the actual descendants of the very roses that bloomed here in the far-off days of Savonarola and the Medici. One finds the usual long, dark refectory and guest-room with tiled floors; the broad grey stone stairway; the corridors with their plain stone cells for the friars and novices and lay brethren. Over all spreads the high-pitched roof of Apennine chestnut beams.

Founded, or rather restored and endowed, by the great Cosimo dei Medici, St. Mark's convent largely owed its prosperity to the bounty and patronage of the Medici, whose familiar coat of arms with the six red pellets shows everywhere conspicuous. Although but a generation old, this small Dominican friary could already boast of great names, both secular and monastic, and especially of the truly angelical painter, Fra Giovanni, from the sister-convent at Fiesole. His exquisite frescoes were then visible in all their freshness of colouring, each cell and many of the large wall spaces being covered with glorious groups of angels and saints. Here, at every turn, one saw the repeated design of St. Dominic embracing the foot of the cross. In the lunettes of the cloister arches Fra Angelico had painted allegorical figures to teach and typify the monastic lessons of prayer, austerity, hospitality, and silence. We see the ghost of all this beauty to-day, a perfect, though faded and lifeless, specimen of an Italian medieval cloister with its atmosphere of aloofness from the impious world outside, and with its many pictorial aids to meditation and self-denial. We are indeed fortunate to possess so precious, and on the whole so little spoiled, a memorial of the historic past.

At the extreme end of the long line of cells upstairs is to be seen the suite of three small rooms reserved for the prior of the community. And these cells still present almost the exact appearance they showed to Savonarola when he first entered the convent. Later he inhabited them as prior. His chair (whose model has been imitated for centuries by the wood-carvers of Florence), his robes, his crucifix, his writing-table are all preserved here. Stern, cramped, and gloomy, the inner study retains its original window with the heavy shutters and ponderous bolts. Everything here speaks with silent eloquence of the ascetic life of its most famous occupant. Indeed, it is impossible to inspect these dingy rooms without an intense feeling of reverence and compassion for one of the most picturesque figures of the Italian Renaissance. Here, at that table, at that desk, with that pen were composed and written the sermons and prophecies that for some years stirred not only Florence, but all Italy, and even Western Europe. In these very chambers dwelled their author, once the all-powerful arbiter of Florentine morals and politics; and from this quiet retreat was the Prior of St. Mark's eventually dragged forth with violence to suffer the cruel and ignominious fate which we see depicted for us in a contemporary painting that hangs on the wall.

Strangely enough, Savonarola's first visit to Florence brought him neither popular favour nor recognition. The rugged sentences and stern piety of the young Dominican made as yet no appeal to the people of Florence. Yet these years of comparative peace proved invaluable to him. He continued to study and learn, not only in his cell at

St. Mark's, but also among his fellow-men ; for much of his time was now spent in missions afield on behalf of his Order to Brescia, Genoa, and to many other towns of Northern Italy. Here, to audiences that showed themselves less critical than the captious Florentines, did the Friar announce his gravest warning, that triple set of ' Conclusions ' which to the last he never ceased to utter. These were (1) that the Church will be scourged ; (2) that she will be regenerated ; (3) that both these events will take place very shortly. The men of Brescia and Genoa believed the warning words of the earnest preacher, and as a consequence he began to acquire a wide reputation, not only as an orator, but also as a prophet of impending woe.

Returning to Florence, Savonarola stepped quickly and with ease into the position of eminence he had failed to attain on his previous visit. All men, including Lorenzo dei Medici, at once recognized the power and influence of the Dominican Friar. With Lorenzo dei Medici, the popular ruler of Florence who hid his tyrannical methods beneath a mask of geniality and culture, Savonarola was quickly brought into sharp antagonism. Two such original and diverse natures as these were bound to clash at close quarters. It is, however, agreeable to imagine that, though so bitterly and radically opposed, the two men must have owned some mutual respect for one another. Within a very short time of Savonarola's return to Florence in 1489, Lorenzo, with his unfailing intuition, measured accurately the rising influence of the friar. All too late he realized it was impossible now to check this troubler of his peace, this merciless but honest critic of his policy. With characteristic Medicean craft he determined therefore to win over, and even utilize for his own ends, this new and unexpected rival. The fiery harangues of the friar, couched in general terms against the prelates and princes of Italy, were not taken, therefore, in a personal sense by the cunning Lorenzo,

who affected to ignore these outbursts against tyranny
and corruption in high places. In 1491 Savonarola was
unanimously elected Prior, or Superior, of St. Mark's ; but
Lorenzo, however much he privately may have disliked the
choice of the friars, offered no objection as patron. He
even refused to show anger on hearing Savonarola's statement that he owed his election to God alone, and to no
earthly prince ; and he brushed aside the new Prior's
refusal to pay him the customary visit of ceremony with a
jest about the proverbial discourtesy of strangers.

It was in this early stage of Savonarola's popularity and
moral influence that the most striking event in all his career
took place. Lorenzo dei Medici had failed to soften the
Prior's hostility by his advances, yet so far he had made no
attempt openly to thwart him. The uncrowned autocrat
of Florence was already ailing with his fatal illness, and
possibly this may account for his strange indulgence or
indifference in this matter. Be that as it may, in March
1492, that climacteric year which may be said to mark the
Rubicon between the Middle and the Modern Ages, Lorenzo
had had the satisfaction of seeing the scarlet hat of a cardinal
publicly bestowed on his sixteen-year-old son Giovanni, the
future Pope Leo X. It was the first time that so high an
honour had been attained by this upstart mercantile family
of Florence ; but what availed all this earthly success when
Lorenzo himself was rapidly sinking to the grave, sick with
a wasting disease that the fashionable quacks of the day
could only aggravate with their absurd nostrums ? Only
a few weeks after the young Cardinal's departure to Rome,
' that sink of all iniquity ', as Lorenzo himself styled it, the
father lay dying at his favourite villa of Careggi outside
the walls of Florence. On his bed Lorenzo reflected on his
past career, and his reflections were by no means all pleasant
ones. His awakened conscience smote him for many past
misdeeds. His humanist deism afforded him scant comfort

at the last : he sighed for the final absolution of the ordinary Catholic penitent. Now, there must have been a score of Florentine priests ready to hear the dying man's confession and to absolve him, but of such sycophantic ministrations Lorenzo had no need. He bethought him of the Prior of St. Mark's, who (I shrewdly guess), was seldom out of his mind. Savonarola was sent for. He came and approached respectfully the bedside. Lorenzo, dismissing his friends to the next room, then began to speak with his visitor and confide to him his tortured conscience. But the Prior would only consent to hear the forthcoming confession on one condition, or rather on a threefold one. First, Lorenzo must have a lively faith in God's mercy, and to this he willingly assented. Secondly, all the money filched at different times from the public treasury and lavishly expended by the Medici for their own ends was to be repaid at once to the state. This second condition was highly distasteful to the dying prince, but after some hesitation he agreed to fulfil it. Last and most urgent of all, full liberty was to be restored to the republic of Florence by Lorenzo and his heir. But this third condition only met with stern silence ; and somehow I cannot but admire Lorenzo for his refusal to surrender in the face of death that which he certainly never would have surrendered in sound health. The Medici groaned aloud and then turned his face to the wall. Savonarola, after vainly waiting a while for an answer, finally left the death-chamber with the illustrious penitent unconfessed and unassoilzied. To my mind this is one of the most picturesque episodes in all history, and also one of the most touching. The incident, related and accepted by contemporary writers, in time grew discredited ; but Savonarola's chief biographer of recent years, Professor Pasquale Villari of Florence, has in my opinion marshalled a sufficiency of evidence to prove its authenticity, and for this alone he deserves our warm thanks. On thinking it all over, how could such a strange interview and duel of opposite minds have ended otherwise ? Both men were by nature unyielding, and though Lorenzo was a sinner and his chosen confessor a saint, on this occasion, I think, the pair parted with equal honours.

With Lorenzo gone, the power and influence of Savonarola waxed ever stronger. In place of the courteous tyrant there was now his son and heir, Piero dei Medici, a hot-headed youth, who owned all the vices and none of the ability of his late father. The Prior might now with safety have taken a personal line of attack against the enfeebled House of Medici. But the final fall of Medicean rule was in no wise directly due to Savonarola. It was due to a purely external political event to which I must now refer—the invasion of Italy by King Charles VIII of France.

This French invasion of Italy marks a new epoch not only in the history of Italy but of all Europe ; for it was the opening move in a coming policy of territorial aggression which, so far as Italy was concerned, lasted till the middle of the nineteenth century. Charles of France had been lightly and selfishly invited by the Duke of Milan, Ludovico Sforza, to seize the crown of Naples from its reigning monarch. After some demur Charles decided to accept this offer, and although the Italian people as a whole did not foresee the far-reaching consequences of such a novel step, a general sense of uneasiness prevailed. But if fear and anxiety were to be found in all the courts of Italy, there was one man at least to whom the news of the impending invasion proved tidings of great joy. This was Savonarola. His strong but narrow intelligence, cast in the medieval mould, could not or would not see ahead ; whilst the mystical vein in his nature urged him to regard this sudden and momentous incident as a direct intervention from Heaven itself. For the last ten years he had in his ' Conclusions ' been prophesying the coming punishment and reform of the Church, and in Charles's swift approach, what did he perceive but a notable fulfilment of his warnings ? In his eyes, therefore, Charles was the Divine instrument chosen to purify the Church in Italy, the corrupt Church that had now sunk to its lowest ebb owing to the recent election of the Borgia Pope, Alexander VI, with its accompanying scandals and bribery. Whilst princes and leaders hesitated or trembled, the Prior of St. Mark's started to hail Charles as the deliverer of Italy, as the appointed servant of the Almighty.

Events moved rapidly. Late in the summer of 1494 the young French sovereign, impelled by designs of military glory and conquest, started to cross the Alps, and then proceeded southwards along the coast. Nor was his army confined to Frenchmen, for it contained many outside mercenaries—Swiss mountaineers, German adventurers, and even archers from remote Scotland. Its artillery aroused the envy and admiration of the Italians, and so formidable appeared this motley host that any suggested schemes of barring its further progress were soon abandoned. As the French approached Pisa, Piero dei Medici in a fever of indecision hurried forward to meet Charles, to whom he weakly ceded the Tuscan frontier fortresses as to a conqueror. This feeble stroke of diplomacy, so unlike the astute dealing of his late father, aroused the fury of the expectant Florentines. Any lingering loyalty to the House of Medici was dissipated by the news of this base surrender of Florentine territory. A civic revolution broke out, and within a few hours Lorenzo's three sons, Piero, the Cardinal, and Giuliano, were all forcibly driven into exile.

This turbulent expulsion of the discredited Medici was, however, no doing of Savonarola's, for he was then absent from the city. He had left Florence to meet Charles on his march, and had been at once admitted to the royal presence, for the French king was not only anxious to see him, but even regarded him already with awe and veneration, so deeply had he been impressed by the reports of his prophetic powers. The Prior entered the royal pavilion in the camp, where Charles sat surrounded by his generals, and without wasting time on the usual preliminaries he started to address the would-be conqueror of Italy:

' O most Christian king, thou art an instrument in the hand of the Lord, who sendeth thee to relieve the woes of Italy, as for many years I have foretold ; and He sendeth thee to reform the Church, which now lieth prostrate in the dust. But if thou be not just and merciful ; if thou shouldst fail to respect the city of Florence, its women, its citizens, and its liberty ; if thou shouldst forget the task the Lord hath sent thee to perform, then shall He choose another to fulfil it. His hand will smite thee, and chastise thee with terrible scourges. These things say I unto thee in the name of the Lord.'

Having delivered his message the Prior returned to Florence, where his presence was sorely needed. In this case it was easy to destroy, but very difficult to reconstruct, for after sixty years of Medicean rule no real executive was ready to hand, now that the reigning family had fled. And it was at this critical hour that the Prior showed himself a true saviour of his adopted city.

In feverish haste the republican machinery of the state, long grown rusty from disuse under the sway of the Medici, was put together again, Savonarola being largely responsible for the necessary measures and alterations required for the purpose. ' He deserves,' says Villari, ' to be ranked amongst the greatest founders of republican states.' By the time Charles approached the western gate some sort of a responsible government was in being, with Savonarola for its guiding spirit. Nevertheless, Charles entered Florence in the guise of a victor. Mounted on a huge charger, clad in black velvet and mantle of cloth of gold and with couched lance, surrounded by the flower of French chivalry, the King made an imposing entrance into Florence. But on his alighting from horseback at the Duomo, general surprise and disappointment were expressed by all at the deformed little creature with the inane face, the dull, staring eyes, the long, thin nose, the tiny trunk and spindling legs ending in feet so enormous that tradition credited their owner with the possession of a sixth toe. ' He was in truth a mannikin,' records the Florentine chemist, Luca Landucci, in his quaint diary ; yet he adds that, as the alleged deliverer and cleanser of Italy, and the ally of their republic, all the Florentine women, old and young, great and small, fell in love with him !

But for the resuscitated Florentine Republic to entertain a King of France who preferred to consider himself the conqueror rather than the guest of the city was a difficult and delicate task. There were moments when a conflict between the foreign occupants and the citizens seemed inevitable ; and in such a crisis could anything have saved Florence from the vengeance of the French monarch with an army of 60,000 men close at hand ? ' If you sound your trumpets,' cried the bold Piero Capponi to the astonished King during one of these hot debates, ' we shall ring our bells ! ' These brave words have passed into history, but (to speak plainly) there could have been only one possible ending to so unequal a conflict between the trained troops of Charles VIII and the Florentine burghers called to arms. But behind the truculent threat of Capponi was the enormous influence exerted by Savonarola over the King, who undoubtedly held the Prior in genuine awe.

The vainglorious monarch seems almost to have cowered beneath the lectures and advice of the spiritual dictator, for in truth this was now the exact position that Savonarola held in the city. When therefore the Prior urged the King under penalty of God's vengeance to quit Florence and resume his interrupted journey to Naples, Charles meekly obeyed, and his army with him. Thus did Savonarola by his firmness and individuality save Florence from the horrors of bloodshed and pillage. Nor was this the only occasion on which Florence owed him her salvation. For, in the following June, Charles, humiliated, depressed, with half his forces scattered, and the remainder infected with a loathsome disease contracted before the walls of Naples, halted on his retreat northward at Siena, only a few leagues distant. There was a strong temptation for the King to approach Florence, and to repeat his visit of the previous autumn. Again only the Prior of St. Mark's stood between the city and unspeakable disaster. De Commines was sent as royal ambassador to confer with Savonarola in his convent. The answer returned to the King's message was that Charles should proceed northward without delay, under threat of the further displeasure of the Almighty. To enforce this piece of advice Savonarola himself proceeded a few days later to the French camp, where he once more rebuked the King face to face. Charles was terrified and convinced. He left Siena, so that Savonarola was able to return to Florence and announce from the pulpit the good news that the imminent danger was past.

Having saved Florence twice from ruin, Savonarola was now at the zenith of his power. He had in the last three or four years changed the whole conduct of the city ; from the immoral epicurean Florence of the Medici it had become a place full of preaching, praying, good works, contempt of vanities. Such a state of things could never last long anywhere, and in fickle, cultured Florence it was bound to collapse quickly. Savonarola's popular dictatorship of the Florentines failed in this respect : that he tried to combine overmuch of the spiritual with the material, and overmuch of the mystical with the practical. In direct political government you cannot mix any two antipathetic elements without seeing there is an equipoise. Only a Cromwell was capable of such nicety of balance. And even admitting that Savonarola's constructive powers were equal to those of the great Protector of England, he laboured under this disadvantage : he was a simple friar, and not a general with a devoted army at his back.

Savonarola's rapid fall came, however, not so much from the Florentines themselves as from Rome.

The condition of the Church had always been the Prior's favourite theme of lamentation and wrath, and he lived to see the pontificate of Alexander VI. His low opinion of that pope was not raised by the secret offer of a cardinal's hat, which he declined with disgust : ' I seek neither hat nor mitre ; I desire only what God has given to his saints, namely, death.' He continued to fulminate against the licentious state of the Roman court, but it cannot be too clearly pointed out that his opposition to the Pope was totally distinct from the attitude assumed a few years later by Martin Luther and the German reformers who claimed him as a forerunner of their own. Savonarola again and again expresses his full concurrence in all Catholic dogma, so that he was in no wise a religious reformer in the usual sense of that term, but merely a rebuker of the flagrant vices and corruption that then sullied the Church, and especially the papacy. Even Alexander later on was unable to accuse him openly of heresy. Indeed, the main argument of the ban of excommunication, which the Pope was now preparing to launch against him, was an alleged refusal on Savonarola's part to report himself at Rome, and his further refusal to accept the Pope's scheme for adding his priory of St. Mark's to a new Tusco-Roman congregation of the Dominican Order. These charges, whether they be deemed serious or trivial, are clearly matters of personal discipline, not of faith or dogma. Possibly Savonarola's partisans in Rome, who were both numerous and influential, might have

placated Alexander but for the Prior's unswerving attitude
of defiance towards the Pope. Although the Prior was
careful to explain that in thus attacking Alexander it was
the man, not the Supreme Pontiff, he was aiming at, the
Borgia Pope naturally writhed under the lash. In May
1497 the papal brief of excommunication was issued, and
after some delay it was pronounced from the leading pulpits
of Florence. It was not unexpected ; and Savonarola, after
publicly protesting his innocence of these papal accusations
of indiscipline and disobedience, bowed dutifully to the
papal command. He ceased to preach, and retired altogether to his quiet cloister-garth in St. Mark's. Here he
spent his days in revising and preparing for the press his
earlier writings, especially his *Triumph of the Cross*, his most
popular work. As he wrote and meditated thus in the
simple apartment that we visit to-day, he may have appreciated this enforced rest from labour, for his fervid orations
in the pulpit always left him unnerved and exhausted. He
owned the feeling too that the majority of the Florentines
sympathized with him in his present conflict with the
papacy, although they dared not raise a hand to oppose the
Pope's policy, and openly dreaded the placing of their city
under a spiritual interdict, that medieval weapon of terror,
which the enraged Alexander was now threatening.

But though this retirement may have been welcome in
itself it formed the first step towards the final catastrophe.
It was in and from the pulpit that the Prior derived his
seemingly magical power over the Florentines ; it was his
earnest eloquence and threats of Divine wrath that had
brought about the late change of feeling among the citizens.
Once that silver tongue was silenced in obedience to the
Pope's command his enemies, the *Arrabiati*, had matters
pretty much their own way. The growing opposition and
intrigue against the Prior were only met by his silence.
When Savonarola did at last decide to defy the papal order

and to restart preaching in the old way, it was too late ; for the whole of the citizens with the exception of the *Piagnoni*, or thick-and-thin followers of the Prior, were now all for treating with Alexander ; and even those who were not ill-disposed towards the Prior put expediency at this juncture before gratitude.

Meantime, negotiations were proceeding smoothly with Rome, the Pope accommodating himself to the wishes of the Republic which was now quite willing to arrest the Prior in Florence, though it still declined to send him to Rome for trial. To put it plainly, an unholy bargain was being concocted between the Florentine government and the Pope ; and when historians abuse the Medici and their rule (which is generally the fashion) it should always be remembered that it was the Florentine Republic and not the Medici that was responsible for one of the meanest political crimes ever conceived and perpetrated. The terms of this bargain were—on the papal side, the arrest, trial, and execution of the Prior by the Florentine Republic, whereby the Pope would be relieved from the prospect of any General Council of the Church and also be avenged for the hard truths spoken of his evil life ; secondly, the detachment of Florence from its present alliance with France, which was specially cherished by Savonarola. For the Republic, there would be no further fear of any papal interdict with its paralysing effects on the social life and commerce of the city ; also the permission for the collection of a clerical tithe which was badly needed for the state coffers. Once the Signory and the Borgia Pope had come to terms, the fate of Savonarola was sealed. On the eve of Palm Sunday, April 7th, 1498, a number of the *Arrabiati*, with the tacit approval of the Signory, stormed the convent of St. Mark's. After a fierce and bloody combat, which he vainly tried to quell, Savonarola and his two most faithful friars, Fra Domenico and Fra Silvestro, were dragged through the streets at midnight and lodged in the condemned, cells of the civic palace, the Palazzo Vecchio. Here for six weeks Savonarola was kept a close prisoner with torture applied at intervals, and was subjected to every indignity and piece of malign treachery which the human mind is capable of inventing. His case was hopeless, for on the very day of his violent arrest his sole remaining champion, King Charles VIII of France, died suddenly of apoplexy at Amboise.

Under the torture, which consisted chiefly of being hung by a rope till he fainted from the pain, and then being revived to consciousness by burning coals held to the soles of his feet, Savonarola · thwarted his tormentors and examiners on every ground except one. That one ground whereon alone he gave out conflicting or repentant answers was the matter of his vaunted powers of prophecy. But here the Prior had himself often been deceived ; he hardly knew his own mind on this very question, so that it is scarcely to be marvelled at that here he gave forth an uncertain note. On politics, Church discipline, questions of faith and morals he never once wavered, though tortured and tempted and urged with every threat and blandishment to deny or admit something that would strengthen his enemy's case. Naturally, he was condemned by a majority of the Signory and sentenced to death. It was a foregone conclusion. By agreement with Alexander two commissioners were now sent from Rome to Florence, who again tried and tortured the Prior and pronounced an ecclesiastical verdict, ordering the three prisoners to be degraded, unfrocked and handed over for punishment to the secular arm. Savonarola received his sentence unmoved ; Fra Domenico received his with ecstasy of joy ; poor Fra Silvestro, a weak, dreamy creature, alone trembled and sobbed and showed himself ready to commit any perjury to save his life. On May 22nd, late at night, the three prisoners were allowed to meet, and their meeting was most affectionate, Savonarola comforting and strengthening the faint-hearted Fra Silvestro. Early next morning, May 23rd, the three Dominican friars were led forth to execution in the great square, which was packed with an immense crowd, mostly hostile and eager to behold the humiliation and agony of the man who had built up and twice saved the new Florentine Republic. A long stage had been erected from the platform before the palace, and it stretched far out into the square. At its farthest end there stood a gallows with three chains and ropes attached; below the scaffold was laid a huge pile of faggots. On emerging from the palace gate the three condemned men were publicly stripped of their black and white Dominican robes, a piece of indignity unexpected at this stage by Savonarola. He was deeply moved by this affront, so much so that he exclaimed, ' Holy gown, how dearly did I long to wear thee ! Thou wert granted me by God's grace, and I have ever kept thee unstained. Now I forsake thee not, but am bereft of thee.'

Savonarola and his two colleagues were now clad only in their woollen tunics—were in fact standing half-naked before the vast concourse in the square. In this condition they were next led before the Bishop of Vaison, himself a Dominican, who formally degraded his illustrious brother-friar from the Church Militant on earth. From the Bishop the trio were next led to the papal commissioner, Cardinal Remolino, who confirmed the sentence, and formally handed them to the public hangman. Amid jeers from the *Arrabiati* close to the scaffold, the three friars were then hanged. Savonarola was in the forty-sixth year of his age.

Scarcely had life left the quivering bodies on the cross-beam than the executioners below ignited the pyre, and the corpses were quickly wrapped in flames and smoke. Some of the mob flung stones at the bodies; others (including several women) sought to obtain pieces of the falling flesh to keep as holy relics. This pious office was soon roughly stopped by the civic guards, and before the flames had wholly consumed the flesh and bones the charred remains were by orders of the magistrates cut down and heaved into carts. The carts were driven to the old bridge over the Arno, and their contents were thence flung into the river. Yet even here, despite the violence of the mob, many of the *Piagnoni* sought to extricate mementoes of their beloved master. Such relics were later enclosed in boxes of gold and silver and treasured in many Florentine families for centuries.

When in due course better times supervened, and men and women needed no longer to conceal their devotion to the Prior of San Marco, the site of his martyrdom was annually, on May 23rd, covered with wreaths. The exact spot is now marked by a bronze plaque in the pavement of the square with a medallion profile of the friar surrounded by the martyr's palm. His memory is still held very dear by the Florentines, and I myself have often seen this historic site heaped with roses and carnations on that anniversary.

> Only the actions of the just
> Smell sweet and blossom in the dust,

is literally true of Savonarola, for each year the dusty piazza becomes redolent of spring blossoms in memory of this uncanonized saint.

. . . . .

Within three weeks of that iniquitous execution there was nominated Secretary of State to the Florentine Republic a citizen hitherto unknown to fame, one Niccolò Machiavelli. He seems to rise phœnix-like from that funeral pile of ashes. I have already said that these closing years of the fifteenth century form the dividing line between the medieval and the modern, between the age of faith and the age of science and scepticism. The world's rapid pace through this stage of transition was marked by many signs and incidents : the spread of printing, the influence of the new learning, the discovery of America, the new wars of aggression, the researches in medicine and astronomy ; but nowhere is the swift transition from the old to the new era so clearly marked out for us as in this particular conjunction of Savonarola and Machiavelli. Yet it is a remarkable circumstance, whilst Savonarola stands typical for the obsolete system of the Middle Ages, and Machiavelli for modern thought and progress, the memory of the pious friar survives to-day fresher and sweeter than that of his brilliant successor. Ten pilgrims to Florence go to visit the rooms of the Prior in St. Mark's to one that pauses with reverence before the great tomb in Santa Croce that political admirers have reared to Machiavelli. The abiding influence of his unique genius and of his patriotic appeal remains, true enough ; but the tribute of personal love is wanting. On the other hand, who could omit a visit to those tiny dark chambers in San Marco's convent, with their sad memories of ' this hero of the eternal tragedy of the human soul,' as Bishop Creighton finely calls Savonarola ? He, or she, must in truth be either a dullard or a hopeless philistine who cannot feel strangely moved in that pathetic atmosphere. For man is compounded of two elements, the material and the spiritual ; it should be his aim to keep a nice balance between the rival claims. No doubt, Savonarola leaned overmuch to the spiritual side ; hence his failure and his martyrdom. But it was a noble error that posterity has condoned with pride and affection.

V

NICCOLÒ MACHIAVELLI

(1469–1527)

LOOKING down the vista of the ages we perceive here and there individuals who stand erect, like Saul, King of Israel, a head and shoulders above their fellow-men. Most of these human giants are, however, later on adjudged but as leaders of their own generation ; their wisdom and their prowess shrink in the eyes of posterity ; their words, their deeds, their writings in time fall into their due place and proportion. But at long intervals there arises a Man whose teaching or example continues with no lack of force, perhaps even with increasing force, centuries after his mortal life has spent its little day. Amongst this scanty band of the world's Immortals must be counted the Florentine thinker and statesman Niccolò Machiavelli. His name is familiar to all, but his reputation remains dubious. Lord Morley has expressed a doubt as to whether Machiavelli has ever been properly understood in this country, although he willingly admits that a strangely modern current of popular sympathy, mingling with all his writings, makes him 'a contemporary of any age and a citizen of all countries'. And the late Lord Acton endorses this estimate by calling Machiavelli 'no vanishing type, but a constant and contemporary influence'. No vanishing type, but a constant and contemporary influence ! To my mind this pithy sentence sums up admirably Machiavelli's present claim to our study, our remembrance, and our respect.

Niccolò Machiavelli was born on May 3rd, 1469, the son of one Bernardo Machiavelli, a Florentine lawyer of good family but of meagre fortune. By a curious coincidence, it is worth noting that the coat of arms of the ancient family of Machiavelli, whose most famous member has for centuries past been vulgarly branded as an atheist and a scoffer, emblazons the Holy Cross and Nails of the Passion ; in heraldic parlance—*On a field argent a cross between four holy nails in saltire azure.* Instinctively, one recalls Kit Marlowe's ' Prologue ' to his play, ' The Jew of Malta ', wherein the ghost of ' Nick Machiavel ' is made to declare, ' I count Religion but a childish toy, and say there is no sin but ignorance.' At the date of his birth Lorenzo dei Medici, ' Il Magnifico ', the untitled and officially unacknowledged sovereign of Florence, was ruling the city with an iron hand concealed in a velvet glove. He was, however, merely carrying out the traditional policy of his grandsire, the wise Cosimo dei Medici, equally father and first hereditary tyrant of his country, who always preferred the internal power to the external pomp of kingship. Taken in one aspect, Florence of the *Quattrocento* was but a large, wealthy, free city of Italy, owning neither the antique prestige of Rome nor yet the colonial expansion of Venice and Genoa. Nevertheless, the true spirit of that brilliant age was more clearly expressed in Florence than in more powerful cities, thanks to the sharp wit of the Florentines themselves. It offers us a fascinating picture, the Florence of Lorenzo dei Medici, and it has perhaps not been over-coloured or over-praised for us by Macaulay in his florid essay on Machiavelli. Yet to the discerning thinker of that day its very existence must have seemed precarious. In Italy the political forces were constantly shifting, thereby requiring all Lorenzo's diplomatic cunning to keep the steady balance of power, on which hung the fate of his own Florence. For there was no Florentine army of defence ; there was much internal unrest among the citizens ; there was ever the vague haunting dread of a sudden invasion of Italy from beyond the Alps. Despite this secret fear in all men's hearts, the cities of Northern Italy, and Florence in particular, continued to lead the van of progress, culture, and civilization to a wondering and imitating Europe, that was perhaps not a little envious. And with the fall of Constantinople in 1453 Italy, and again Florence in a special degree, added to her intellectual wealth the liberated stores of Greek learning and science. Thus Niccolò Machiavelli had the honour to be born a citizen of the most cultured, the most artistic the most critical city of Europe, then at the zenith of its fame and beauty. No wonder, then, that Machiavelli, like his equally famous contemporary and fellow-countryman, Michelangelo Buonaroti, always bore and displayed the utmost affection and loyalty to Florence.

What events can the boy Niccolò Machiavelli have recalled in his infancy? Perhaps only a vague recollection of the fêtes and processions of the genial Lorenzo dei Medici, who wrote tolerable verse himself and strongly encouraged his quick-witted subjects to compose love poems rather than polemical tracts. It may well be that the boy when in his seventh year heard talk of the birth of another son to Lorenzo, a singularly ugly baby with squinting eyes, christened Giovanni, and afterwards destined to become His Holiness Pope Leo the Tenth. He must certainly have remembered all the pother, and perhaps may have seen the actual affair, of the attempted assassination of Lorenzo and his brother Giuliano at the Easter Mass in the cathedral, 1478, for he was about nine at the date of the historic Conspiracy of the Pazzi. He may have watched the boyish sculptor, Michelangelo Buonaroti, at work in the gardens of the Medici palace, feverishly making copies of the classical busts and fragments brought by Lorenzo from the ruins of Rome. Doubtless he went to hear the new preacher, Girolamo Savonarola, in the cathedral, whose vast nave proved hardly sufficient to contain the audiences that hung intent on the sermons of the bold, impassioned friar. Did he, I sometimes wonder, form one of that crowd which went to meet the young Giovanni dei Medici on his return from the neighbouring abbey of Fiesole, where the Pope's envoy had just bestowed the scarlet hat of a cardinal on this lucky youth of sixteen ? Perhaps young Niccolò, now in his twenty-third year, was on that occasion filled with seething discontent, as he observed the ease wherewith a mere stripling, provided he be born a prince, can obtain the highest earthly honours ; perhaps he speculated bitterly as to whether his own genius—for genius always recognizes itself—would ever be appreciated. He must have been excited by the news of the great Lorenzo's death, with its accompanying gossip concerning the visit that Savonarola paid to the dying tyrant's bedside. He must have watched with contemptuous disgust the feeble policy of Lorenzo's heir, Piero il Pazzo, ' the headstrong ', whose incapacity quickly broke the mutual bond between the Medicean House and the Florentine people, so delicately welded by his father and forefathers. He saw for the first time in the autumn of 1494 the awakened fury of a Florentine mob, and the violent expulsion of the three Medici brothers, Piero, Giuliano, and the Cardinal Giovanni. No doubt he was among the sightseers who watched the miserable and vainglorious King Charles VIII of France, and his powerful army enter the gates. It may well have been that (like his intrepid fellow-citizen Piero Capponi) he played a bold and patriotic part during this curious foreign occupation of Florence, wherein the French king called himself a conqueror, whilst the civic magnates with plucky obstinacy persisted in treating the uninvited French monarch as their guest. Later, Machiavelli must have witnessed the religious revival under the new popular dictator Savonarola. I can imagine his mental attitude towards this spiritual tyrant's actions and theories, finding something to approve, some-

thing to denounce, and a good deal to ridicule. How, for
instance, Machiavelli must have smiled at the bonfires
lighted in the streets for the obedient public to immolate
their cherished vanities—lascivious pictures and statues,
bottles of perfume, false hair, cosmetics, ribbons. And last
and most lurid scene of all, he must surely have attended at
a very different sort of bonfire in the broad space before the
civic palace, when the fickle Florentines slew at the stake
their late spiritual dictator. What a practical lesson on
the rise and fall of a popular favourite ! What a satire on a
religious revival, first to burn the gauds of sin and then to
burn the preacher who had denounced them ! We may
feel sure these later events were all carefully noted and
docketed within that shrewd, capacious brain.

I have described this list of leading events in Florence
at some length, and for this reason—that the name and
personality of Machiavelli only emerge for the first time
from obscurity after the burning of Savonarola by the
Florentine ' Signory ', or Government, of the Republic.
For of his early life practically nothing has hitherto been
discovered beyond the fact that he was a simple Florentine
citizen, and must have known intimately, and probably
have witnessed, all the events I have just recorded. He
was now—that is, May 1498—just twenty-nine years of age,
and this plain circumstance is itself well worth noting.
Nowadays twenty-nine is reckoned a very suitable age for
the promising aspirant to start in political life. It was far
otherwise in the era of the Italian Renaissance. Age owned
then a totally different significance or value from its present-
day acceptance. You were a young man in your teens—
witness Giovanni dei Medici created a cardinal at sixteen.
You were a man in the twenties, like Caesar Borgia ; you
were regarded as middle-aged at thirty, like the humanist
Pico della Mirandola, Machiavelli's own contemporary ;
you were old at forty—Lorenzo dei Medici had died almost

of senile decay in his forty-second year ; you were deemed
a fossil at fifty, or if you were still active at that advanced
age you were considered a miracle of health and vigour.
Nor is the reason far to seek. Existence was painfully
strenuous, and human life held very cheap in those stirring
days. To realize this fact one has but to read that wonderful
human document, the autobiography of Benvenuto Cellini,
who is himself but a generation behind Machiavelli. Add
to this the fact that the science of medicine had sunk to its
lowest ebb at this period. The old classical teaching was
lost ; the learning of the medieval Arab physicians was
forgotten ; such doctors as there were—and apparently
they existed in plenty—were almost without exception
impudent and unscrupulous quacks, who only gave their
unfortunate patients filthy or fatal prescriptions : a sapphire
pounded up in white wine, hot pigeon's blood dropped on
the soles of the feet, a frog's bowels stirred with a splinter
of the true Cross, or some other recipe equally repulsive or
absurd. Indeed, medicine in Western Europe in the days
of the Medici was on a level with the witchcraft of tropical
Africa to-day ; the rise of Vesalius and the anatomical
school of Bologna lay still far ahead in the future. It is
such a fantastic medley of learning and ignorance, of
splendour and squalour, this marvellous Italian Renaissance.

Savonarola was executed publicly on May 23rd, 1498,
and on June 10th following Niccolò Machiavelli received his
official appointment as secretary to the *Dieci di pace e di
libertà* (the Council of Ten for Peace and Liberty), which
may be described as the Foreign Office of the Signory, or
Government, of the Florentine Republic. It was a subordinate post ; its holder was but a paid clerk ; yet it is
important to note that this modest appointment marks the
limit of public trust Machiavelli ever contrived to attain,
though he had nearly thirty years of life still to run. Now,
this Council of Ten was largely concerned with the relations

of the Florentine Republic to the other states of Italy, and its duties frequently compelled its members to proceed not only to the various capitals but even to the camps of campaigning armies. Such journeys afield, and especially that to the camp of Caesar Borgia, gave Machiavelli a rare opportunity to perfect his study of men, and assuredly he made the most of all he saw and heard. Hitherto his outlook had been restricted to his native city ; now in an official capacity he was to observe mankind and its leaders in Rome, Milan, Venice, Ferrara, and elsewhere. From his obtaining of this confidential post it is therefore evident that his native genius must have been recognized, however faintly and imperfectly, by his fellow-citizens. For he was not learned according to the pedantic standard of his day ; like all true men of genius he drew his inspiration not so much from books as from meditation and experience.

In a certain sense Machiavelli was now living a double life. There was Niccolò Machiavelli, the conscientious servant of the state, taking his duties very seriously, deferential to his masters whilst secretly laughing at their foibles ; drawing his modest salary of about one hundred golden florins, which he doubtless found a most welcome addition to his meagre patrimony, for he was already a married man with a growing family. On the other hand, there was Niccolò Machiavelli, the deep and prescient thinker, hungry to add to his store of practical knowledge and experience ; watching with furtive eyes the princes, politicians, and generals that passed before him ; studying the trend of the movements of the day ; and ever attuning each fresh adventure to his own innate gift of vision.

It was during these first few years of this peripatetic diplomacy that Machiavelli was brought into close contact with a certain young prince, whose name has been coupled by posterity with his own. I mean, of course, Caesar Borgia, who was the favourite son of the reigning Pope

Alexander VI, a Spaniard. To say outright that Caesar Borgia was Machiavelli's ideal prince, which is still not an uncommon assertion, is less than half the truth. Certainly, Machiavelli in his most famous treatise, *The Prince*, praises Caesar, but only for certain definite qualities and definite actions. For already he was beginning to perceive the dire necessity for the foundation of a new state in Italy—*the* new state—which should be powerful enough to prevent or repel a second invasion from France or the Empire. And in this precocious young man, who owned a heart to resolve, a head to contrive, and an arm to execute, he found not a little to admire. In spite of a natural prejudice against his papal and alien birth, Machiavelli was too generous and too shrewd a critic not to admit that Caesar had the stuff of a great ruler and organizer in him. At this time, with the help of his father Pope Alexander, he was busily erecting a new principality in the Romagna on sound and definite lines. Like our first Tudor king, Henry VII, now on the English throne, the young Borgia was stamping out the embers of feudal tyranny ; he was encouraging commerce ; he was promising justice and security to the oppressed farmers and artisans ; he was also arranging for an adequate militia of defence. All these truly sound traits of administration Machiavelli saw, noted, and praised. That in his pursuit of this desirable end Caesar employed such means as treachery and the assassin did not in the least affect Machiavelli's judgement. Trickery and the dagger were recognized weapons of statecraft at that time, and nobody protested at their employment or was scandalized by their success.

This Borgian phase, if I may so term it, of Machiavelli's early career came to an abrupt ending in 1503, for in the summer of that year Pope Alexander expired suddenly in Rome—not, as vulgarly supposed, of a dose of poison, but of a feverish chill aggravated by the doses of his own physician. Caesar Borgia himself, also a victim to malarial

fever, was lying helpless on a sick-bed. As a direct consequence of this double misfortune the Borgian realm, which
was to become the nucleus of a national Italian state,
quickly collapsed, and its youthful artificer had to fly from
Italy, an exile never to return.

The changes that followed on Alexander's death were in
Machiavelli's eyes greatly for the worse. After a short
interval, the Sacred College (of whom Medici was now a
prominent member) elected Cardinal Giuliano della Rovere
for Pope, with the title of Julius II. This famous pontiff
(quite unintentionally, it is only fair to state) wrought an
immensity of mischief to Italy; for he was the practical
founder of the States of the Church, whereby the popes,
hitherto regarded mainly as spiritual potentates, became
henceforth definitely temporal sovereigns, who freely and
openly mingled in the political intrigues of Europe. Old,
ignorant, rough, coarse, yet withal energetic and far from
unpopular, Julius II may be taken as representing the
secular papacy in its most dangerous aspect. At the opening
of his reign he helped to reduce Venice, now the leading
Italian state, to impotence by calling in the French under
Louis XII; he proceeded to grab Venetian cities and
districts to add to the new papal dominions; he set a
shocking example of indifference to religion—far worse
than the execrated Alexander; his love of military pomp
and power was an open scandal in any priest, let alone a
pope. Such a spectacle aroused the anger and loathing of
Machiavelli; and it is specially interesting to note that his
only contemporary intellectual peer, Erasmus of Rotterdam,
evidently shared his feelings in the matter. The great
Dutch scholar was actually present at Julius's triumphal
entry into Bologna, which city he had annexed in 1507.
Erasmus was so appalled by what he saw on this occasion
that in the *Dialogue*, called ' Julius Exclusus ', or ' Pope
Julius excluded from Heaven ', the great northern humanist

makes the warrior-pope thus boast to the horrified St. Peter :

> ' Would that you had seen me carried in state in Bologna, and afterwards in Rome ! Carriages and horses, troops under arms, generals prancing and galloping, handsome pages, torches flaming, dishes steaming, pomp of bishops, glory of cardinals, trophies, spoils, shouts that rent the sky, trumpets blaring, cannon thundering, largesse scattered to the mob, and I borne aloft, the head and author of it all ! Scipio and Caesar were nothing in comparison with me ! '

But this was only part of the mischief. Having discomfited Venice and having gained Bologna by aid of the French, Julius next conceived the fatal notion of expelling the French from Italy by calling in the Spaniards. For this new purpose Spanish troops arrived by sea, and after the battle of Ravenna on Easter Day, 1512, the French, it is true, had unwillingly to retire across the Alps. But the victorious Spanish troops remained, and from that day almost to our own time portions of Italy have been permanently occupied by foreign armies. Thus the double legacy of Julius to his native Italy was the settled domination of the foreigner, and the creation of the Papal States as a third-rate European power. We can imagine Machiavelli's righteous detestation of the obstinate, greedy, disreputable, short-sighted old Julius, whose misdeeds have been painted in the halls of the Vatican by the divine Raphael ' with matchless art and with matchless unveracity '. How bitterly in his *Discorsi*, or Lectures, does he upbraid the timid, superstitious lord of Perugia, Gianpaolo Baglioni, for not massacring Julius and his whole train of cardinals and courtiers when he had a unique opportunity of so doing. It is a famous passage this, in which Machiavelli lashes the Perugian despot for his

rank moral cowardice, the human vice that of all others
Machiavelli most hated and despised.

' Men know not either how to be splendidly wicked or
wholly good, and they shrink in consequence from such
crimes as are stamped with an inherent greatness, or
disclose a nobility of nature. Thus Gianpaolo Baglioni,
who thought nothing of incurring the guilt of incest or of
murdering his kinsmen, could not, or more truly durst not,
avail himself of a fair occasion to do a deed which all
would have admired ; which would have won for him a
deathless fame, as the first to teach the Prelates how little
those who live and reign as they do are to be esteemed,
and which would have displayed a greatness far trans-
cending any infamy or danger that would attach to it.'

By a most unfortunate chance the Florentine Republic,
which Machiavelli served with eager fidelity for over fourteen years, was committed to an official sympathy, hardly a
formal alliance, with France. This was a survival of the
eccentric policy of Savonarola, who always chose to regard
the French king as God's chosen instrument to chastise the
corruption of the Church in Italy. So illogical and unpat-
riotic a view must have been most hateful to Machiavelli,
but the Signory persisted in this mischievous attitude. As
a direct consequence, after the battle of Ravenna the
Republic found itself placed in a dangerous and difficult
position, especially when Julius, at the request, no doubt, of
Cardinal dei Medici, decided to restore the exiled family of
Medici to their native city by means of the Spanish troops
at his disposal. Florence was thoroughly alarmed at the
prospect ; there was talk of compromise, even of surrender ;
the dormant faction of the *Palleschi*, or Medicean party,
started to agitate. But the meaning of fear was unknown
to Machiavelli. In this critical situation he saw only a

golden opportunity of putting one of his cherished schemes into effect, namely, self-defence by the whole people against any outside attempt at interference. He had already induced the Signory to raise a militia and train-bands, and, thanks to his own infectious enthusiasm, the order was given for more men to be equipped and drilled. But, alas! a capable army of defence cannot be raised in a few weeks, and in spite of Machiavelli's exertions and high hopes this hastily levied force of Tuscan peasants and citizens was easily routed by the Pope's Spanish veterans at Prato, a little walled city only eight miles north of Florence. The victory was followed by the sack of Prato, of impious memory, with its long tale of butchery and sacrilege. So terrified was the Signory that it decided to surrender Florence practically without conditions. The leading members of the republican government fled, the Medicean faction seized the city, and there was a general sense of impending vengeance from the approaching Medici. With the Cardinal at Prato were his brother Giuliano, a mild, cultivated gentleman; his nephew Lorenzo, an arrogant young prince who rejected all the old burgher traditions of his House; and his bastard cousin Giulio, who was afterwards to become Pope Clement VII. In due course these four distinguished exiles entered in triumph the city which had expelled, and even outlawed, them eighteen years before.

Thus Machiavelli failed completely in his efforts to save Florence from the despotism of the Medici.

Here, then, was a fine test for the mettle of a man. What was Machiavelli's attitude at this crisis? No doubt he reasoned out the situation, and it is easy to gather his conclusions from his subsequent conduct. He did not sneak away, like other members of the late Signory. On the contrary, he decided to remain; and not only to remain but to offer his services to the new masters of Florence.

After all, the Medici *were* true Florentines ; the Cardinal's father had been the acknowledged ruler of Florence ; the old executive was gone, and with it his old official post ; then why not a new post under Medicean rule ? This line of argument seemed easy and natural enough to Machiavelli's quick brain, but how would it appeal to the Cardinal ? That was the question. And here let me pause for a moment to discuss this attitude of easy adaptation to changed circumstances. Why should not a citizen serve his city or state under any existing form of government ? Why not indeed ? That was Machiavelli's point of view, and in later times such a theory was upheld and acted on by Talleyrand, who served France as priest, bishop, deputy, minister, ambassador, and (by no means least) as simple citizen. Thus both Machiavelli and Talleyrand believed only in governments *de facto* ; both were ready to serve any government loyally so long as it existed, and to transfer that same loyalty intact to the next stable executive. How far such an attitude is morally defensible must be left to individual judgement.

For this purpose Machiavelli drew up for the Cardinal a carefully worded letter, wherein he ventured to give His Eminence some sound advice, whilst at the same time professing his earnest desire to serve the House of Medici. So admirable was the tenor of this document that Medici, though he must have regarded its author with grave mistrust, certainly acted on some of its hints. Amongst other thoughtful suggestions, Machiavelli particularly warned the returning Medici not to attempt the recovery of their confiscated family estates, which had in many cases been bought and sold more than once in good faith, but rather to recoup themselves for their old losses out of the public treasury, which was wholly at their mercy. ' For,' he added, ' men will sooner forget the death of their father than the loss of their farms.'

But although this ingenuous appeal brought the ex-secretary of the late Council of Ten to the favourable notice of the Cardinal, yet it did not save him altogether from certain unpleasant consequences of the recent fall of the Republic. Machiavelli was arrested, imprisoned, and examined, this last stage including, according to the almost inevitable practice of the day, some turns on the rack. There was, however, no vindictive cruelty in all this ; it was merely the contemporary method of refreshing the human memory. On the whole, the late republican official came off lightly, and ere long he was permitted to go and reside on his small estate at San Casciano outside the city gates. He was, in fact, placed on parole, for he was not allowed to pass the walls of Florence. In this mitigated exile, then, still aching from the torture, we must picture to ourselves the author of *The Prince* moodily pacing the lanes and pathways of the Tuscan country-side ; perhaps walking to some lofty point of vantage so as to gain a glimpse of the great dome and the towers of Florence ; eating out his heart in poverty and enforced idleness. He was now forty-three, and we can depict him as middle-aged to elderly in appearance, wearing the long, loose robe with the round cap and flowing crimson veil, or *lucco*, which the older citizens of Florence usually affected. But we cannot, alas ! conjure up his face and features, for, as I was once told by one of the two greatest authorities on Machiavelli, there exists no authentic likeness of him, either in stone or on canvas. Indeed, the only genuine portrait we have of him is the miserable little woodcut on the title-page of the so-called ' Testina ' edition of his collected works, which was not published till 1550, more than twenty years after his death. Certainly, out in Italy you will often come across pictures and statues of this illustrious Florentine, but I fear the face in all cases is more or less fanciful.

Machiavelli was now thrown on his own resources. He

had his small estate, or rather farm ; he had his wife, Marietta Corsini, and his children, of whom he seems to have been moderately fond ; he had his library ; and, above all, he had the interior life of his own fertile mind. To me it always seems especially wonderful that this man, who in his most fortunate phase was but the paid clerk of a petty republic, and was now poor, neglected, discredited, and an exile, should even in his own day have shed such a pervading influence. Despite all, the sheer genius of Machiavelli broods, as the historian Bishop Creighton finely observes, like a thundercloud over the whole of this pregnant period of history.

As to his manner of spending the long, long days of this enforced retirement we fortunately have first-hand evidence. This is contained in a letter dated December 10th, 1513, sixteen months after the surrender of Florence to the Cardinal dei Medici, now reigning in Rome as Pope Leo the Tenth. This was written by Machiavelli himself to his friend, Francesco Vettori, on whose good offices he was relying to obtain the confidence of the suspicious Medici.

' I am at my farm. . . . I rise with the sun, and go into a wood of mine that is being cut, where I remain two hours inspecting the work of the previous day and conversing with the woodcutters, who have always some trouble on hand among themselves or with their neighbours. When I leave the wood I proceed to a well, and thence to the place which I use for snaring birds, with a book under my arm—Dante or Petrarch, or one of the minor poets, like Tibullus or Ovid. I read the story of their passions and let their lives remind me of my own, which is a pleasant pastime for a while. Next I take the road, enter the inn-door, talk with the passers-by, inquire the news of the neighbourhood, listen to a variety of matters, and make note of the different tastes and humours of men. This brings me to dinner-time, when I join my family and eat the poor produce of my farm. After dinner I go back to the inn, where I generally find the host and a butcher, a miller and a pair of bakers. With these companions I play the fool all day at cards or back-gammon : a thousand squabbles, a thousand insults and abusive dialogues take place, while we haggle over a farthing, and shout loud enough to be heard from San Casciano.—But when evening falls, I go home and enter my writing-room. On the threshold I remove my country habit, filthy with mud and mire, and array myself in courtly garments ; thus worthily attired I make my way into the ancient courts of men of old where they receive me with love . . . and for four hours' space I feel no annoyance ; I forget all care ; poverty cannot frighten, nor death appal me.'

Later, he writes wistfully again to Vettori :

' I wish these lords of the House of Medici would begin to make some use of me, were it only to the task of rolling a stone.'

And of his many attempts at this period to ingratiate himself with Leo X we may mention a sprightly comedy, the ' Mandragola ', or ' Love Potion ', one of the earliest and (being Machiavelli's) one of the wittiest and boldest of Italian farces. Much as the court of Versailles in after years made merry over the seeming absurdities of Beau-marchais' ' Mariage de Figaro ' on the eve of the French Revolution, so now were Leo and his frivolous prelates convulsed with laughter at the grim jests, the biting satire, and the merciless exposure of Italian priestcraft and the abuses of the confessional contained in the ' Mandragola '. But the success of his play only won him the applause and not the political confidence of Leo and the Medici.

Nevertheless, though he was thus left severely to himself, this compulsory isolation bore perhaps more valuable fruit than if Machiavelli had been graciously restored to the public life that his restless soul craved. Here, in his solitude, his active mind worked the more vigorously ; his states-man's vision grew clearer ; his detachment became more complete. Here it was that he began to perceive a new opportunity for the liberation of Italy. With all their faults the Medici were true Italians ; their head was not only master of Florence and Urbino, but was also pope of Rome and ruler of the Roman realms that the late Julius had consolidated. Was there not in this double concentration of power, both secular and spiritual, a rare chance for a member of the House of Medici to arise, to found the new state that would in time absorb all Italy ; that might in due course and with good fortune become even a UNITED ITALY ? And this United Italy of his dreams and aspirations, might it not grow sufficiently powerful to expel the foreign invader and revive the sunken glories of ancient Rome ? Could not this ideal prince of the House of Medici call his laggard countrymen to arms with a rousing appeal to Italian patriotism and unity ? At the very time Machiavelli was meditating thus at San Casciano, the Frenchman and the Spaniard and the German were beginning to treat Italy as a future cockpit in their wars for the mastery of Western Europe ; and it was to save his unhappy country from such a fate, not merely as a Florentine but as an Italian, that Machiavelli now decided to appeal direct to the one and only reigning Italian House that might possibly prove ambitious or patriotic enough to listen to his words. For his immediate purpose he now addressed himself to the heir of the family, the young Lorenzo dei Medici. This youth was already Duke of Urbino and he was heir to Florence ; whilst his uncle Leo held Rome and the Papal States. True, Lorenzo was not a very promising pupil, but he was at least an Italian by birth, being half Florentine and half Roman. Though haughty and licentious, he had brains, like all the Medici ; he was a soldier ; above all, he was young, and youth itself offers (to a sanguine temperament like Machiavelli's) unending possibilities. To Lorenzo dei Medici therefore he decided to dedicate a certain treatise on statecraft he had been for some time composing. I am not going to comment on *The Prince* ; any criticism of mine would be not only valueless but superfluous. But I will say this. If *The Prince* be reckoned, as is usually the case, a practical handbook for an intending tyrant, and is therefore to be shunned as rank political poison, I would point out that it is a poison that carries its own antidote within itself. For, if in its pages it explains to the Prince the most forcible means of reigning as a tyrant, it also reveals those very aims and methods to the general reader. *The Prince* ranks therefore at once as an exposition and an exposure of the political science of Tyranny. The whole machinery of despotism is laid bare in its pages.

At present the work was safe in manuscript, and as such it would be used cautiously and discreetly by the one person or one family to whom it was addressed. Later, it was bound to be published to the world at large, and the world would then obtain a full insight into all the secret arts and aims of a would-be autocrat, and would thus get to know how best to defend its threatened liberty. Now, *The Prince* was primarily written with the sole object of freeing Italy from the yoke of the invader. What the fatal hour and the special circumstances needed was a Man, a Prince, who would weld together the jarring elements and the disunited cities of Italy into a true nation ; and with a national army at his back would drive the foreigner across the Alps or over sea, nevermore to return. For this one urgent and immediate purpose, Machiavelli felt that a patriotic tyrant, an ideal prince, was an absolute necessity.

That supreme task once accomplished—well, it would rest with Italy herself to decide on her own internal form of government for the future.

As it stood at the moment, this consummate treatise of cold, clear reasoning finished with an impassioned appeal to the young Lorenzo dei Medici to rely upon the awakened loyalty of a grateful nation, to offer himself as a national leader, and to liberate Italy once and for all.

' Let your illustrious House of Medici therefore take upon itself this enterprise with all the courage and all the hopes with which a just cause is undertaken. . . . This opportunity then for Italy at last to look on her deliverer ought not to be allowed to pass away. With what love he would be received in all those Provinces which have suffered from the foreign inundation, with what thirst for vengeance, with what fixed fidelity, with what devotion, and with what tears, no words of mine can declare. What gates would be closed against him ? What people would refuse him obedience ? What jealousy would stand in his way ? What Italian but would yield him homage ? This barbarian tyranny stinks in all nostrils.'

But again Machiavelli failed. The Medici were too cautious and suspecting ; one can imagine the puzzled expression on the fleshy face of the jovial Leo, as through his spyglass he perused this enigmatic document of his enigmatic fellow-Florentine. And in the midst of this fatal but scarcely unnatural hesitancy on Leo's part, young Lorenzo dei Medici himself died at Florence, leaving behind him only a sickly baby girl, the heiress of her House, the future Catherine dei Medici, Queen of France. How strange it is to reflect that this dissipated youth, Lorenzo, almost the least worthy of remembrance of all the Medici, should have been immortalized by the pen of Machiavelli, by the brush of Raphael, and by the chisel of Michelangelo, for the famous statue of the seated warrior, ' Il Pensieroso ' (the Thinker), that adorns the Medici chapel in Florence, is an idealized effigy of the young Lorenzo dei Medici.

With this collapse of his hopes in the young Lorenzo's premature death, curiously enough Machiavelli's private affairs began to improve. For Leo now sent his cousin, the Cardinal Giulio dei Medici, to act as his viceroy at Florence in 1519. Despite his odious character, Giulio dei Medici owned an unerring instinct for genius in art and literature. On his arrival in Florence he at once proceeded to treat Machiavelli with marked favour ; he removed all galling restrictions on his personal freedom ; he invited him to lecture to the Florentine Academy in the pleasant Oricellari Gardens within the city walls. Doubtless the Medici cardinal held not a few intimate conversations and discussions with the author of the unpublished *Prince*, which he must have read in manuscript. But the Cardinal Giulio dei Medici, growing daily more selfish, crafty and timid, was the last type of personality to appeal to Machiavelli. Their close intercourse, indeed, ended in nothing better than a commission from the Cardinal to write a history of Florence and a paltry diplomatic errand. Machiavelli's genius was too vast to suffer contact with the mediocre or conventional. Real genius, in truth, must always stand alone, for it is ever in advance of the average and admitted views of the day. It is only the glib, commonplace politician that can win praise or rewards from his own generation ; genius itself can only look to posterity for due recognition.

There is reason to believe the last few years of his life were passed happily. He was growing older and less active ; possibly he confessed his past failures to himself, and was content to watch with cynical calm the headlong course of Italian and European politics. He knew the lethal path Italy was treading ; he had done what he could in the past to avert disaster; and, well, no one would listen to him. ' *Pazienza !* ' That is what he probably thought and very likely spoke aloud, that simple untranslatable Italian word *Pazienza !* which expresses a whole volume of melancholy resignation to the inevitable. No doubt he appreciated the Cardinal Giulio's patronage and payment; he was flattered by the reception of his *Discorsi*, or Lectures, to the members of the Florentine Academy; he still enjoyed his intimate and not always very edifying correspondence with his old crony Vettori; also he wrote private letters in friendly vein to Francesco Guicciardi, the Florentine historian. Till within a few months of the end of his life existence flowed smoothly enough; still, it was but a mild compensation for past neglect and failure.

Machiavelli lived to see the sack of Rome, that crowning catastrophe whose coming he had probably foreseen. Leo X had died in 1521, and less than two years later his cousin Giulio, the bastard Medici, was elected Pope with the title of Clement VII. It would seem that at first the new Medicean Pope certainly paid Machiavelli the compliment of consulting him, for the latter spent some time at Rome about this period. It is clear enough, however, from the subsequent trend of events that Pope Clement, always irresolute, cannot possibly have followed any advice given to him by so shrewd and long-sighted a counsellor as Machiavelli. Torn between the claims of the young Emperor Charles V and King Francis I of France, Clement continued to intrigue, to shuffle, to lie, seeking vainly to meet military supremacy with Medicean cunning. Steadily the inevitable result of this tortuous policy drew nigh. In 1525 the French were utterly routed at Pavia; two years later, and Rome itself was in the hands of a motley army composed largely of Spanish and German mercenaries, and the Pope a prisoner. Clement's cup of humiliation was finally filled by the ensuing revolt in Florence, and the establishment of the third and last Florentine Republic in the early summer of 1527.

At this juncture Machiavelli, aroused momentarily from his political lethargy, was tempted to apply to the new republican Signory for his old congenial post of secretary of the Council of Ten of Peace and Liberty. His request was refused. This refusal was on June 10th, 1527, the twenty-ninth anniversary of his first elevation to this office. I think the rebuff must have broken his heart. A week later he took to his bed at his house in the narrow, gloomy street that leads from the Old Bridge, the historic ' Ponte Vecchio ', that modest dwelling which is now adorned with a flamboyant tablet to his memory as ' Prophet of United Italy '. His wife and family gathered round his sick-bed. ' He consented to confess his sins to Fra Matteo, who stayed with him to the end,' so writes his son, Piero Machiavelli, to a member of the family. He died on June 22nd, aged fifty-eight. The spiteful tradition that he died blaspheming owns no basis whatever ; it is hardly less absurd than the vulgar legend of the devil being seen to enter the dying man's chamber and carry off his soul.

. . . . . .

But Machiavelli has never died in the hearts of his Italian countrymen. In their gratitude and affection his sole rival is Dante. His memory and writings served to hand on the torch of Italian unity and freedom across the three intervening centuries of foreign domination. It was Machiavelli's books that inspired the first Italian patriot of the ' Risorgimento ', that great modern Italian political Renaissance. This was none other than Count Vittorio Alfieri, the Sardinian tragic poet, who himself confesses this influence—the very influence that a little later drove the lyric poet, Ugo Foscolo, to become the first Italian patriot to seek a voluntary exile. And his too was the guiding spirit in those degenerate days when the Spanish Bourbons were seated at Naples and Habsburgh grand dukes reigned at Florence ; when the Papal States, that uncomfortable legacy of the warrior-pope Julius II, stretched from the Adriatic to the Tyrrhene seas ; when the Austrian had his heel firmly planted on Venice and Milan. Indeed, it was in the darkest hour of those dark days that there arose the true Prince for whose coming Machiavelli had appealed in the far distant times of the Medici. This of course was Victor-Emmanuel, of the House of Savoy, the most venerable and illustrious of Italian reigning Houses. Like his Sardinian compatriot, Vittorio Alfieri, this young monarch drew much of his patriotic inspiration from the pages of the long-dead Machiavelli, whose works he constantly studied, even placing the beloved volume nightly beneath his pillow. And to aid him in his heavy task of unification and deliverance, Victor Emmanuel found the ideal diplomatist in Count Camillo Cavour and the ideal democratic leader of men in Giuseppe Garibaldi. Thus did a true Italian prince, an Italian noble, and an Italian peasant, working in unison, succeed in expelling the alien dynasties and the Austrian troops so as to found the modern kingdom of United Italy, ' Italy Redeemed ', the actual completion of the great task having been only consummated in our own days. We can recall with pride and pleasure in this country our own historic sympathy for this movement, which resulted in the birth of another Great European Power. ' Every Englishman ', once said the late Lord Kitchener, ' has two loves : Old England and Young Italy.'

Thus that ardent call to national unity and action, which fell on cold hearts and deaf ears in the far-off days of the Renaissance, echoed across the centuries and was heard and responded to by a new generation of Italians in the nineteenth century. The torch that Machiavelli had lit in the days of the Medici had never been wholly extinguished, and under favourable auspices it had flamed once more into burning brightness. Truly do we reverence that superb tribute engraved on the monument of Niccolò Machiavelli in the world-famous church of Santa Croce in Florence. For it is the due of a great forerunner of Italian unity, of the pleader and the prophet of a United Italy in an age when Italy itself was but a geographical expression. '*Tanto nomini nullum par eulogium*', so runs the epitaph, which I venture to translate: 'It is impossible to over-praise so great a name.'

THE ADORATION OF THE MAGI, WITH PORTRAITS OF THE MEDICI
From the Painting by Botticelli in the Uffizi Gallery, Florence

POPE CLEMENT VII
*From the Painting by Bronzino,
Uffizi Gallery, Florence*

COSIMO I, GRAND DUKE OF
TUSCANY
*From the Painting by Bronzino,
Pitti Gallery, Florence*

PIERO I DEI MEDICI
*From the Bust in marble by Mino
da Fiesole, Bargello, Florence*

GIULIANO DEI MEDICI
*From the Painting by Allori (after
Raphael), Uffizi Gallery, Florence*

POPE ALEXANDER VI
From the Fresco by Pinturicchio in the Borgia Apartments of the Vatican, Rome

LUCRETIA BORGIA, DUCHESS OF FERRARA
From the Fresco by Pinturicchio in the Borgia Apartments, Vatican

HIERONYMI·FERRARIENSIS·A·DEO·
MISSI·PROPHETÆ·EFFIGIES·

SAVONAROLA
From the Painting by Fra Bartolommeo in the San Marco Museum,
Florence

LORENZO II DEI MEDICI, DUKE OF URBINO
Statue and Tomb by Michelangelo in San Lorenzo, Florence

POPE SIXTUS IV WITH PLATINA AND THE PAPAL NEPHEWS
From the Painting by Melozzo da Forli in the Vatican, Rome

THE PERSEUS OF CELLINI

From the Statue in Bronze in the Piazza della Signoria, Florence

PALLAS AND THE CENTAUR
From the Painting by Botticelli in the Pitti Palace, Florence

THE VIRGIN, ST. ANNE, AND THE HOLY CHILDREN
From the Cartoon by Leonardo da Vinci in the Diploma Gallery of the Royal Academy, London

POPE JULIUS II
From the Painting by Raphael in the Pitti Gallery, Florence

THE SISTINE CHAPEL IN THE VATICAN, ROME
With the Ceiling and Frescoes by Michelangelo

HELIODORUS DRIVEN FROM THE TEMPLE

From the Fresco by Raphael in the Stanze of the Vatican, Rome

THE LOGGIA OF RAPHAEL IN THE VATICAN, ROME

CATERINA SFORZA

THE Italian Renaissance produced several famous women, but of these the majority belong either to the categories of *donna intellettuale*, or blue-stocking, or else of saint. Some of them fall between these two types. Women of action and political women are comparatively rare. Yet of this latter class there stands out at least one conspicuous example in Caterina Sforza, ' the Lady of Forli ', who still remains, even to-day, one of the popular heroines of Italian history and tradition. She is far removed, as I have just said, from that type of which the learned and virtuous Vittoria Colonna, Marchioness of Pescara, the beloved lady of the great Michelangelo, is the most shining instance ; yet Caterina Sforza has undoubtedly left behind her a wider reputation and popularity than the famous Lady of the Rock of Ischia, who wrote graceful sonnets and corresponded with the intellectual luminaries of her day. The whole of the last quarter of the fifteenth century, or *Quattrocento*, is closely bound up with the chequered career of Caterina Sforza, which gives us a vivid picture of the lives and courts and atmosphere of the Italian petty tyrants of that period. For the Lady of Forli enters largely into the doings of the Sforzas of Milan, the upstart papal families of Riario and della Rovere, the Medici of Florence, and the Borgias ; whilst her personality, her power, her valour, and her misfortunes alike claim for her not only a prominent place in the history of her own time, but also demand our remembrance to-day.

The House of Sforza of Milan, ranking amongst the historic dynasties of the Renaissance, were originally Attendoli of the Romagna, that debatable low-lying district nominally under papal rule, but in the hands of a number of reigning dynasties, which stretches from the Apennines to the Adriatic. Situated between the states of the Venetian Republic and the territories of the King of Naples, this country of the Romagna formed the main road on the eastern side between North and South Italy. From its critical position it lay open to constant invasion and occupation, with the result that it bred a turbulent race, whose antique reputation for violence and discontent seems to have lasted well into our own times. Caught between the conflicting powers of north and south Italy, the inhabitants of the Romagna were—indeed, they had to be—always on the alert.' The Attendoli, dwelling at Cotignola, were a family of *condottieri*, or paid leaders of mercenary troops, ready to fight for any master who would employ them ; but they were in no sense a princely House. Muzio Attendoli, a famous *condottiere* in his day, prepared the future greatness of the family. He had served with success and éclat under various masters, including Queen Joanna II of Naples, who reckoned him amongst her many lovers. This queen had fastened upon Muzio Attendoli his own soldiers' nickname for their intrepid leader, that of ' Sforza ', which refers equally to the violence of his mental and his physical powers. Henceforward, the whole family assumed this ominous name, which they evidently accepted as a high compliment. Muzio died in 1424, leaving a son, Francesco Sforza, who as a successful soldier of fortune completed the aggrandizement of his House by finally marrying Bianca Visconti, daughter of Filippo, last Visconti Duke of Milan. Francesco died in 1466, and his son and heir Galeazzo Visconti-Sforza now quartered in his arms the serpent crowned and holding a baby in its mouth, the famous bearings of the Visconti, together with the black eagle on a gold ground, the coat of the new-sprung Sforzas. These plebeian fighting Sforzas were now undisputed reigning Dukes of Milan, and Galeazzo took to wife a real princess, Bona of Savoy. Duke Galeazzo was the father of Catherine, the Lady of Forli; but the Duchess Bona was not her mother, for she was a natural daughter of Duke Galeazzo's by one of his mistresses, Madame Lucrezia Landriani, wife of a Milanese citizen, one Pietro Landriani. This Madame Landriani must have been a woman of a light, or at least over-sympathetic, nature, for she seems to have had children not only by her husband and the duke, but by others as well.

Now, fortunately for the little Catherine the age wherein she was born was less squeamish and more benevolent than our own in regard to bastardy. The good Duchess Bona not only took an interest in the child, but received her into the palace at Milan and educated her with her own children, and there seems to have existed some degree of genuine affection between the duchess and Catherine, her husband's love-child. What strikes one as being even more remarkable is that in after years Catherine is found on intimate terms with the Landriani, whom she took to live with her at Forli, including her mother's husband, Pietro Landriani. In spite of her being the daughter of a married man and of a married woman, Galeazzo of Milan declared Catherine legitimate with the full consent of his duchess, and nobody seems to have found anything unusual in such an edict. Perhaps it would be better to regard it as a case of *adoption* by both duke and duchess. It was a curiously lax age in family arrangements, as appears again and again. Highly educated and esteemed at the court of Milan, Catherine grew up handsome, clever, and agreeable. She was intensely proud of her birth, and especially of her descent from Muzio and her fighting forefathers of the Romagna, whose deeds of force in after years she was always ready to quote on occasion. She undoubtedly possessed to the full the martial spirit of the Attendoli, now Sforzas. Her base birth seems to have sat very lightly on her, and indeed scandals of this sort were common enough amongst the reigning families of Italy, whose pedigrees still puzzle the historian. Of her relations, we may name her young half-brother, Gian-Galeazzo, afterwards Duke of Milan ; another brother, Hermes ; and her two half-sisters, Bianca and Anna, who were wedded respectively in due course to the Emperor Maximilian and to Alfonso d'Este, Duke of Ferrara. There were also her two uncles, Ludovico (' Il Moro '), afterwards famous as the usurping Duke of Milan and more famous as the patron of Leonardo da Vinci, and the Cardinal Ascanio Sforza ; also her aunt, Ippolita, Queen of Naples. Thus, as a recognized daughter of the House of Visconti-Sforza the little Catherine was powerfully connected.

An early marriage, and an even earlier betrothal, was the inevitable fate of most daughters of royal or princely Houses, and Catherine was therefore affianced at the age of ten to young Girolamo Riario, nephew of the reigning Pope, Sixtus IV. It was of course a purely political match, undertaken with the object of bringing the duchy of Milan into closer contact with the papal court.

And now a word as to the Riario family, with whose good and ill fortunes the future career of Catherine Sforza was to be so closely entwined. If the Sforzas of Milan could fairly be described as upstarts and adventurers, they had at least carved their own way to political power and princely rank by force of their brains and their swords. They had already proved themselves fine soldiers and tolerable statesmen. But this was not the case with the Riario and della Rovere families, which owed their sudden rise to importance and wealth solely to the accident of the election

of their uncle, Cardinal Francesco della Rovere, to the
papal throne in 1471. The new Pope was a man of obscure
birth, the son of a humble fisherman of Savona, near Genoa.
Francesco had become a Franciscan friar, and owing to his
learning, his capacity, and an apparent but insincere
humility had risen to be a cardinal and the General of the
Franciscan Order. On the death of Paul II, Cardinal della
Rovere had sufficient influence to become the rival of the
learned Cardinal Bessarion for the vacant tiara. His
chances of election by the conclave were largely increased
by the shameless promises to many of the more unscrupulous
cardinals made by della Rovere's favourite young nephew,
Pietro Riario, son of his sister, Bianca Riario. Eventually,
della Rovere was elected and assumed the name of Sixtus IV.
He promptly showed himself to be the proverbial ' beggar
on horseback '. The cloak of modesty, poverty, and piety
was hastily flung aside, and the new Pope began to make full
use of his new powers, and especially of the papal treasury,
as a means of advancing his various nephews, and in particular that young libertine, Pietro Riario, his favourite of
them all, to whose base tactics he largely owed his recent
election. Sixtus, in short, laid down that policy of papal
nepotism and of secular behaviour that lasted in Rome
with scarcely a break for nearly eighty years, and was to
a great extent responsible for the Reformation. Of these
nephews of Sixtus IV there were four della Rovere youths,
all sons of his brother Raffaello della Rovere, and two young
Riarios—the already mentioned Pietro, who was absolutely
overwhelmed with bishoprics and abbeys by his doting
uncle, and Girolamo, who now sought the hand of Catherine
Sforza. Besides these there was the lad, Raffaello Sansoni,
son of the Pope's younger sister, Violante Sansoni, who was
also made a cardinal in his 'teens.

This then was the delectable family circle which now received Catherine when she had attained the age of fourteen.

Foremost amongst the papal nephews was of course Pietro Riario, who arranged the match. His extravagance, vice, and ambition made the talk of the hour, and it was fortunate for the Church that this greedy and odious young man died within three years' of his uncle's election, utterly worn out with excesses at the age of twenty-eight, yet not before he had managed to secularize the court of the Vatican, and to change its atmosphere from a traditional respectability to 'a sink of iniquity', as Lorenzo dei Medici did not hesitate to call it. It is only fair to add that Sixtus, with all his crimes and faults, was a true patron of the arts. It was he who built the Sistine Chapel, and with a kinder purpose erected the great hospital of Santo Spirito in Rome. He also founded the famous library of the Vatican, where to-day there exists a most interesting picture by that rare and admirable master, Melozzo da Forli, of Pope Sixtus seated in state, with the papal historian Platina kneeling at his feet, and surrounded by four of his worthless nephews. Pietro and Girolamo are shown wearing rich robes and watching the affair with a contemptuous expression; whilst Giovanni della Rovere (the founder of the ducal line of Urbino) stands behind the papal chair. The Cardinal Giuliano della Rovere, then a young man, bends over the Pope. He was at that date considered a rather dull and obtuse person, and few foresaw in him the great warrior-pope Julius II, who was to succeed some twenty years after his uncle's death. It is one of the finest portrait-groups in existence, and has been well reproduced by the Arundel Society in their series of colour prints.

Naturally, Catherine Sforza did not go empty-handed into matrimony. For her dower she received from her father the town of Imola in the Romagna, one of the places which her grandfather had gained by right of conquest, and which the Duke Galeazzo, her father, held as papal vicar, or feudal tenant of the papacy. To this Sixtus proposed to

add the more important town and fortress of Forli also in
the Romagna, from which he had driven out the local ruling
family, the Ordelaffi, to make room for his nephew, who
was appointed captain-general of the forces of the Church.
In April 1477 Catherine, who was already wedded by proxy,
set out with a gay train from Milan to join her husband,
who awaited her in Rome. She did not, however, travel
direct thither, but turned aside in order to spend some few
days both at Imola, her own town, and later at Forli, of
which she was now countess in right of her husband, the
Count Girolamo of Forli and Imola. She was well received
at both places; indeed, these receptions and fêtes in that
period constituted a regular part of the pleasures of the
populace, who could feast and be entertained at the expense
of their ever-changing sovereigns. After receiving the
homage of the two towns Catherine and her suite travelled
southward to Rome, where Girolamo and the leading personages of the papal court advanced to meet and greet
her. Finally, she entered Rome by the Porta Angelica,
and was taken into the presence of the Pope, who warmly
welcomed his niece-by-marriage.

For the next seven years Caterina Riario-Sforza, Countess
of Forli and Imola, resided in Rome, where her beauty, her
high spirits, her evident political capacity, her horsemanship,
and her strength of character won her many admirers. As
the chief lady at the Roman court, Catherine enjoyed an
existence of splendour and extravagance. Yet she was ever
learning and studying the political position of Italy, and of
the Sforza and Riario families in particular, during this
period of her life. She soon grew to realize, after the Pazzi
conspiracy of 1478, that Lorenzo dei Medici was a deep
and unforgiving enemy of her husband and his House;
and yet, strangely enough, Catherine was always drawn
towards Florence and the Medici. This attitude bred in
her a peculiar policy of her own, quite apart from the line

pursued by her unpopular and indolent husband. Of
Girolamo it is not easy to speak with any certainty. He
owned a bad reputation, which no doubt he deserved ; yet
it is hard to discover anything like the exact truth concerning these personages of the Italian Renaissance. Vulgar
and malicious gossip was so rife ; there was so much vague
and indiscriminate abuse in that age of violence ; it may
well be doubted whether Girolamo Riario, Count of Imola
and Forli and captain-general of the Church, was the
monster of iniquity, cowardice, and vicious habits that he
is usually described by subsequent historians. No doubt,
as the learned Dr. Creighton suggests, he was 'not a
gentleman ', to start with ; he was an arrogant upstart,
pitched suddenly into a high position for which he had
received no previous training or education. Though still
young, he was several years senior to his high-spirited wife ;
he was fat, lazy, and sensual ; he was certainly no soldier
or strategist, even if he were not an actual coward ; but
it is difficult to believe him guilty of the gross acts of sacrilege whereof he stands accused.

Except for their mutual ambition to rule and to extend
their power, Girolamo owned little in common with his wife,
the haughty descendant of Sforzas and Visconti. That
Girolamo treated Catherine with much harshness in the
early days of their marriage is probable enough. There
exists a letter from the young countess to her brother, Gian-
Galeazzo, Duke of Milan, in which she alludes pretty plainly
to her husband's brutality in these first years of wedded
life. But I think we may take it for granted that with time
and growing experience the bride of the Sforzas soon learned
to hold her own against her weak but violent husband, and
probably returned him pretty much as good as he gave.
She was essentially a *virago*, a masculine woman, and one
not likely to be bullied by a man for whom she held no small
degree of contempt as being her inferior in birth, breeding,

ability, and judgement ; yet the match does not seem to
have been an unhappy one on the whole. The pair worked
fairly well in harmony, though all the time Catherine held
broader and sounder views of policy than her husband.
As Catherine gloried constantly in the martial deeds of her
male ancestors, so also did she follow in the steps of the
Sforza wives, for she was prolific, and each year presented
her lord with a child, generally a son. Her many confine-
ments sate easily on her ; she thought nothing of riding at
full speed for whole days at a time, even when she was far
advanced in pregnancy.

In the summer of 1484 Pope Sixtus expired, and for the
time being the Houses of Riario and Rovere were thrown
into the shade. No more largesse from the papal treasury,
for Girolamo ceased to be captain-general of the Church on
the election of Cardinal Cibò as Pope Innocent VIII. He
and his countess now retired from Rome, and started for
their little principality in the Romagna. The new Pope
confirmed Girolamo's title as papal vicar, or Count of Imola
and Forli. They took up their residence at Forli, and here
Girolamo and Catherine for nearly four years lived the usual
existence of the petty despots of their age. It seemed a
paltry and anxious life after the ease and luxury of the
Roman court. So long as the count's treasury was well
stocked, things went smoothly enough for the pair ; the
nobles and people of Imola and Forli were quite satisfied
with their rule so long as taxes were not enforced and they
were being entertained by their reigning prince. But ere
long the coffers of Girolamo became empty, and in spite of
windy promises of freedom from taxation made in past
days of prosperity, the taxes had to be reimposed. Hence
there arose the usual discontent and plots, which were the
daily portion of nearly all these petty princes of Italy.
There was a revival of attempts to restore the deposed
Ordelaffi, former Counts of Forli, whose heir was hovering

unpleasantly near in the hope of recovering his lost dominions. So far as can be seen, Girolamo as well as Catherine did all that was possible to retain the good-will of their turbulent and discontented subjects. It was a somewhat hopeless task, and of the pair at least Girolamo was utterly incompetent to combat such difficulties. The general unrest at last came to a head in the conspiracy of the noble family of Orsi, who had some special grudge against the count. A plot of assassination was carefully concocted by Checco Orsi, and on April 14th, 1488, it was put into execution. The time chosen was the hour after dinner when the count remained in the great Hall of the Nymphs, so called, the chief chamber of the palace. It is ominous that special arrangements were made by the conspirators to guard the entrance of the staircase leading to Catherine's bower, whither she always retired with her ladies and children after the meal. Checco Orsi entered the palace unchallenged, and walked up to the Sala dei Ninfi, where he found Girolamo lounging in the embrasure of a window with one arm on the sill. Suspecting no harm, the count welcomed him.

' How goes it, Checco mio ? ' he called out kindly, extending his hand to the new-comer.

' That way it goes ! ' was the brutal reply, as Orsi plunged his dagger into the count's stomach, mortally wounding him.

All was now confusion in the palace. Other members and friends of the Orsi family rushed into the Sala dei Ninfi, occupied the palace, flung the corpse of the murdered count into the square below, and finally rushed up the inner staircase to seize Catherine and her children. For the first time the Lady of Forli, now a widow with six children (one being still at the breast), and also pregnant, was called on to face imminent danger, for which she needed all her wit as well as her courage. She barricaded her door with furniture, but eventually the band of assassins broke in

and captured Catherine and her children. Through all this
tumult (in which, as Catherine afterwards declared, there
was no time for tears), the Lady of Forli comported herself
with admirable dignity and calm. She managed somehow
to send a secret message to the governor of the Castle of
Forli, Tommaso Fèo, whom she knew she could trust, on
no account to surrender the castle to the Orsi. She then
descended into the square in the hands of her captors. Her
children were now removed as hostages and taken to a
certain gateway of the town and lodged there. She herself
was led to the entrance of the castle, where Monsignor
Savelli, the papal legate, who favoured the designs of the
Orsi, asked her to order its surrender to himself as the
representative of the Pope, who was overlord of the whole
Romagna and suzerain of the late Count Girolamo.

The governor, Tommaso Fêo, refused to surrender save
to the widow of his late master, the murdered count.
Catherine, who was as cunning as she was brave, now
turned to Monsignor Savelli, and offered to enter the castle
alone and confer with the governor, in order to persuade
him to open his gates. The Orsi, suspecting a ruse, de-
claimed against this suggestion, but Savelli after some
demur assented to it. So Catherine walked forward alone ;
the portcullis was lowered, and she entered the castle.
Three hours was the time allotted by Savelli to this interview of Fèo and the countess, but that time was already far
exceeded when Savelli and the Orsi began to shout for her
return. Catherine then appeared on the battlements, and
in reply to Savelli's demands declared she intended to
remain in the castle, nor would she stir thence till she
received help from her relatives, the Sforzas of Milan.
Savelli and the Orsi now saw how they had been outwitted
by this intrepid woman, and became a prey to mingled fear
and fury. In vain Savelli urged the claims of his master,
Pope Innocent, who through Girolamo's death was now

legal sovereign of the city of Forli. Catherine only retorted she was Regent of Forli during the minority of her eldest son, Ottaviano Riario. The Orsi went further: they threatened to massacre Catherine's family of six children. Even this threat failed to move the Lady of Forli. ' I am pregnant now,' was her reply. ' Besides, I am young and I can marry again.'

Such are Catherine's reported words, and it seems not improbable that she really did utter them. In any case, they would be characteristic of her. Perhaps she felt certain that, despite all threats, Monsignor Savelli, even in that age of iniquity, would shrink, as the legate of the Pope, from condoning the murder of helpless young children— children, by the way, who had powerful relations amongst the reigning Houses of Italy, and were even nephews of the Empress Bianca, Catherine's half-sister. Even when these unfortunate infants were brought by the cruel Orsi up to the entrance of the castle, and at the instance of their captors implored their mother to save their lives by surrendering the castle, never did Catherine flinch for a moment. And her bravery and determination won their due reward, for four days later, on April 18th, the army of the Duke of Milan, sent to her rescue, arrived within easy distance of Forli. At the same time the fickle people of Forli had begun to turn against the Orsi and the papal legate; a counter-revolution was in progress. There was scarcely need of the Milanese troops, and indeed it required all Catherine's subsequent skill to prevent the sack of Forli itself by this assisting army. The Orsi fled; the people rose and shouted for Catherine, their lady ruler; they cheered the released children, and amid great rejoicing the Lady of Forli was restored to her full powers of Regent of Forli in the name of her son.

Caterina Sforza had now reached the highest point of her career. All Italy was ringing with praise and admiration

for her valour and cleverness. She was acknowledged
henceforth as Countess of Forli and of Imola, and as such
she remained for nearly twelve years one of the recognized
petty sovereigns of the Italian states. On the whole, the
Lady of Forli used her victory with moderation, according
to the lights of that time. She refused to take measures
of reprisal against the wives and children of the Orsi and
other rebels, in spite of the treatment she had received and
the threats that had been launched against her own helpless
family. Yet many cruel deeds were done, more, it seems,
to please the people of Forli than to glut her own vengeance.
The younger male conspirators had fled in haste and managed
to keep out of harm's way ; but old Andrea Orsi, over
eighty years of age, the head of the Orsi family (and it must
in fairness be added the most bloodthirsty of the whole crew),
received a terrible measure of revenge. First of all, he had
to stand by and watch his palace sacked by the mob and
then razed to the ground—a fearful humiliation for a proud
baron ; and after this the old man was strapped to a plank,
tied to a horse's tail, and dragged thrice round the square
till he was torn in pieces. The spectacle delighted the
populace of Forli. It was a barbarous age, and this type
of punishment commended itself to popular feeling. To
those who had remained faithful to her cause and that of
her infants Catherine showed innumerable favours.

As dowager countess and regent for her young son,
Ottaviano Riario-Sforza, Catherine was now a prominent
and even an influential figure in Italian political life. Forli
became the centre of much military activity, and the troops
of the countess, in whose training and equipment she took
a close and personal interest, were in high demand as
mercenaries. In 1492 her position was made still more
secure by the death of Lorenzo dei Medici, her husband's
old enemy, who was strongly suspected of having stirred up
the late conspiracy of the Orsi against Count Girolamo.

In the same year she was pleased by the election of Cardinal Rodrigo Borgia as Pope Alexander VI, for the Borgia had always shown himself her good friend during her Roman residence. She was able also to form an alliance between her daughter Bianca and the young Astorre Manfredi, tyrant of Faenza, though owing to the tender age of the bridegroom, then only ten, the actual marriage had to be postponed. Everything now seemed to smile on the Lady of Forli. But if Catherine was by nature a warrior, she was also very much a woman. Her marriage with Girolamo Riario had been loveless, though she had shown herself a good wife and helpmate. Now for the first time she was apparently smitten with a love-passion. The object of her affections was the youthful Giacomo Fèo, a younger brother of that Tommaso Fèo who had so loyally held the castle of Forli in her behalf. Fèo was hardly a suitable match for a reigning princess, so Catherine, who was certainly virtuous, had a secret marriage performed ; nor was Fèo openly recognized as her husband. In short, it was a morganatic marriage, and besides the humble birth of the bridegroom, there was also the question of the regency of Forli, which in reality she could claim only so long as she remained a widow and her son a minor. Nobody seems to have cavilled at first at this match, and for a time at least Fèo had the good sense to behave with modesty and discretion. But after a while his good fortune began to turn young Fèo's head. He grew arrogant and interfering. He began to meddle in affairs of state, and even on one occasion he openly struck the true Count of Forli, Ottaviano. The people of Forli began to murmur, and plots were started against the detested favourite. In August 1495 one Antonio Ghetti, who was filled with bitterness against Fèo, set upon him openly in the street and stabbed him to death, flinging the body into a ditch. Catherine was riding close by, and turned to hear her husband cry aloud, ' Oh,

madame, I am assassinated ! ' whereupon she saw the foul
deed. It was the second time she was called on to see a
husband brutally murdered, practically in her presence.
Again there arose a tumult in the city, but the people of
Forli stood by their sovereign, though doubtless they
rejoiced in the death of the unpopular Fèo, for ' a favourite
has no friends ', as the poet truly says. On this occasion
Catherine, who was undoubtedly enamoured of Giacomo
Fèo, did not exhibit any of the clemency she had shown on
the previous occasion of Count Girolamo's murder. As a
writer of the time expressed it, she became like a tigress
thirsting for blood after her lover's murder. She acted
without pity or mercy. Ghetti himself had already been
slain by a zealous soldier, so was at least out of the range
of her vengeance. But no fewer than fifty-eight persons
are said to have been executed for a share in this assassination, some of their number being mere children, and some
of them women. The dungeons below the palace were
long filled with victims of the countess's fury, and their
cries from starvation or torture used to mingle audibly
with the concerts and banquets held in the upper rooms.
Even Catherine's own children expostulated in vain with
their enraged mother. It is a horrible story, and her
brutality towards the innocent women and infants of the
miscreants is inexcusable. No wonder contemporary historians called her ' *virago crudelissima* '; they were certainly justified.

What made the occasion the more bitter, and even more
humiliating to Catherine was the knowledge that her own
son Ottaviano and his brothers privately rejoiced in Fèo's
fall and end. Ottaviano was now seventeen, and therefore
old enough to be betrothed and even married ; also old
enough to assume the rule of Forli. But political power
was life to Catherine ; she never meant to surrender her
principality to her heir so long as she lived. Probably she

realized that Ottaviano was quite unfit to rule; indeed, her sons by Girolamo took after the pattern of their sluggish Riario father, much to Catherine's disgust. Still, the fact remained, the Lady of Forli was an usurper, whatever excuses she might have for thus clinging to power. But she continued to drill her soldiers and to govern her turbulent cities, and to lend out her troops on pay, especially to the revived Florentine Republic, with which she always showed herself in sympathy. So poor Ottaviano, who was fat and lazy and loved comfort like his unlamented father, was sent off to fight in the service of the Florentines, whilst Catherine remained ruler of his patrimony.

In 1496 the Florentine Republic sent Giovanni dei Medici on an embassy to the court of Forli. He was a cousin of the exiled Medici princes but professedly not a Medicean partisan; indeed, he had even changed the hated name of Medici to 'Popolano' in order to curry favour with the ruling republican party in Florence. Giovanni was thirty years old, a little younger than Catherine; he was handsome, agreeable, and talented. It is clear there was mutual attraction. They were married, but without any ostentation, and the Signory of Florence, in approving of the match, decreed that the countess should be reckoned an honorary citizen of Florence, and also any children of the marriage should likewise be deemed citizens. But her third period of married life was of very short duration. Giovanni dei Medici fell suddenly sick at the baths of San Piero-in-Bagno. Catherine hastened to the bedside of her third husband, only to find him dying, and indeed he expired in her arms on September 15th, 1498. There was one son of this short-lived union—Giovanni, the celebrated Giovanni delle Bande Nere (' John of the Black Bands '), the great general and strategist, the only warrior of worth who ever owned the name of Medici. But it is evident that his military talents were inherited from the distaff side, for

Giovanni delle Bande Nere was in years to come destined to prove himself a true child of Caterina Sforza, the descendant of a long line of fighting soldiers.

Shortly before her husband's death, and possibly with his advice or approval, the Lady of Forli had declined—and declined with some asperity—a proposal from Pope Alexander to form a match between her son and heir Ottaviano, now about twenty, and his daughter, the celebrated Lucretia Borgia, the recently divorced wife of Giovanni Sforza, Lord of Pesaro. Already Alexander was beginning to scheme for the aggrandizement of his son Cesare Borgia, and he was anxious to get Forli into the grip of the Borgia influence. This tart refusal on the part of Catherine, who saw the political danger of the proposed match and also the certainty of her own speedy removal from power, destroyed whatever friendship still existed between the Pope and the Riario-Sforza House; it would have been more politic on Catherine's part to have temporized with the suggestion. As it was, she now had the Borgias for definite enemies.

The sudden death of her husband, Giovanni dei Medici, was a political as well as a private loss to Catherine. She now stood defenceless when Italy was on the eve of vast changes. The second invasion of Italy under Louis XII, the new King of France and formerly Duke of Orléans, was now imminent. The Sforza family were deeply involved. It is too long a story to tell here. But Ludovico (' Il Moro '), the usurping Duke of Milan, ultimately lost his throne and was carried a prisoner to France, and his younger brother, the once-powerful Cardinal Ascanio Sforza, was also captured. The Florentine Republic was allied with the invading French; the Pope was not only hostile, but had already marked out Forli as a suitable starting-point for his son Cesare's career of conquest. At the close of the century Caterina Sforza stood almost alone.

She had only a small principality and a small though excellent army. She was in reality helpless in the face of the political storm. A man—a wise man—would have yielded, and retired in the hope of better times returning. Not so the Lady of Forli. First of all, she turned hither and thither to find allies, and when these were not forthcoming, she decided to stand solitary, whatever might befall. She faced the dark situation with courage, but without discretion. It is difficult to say whether she should be blamed for her obstinacy or admired for her pluck. In any case her chances of retaining Forli were almost hopeless.

For the last year or two the Pope had been preparing for his campaign of seizure of the Romagna, so as to found a duchy and dynasty for his son, the young Cesare Borgia. That youth had lately been released from his ecclesiastical vows, and had become a layman. He had gone to France in great state, had married the King's niece, the Princess Charlotte d'Albret, sister of the King of Navarre ; he had been created Duke of Valentinois by King Louis. Cesare was only twenty-three, but he owned real gifts of mind and an iron will to succeed. His aim and intention were, with all the aid that the Pope could bestow in men, money, and spiritual threats, to seize the various principalities of the Romagna, being nominal fiefs of the Church, and out of these to erect for himself a duchy of the Romagna. Beyond this his ambition did not for the moment extend ; no doubt, if fortune favoured his plan his future realm could be enlarged indefinitely. Forli was marked out as the most suitable point for beginning this proposed campaign of conquest. In July 1499 Catherine had received an embassy from the Florentines, headed by no less a personage than the rising young statesman, Niccolò Machiavelli. It was his first mission, and this of itself constitutes an interesting episode in Catherine's career, though their interview does not seem to have led to any definite result. It was on the eve of the final scene in Catherine's dramatic career. Machiavelli may or may not have warned the famous Lady of Forli of the extreme danger of her position, for he must have seen that she owned something of the vixen as well as of the lioness, a combination which he openly advocated in his famous treatise of *The Prince*.

With a fine force of picked men and backed by Yves d'Allègre and a section of the invading French army, the papal leader advanced against Forli. Imola had already opened its gates to Cesare, fearing pillage and massacre. Forli was anxious also to admit Cesare, whose name was already a terror to Italy, but Catherine would not hear of either surrender or compromise. Finally the citizens (and really one cannot blame them) took the matter into their own hands. Catherine had already retired into the castle with her most faithful soldiers and retainers, and had taken measures to defend the city of Forli as well, by clearing the ground, cutting down trees, and generally leaving a circle of open waste round the town. But in their growing alarm the people of Forli at the last moment refused to be associated in a forlorn hope with their countess. Cesare entered the town unopposed, and after a while proceeded to the castle to parley with the Lady of Forli. This was in the latter part of December 1499. It would seem that Catherine appeared on the battlements, much as she had shown herself some twelve years before to the murderers of her first husband, the Count Girolamo. Cesare, who was handsome and could show himself graceful and gracious enough when he chose, harangued the Lady of the Castle at some length, pointing out to her the folly of resistance, and promising to provide her son Ottaviano with some other principality in due course. This he promised on the oath of himself and the Pope. Unfortunately, the word of the Borgia was never taken seriously, and in any event Catherine intended to stay and rule in Forli, and flatly told Cesare Borgia as much in fairly polite but quite firm language. Again Cesare tried to reason and argue with the obstinate countess, but only met with a blank refusal. And yet the position of Catherine was hopeless; she might delay and inconvenience Caesar Borgia, but sooner or later the castle of Forli was bound to fall. Of her faithful troops and attendants shut up in this death-trap with their mistress, Catherine does not seem to have thought at all. Yet of the Borgia, it is only fair to say that he warned her of the inevitable consequences, which for many reasons he was anxious to avoid. Cesare Borgia was an able and unscrupulous adventurer, but he was not the wanton monster of slaughter and iniquity that historians of a later generation (not of his own) have painted him. He did not like making war on a woman; he was, to use a homely expression, eager to let her down as easily as he could afford. But Catherine perhaps relied on this occasion too much on her sex. She knew that Yves d'Allègre and the chivalry of France were not pleased at being implicated in this attack on a woman's castle. Perhaps this was her secret reason for holding out against overwhelming odds. If she did cherish any such hope she was destined to be grievously disappointed. Still, such a notion may have partly accounted for her intense, one may almost say her criminal, determination on this occasion. In any case, she refused Cesare's offer, and determined to fight to a finish.

Cesare's army was far superior both in numbers and in skill to the garrison of the castle of Forli. The first attacks certainly failed, but with the help of his engineers Cesare soon bridged the moat and led his forces to the walls. Having crossed the moat, the rest was easy work. At the end of three weeks from the date of his arrival at Forli on January 12th, 1500, the fortress was carried by assault. A soldier waved a white flag, but this act of formal surrender passed unheeded. Fierce hand-to-hand fighting took place within the castle courtyard, which was soon turned into a veritable shambles. Catherine was seized and carried to the presence of Cesare Borgia and Yves d'Allègre. She seemed quite indifferent to the massacre that her obstinacy, or her valour, had caused. She acknowledged herself a prisoner not of the Borgia but of the King of France, whose code of military chivalry took no cognizance of female prisoners of war. She was therefore, according to her feminine reasoning, a free woman. Yves d'Allègre was placed in an awkward dilemma, yet he finally handed the Lady of Forli over for honourable keeping to Cesare, who promised to conduct her safely to Rome as a hostage and a French subject rather than as a prisoner. She was treated with distinction, and though no doubt during the next few days Catherine endured humiliation and even some hardship, such results were inevitable. Cesare is accused by later chroniclers of having behaved with revolting bestiality towards his captive. It is highly improbable. In any case, we must remember that Catherine was now a middle-aged woman approaching forty, whilst the Borgia prince, 'beau et blonde', was but three-and-twenty. Charms and beauty that might once have aroused the conqueror's evil passions had long disappeared ; Catherine Sforza had by this date become in very truth merely the '*femina quasi virago, crudelissima e di gran animo*' that the Venetian ambassador had once described her.

On her arrival at Rome, Catherine was received not unkindly by Pope Alexander. She was assigned the Belvedere, or summer pavilion in the Vatican gardens, for a residence. Her faithful chaplain, Fra Lauro, was allowed to accompany her. Here Catherine remained till the spring, the Pope continually trying to obtain from her a formal renunciation of her sovereign rights and those of her sons to Forli and Imola. But Catherine remained obdurate to threats or entreaties on this point. She made an attempt to escape from Rome, and this effort on her part gave Alexander the needed excuse to imprison her in the gloomy and dreaded castle of Sant' Angelo. She was accused also of having conspired to kill the Pope by means of a poisoned letter. The charge was undoubtedly trumped up, and Catherine denied it with energy. Her Riario sons, all of whom had now entered the secure service of the Church and were clamouring for benefices, made no attempt to obtain their mother's release for fear of offending the Pope, the source of all ecclesiastical patronage. She seemed abandoned by all. In the castle of Sant' Angelo she was kept in strict and indeed cruel confinement. Her life was in constant danger, yet never would she abate one jot of her claims to Forli. Her hair turned white with anxiety and sorrow ; her conscience smote her for the bloodthirsty massacre of those poor women and children, whom she had sacrificed in her rage simply because they had been related to the assassins of her second husband, Giacomo Fèo. It had all happened six years before, but the memory of the foul deed returned so that Catherine, with her life now hanging on a thread, suffered agonies of remorse in her Roman prison for her past misdeeds.

In the summer of 1502 the French were again in Italy, and Yves d'Allègre was marching on Rome. At Viterbo he heard for the first time of the Pope's ill-treatment of Catherine Sforza, the nominal subject of France and of his master King Louis. Hurrying to Rome, he demanded Catherine's prompt release. The Pope did not dare disobey, and Yves himself sought the cell of the Lady of Forli, who had now languished for over a year in close captivity. The gallant French general was shocked to see the changes that misfortune had wrought in the proud *virago* of Forli, whom he had in all good faith handed over to the Borgias two years before. Catherine gratefully accepted Yves' good offices. It was arranged that she should proceed to

Florence, where her youngest boy, the little Giovanni, the only son of her third husband, Giovanni dei Medici, was now being brought up by his father's family. She herself was also an honorary citizen of Florence, so she could fairly claim the hospitality of that city. Even Alexander sent her a letter of recommendation to the Signory of Florence styling her ' Our dearly beloved Daughter in Jesus Christ '. What a contrast human deeds and human words present! Letters are often only written lies.

So Catherine departed by sea from Rome. Her career was definitely over ; she was now prematurely old and worn ; even she realized at long last that she would nevermore become a sovereign. As she approached Florence she was met by all her sons, including young Fèo, the child of her second marriage, and the infant Giovanni dei Medici. With her Riario offspring she now owned nothing in common, just as they had inherited none of the Sforza qualities of mind or body. Her whole being went out to her youngest son, the little Giovanni dei Medici. The last seven years of her life were spent in Florence, educating this child according to Sforza notions, and later on she confessed to feeling an access of intense joy when his despairing tutors informed her that Master Giovanni dei Medici cared for nothing and thought about nothing save the art of war and horsemanship. It seems a pity, and perhaps a punishment, that Catherine did not survive to see her favourite boy develop into the most famous warrior of his day. How it would have delighted the heart of the Lady of Forli ! Also to have known that her grandson was to become first Grand Duke of Tuscany, a throne which was beyond her wildest dreams. For Catherine Riario-Sforza only survived her release some seven years. She made an edifying end in the convent of the nuns of the Murate in Florence, dying on May 28th, 1509, aged about forty-six, for the exact date of her birth is lost in obscurity.

There are several portraits of the Lady of Forli. The best is probably that by Palmeggiani (the worthy pupil of that excellent master, Melozzo da Forli), which hangs in the little gallery of Forli. It was painted in early life, perhaps at the date of her marriage to Girolamo Riario. It shows us a buxom girl, fair but not strikingly beautiful, holding a bowl filled with jessamine in her hands. It suggests nothing of the conventional *virago*, of the future warrior-Countess of Forli. It is interesting to contrast this calm picture of youth with the later portrait in the Uffizi Gallery at Florence, where she appears amongst the many likenesses of the later Medici, Grand Dukes of Tuscany, her descendants through her third marriage. She is shown therein as an elderly woman in black dress and wearing the widow's white coif of the period. The face wears an old and weary look, but is not without attraction, nor does it again suggest the *virago* of history with a stormy past.

What is Catherine Sforza's exact place in the roll of history? Her name is certainly remembered, but chiefly as the mother of John of the Black Bands and ancestress of that long line of Medici sovereigns who ruled Florence and Tuscany for two centuries. But in reality she has a greater claim than this upon our interest and attention. Says her chief modern biographer, Count Piero Pasolini, on whose great work this study has been largely based, Catherine Sforza ' represents the heroine of the chivalry of the Middle Ages. She is prominent in history, not as the representative of a new era, but as a detached figure from an age already passed and gone '. This estimate is, however, only partly true. Catherine is certainly not a *typical* figure of the Italian Renaissance : she was no blue-stocking or fascinating dame, like Isabella d'Este or Vittoria Colonna. Yet she was thoroughly steeped in the statecraft of her day ; she showed herself the political rather than the learned great lady. She was the first to cross diplomatic swords with Machiavelli, who seems to have regarded her with approval. Although she wore armour and trained troops, she had evolved a policy of her own, and a shrewd if selfish policy too. She was not a whit inferior to the average Italian tyrant of her day. That her outstanding personality made a deep and lasting impression on her own generation is clearly proved by the fact that Catherine became a popular figure in the contemporary ballads of the people. On the rude stages of village concerts or booths at fairs the melancholy figure of the Lady of Forli was often introduced, to sing her story or tell her tale of woe ; and all Italy in time grew to learn her tragic career from these rough verses that were composed about her. Count Passolini quotes one long poem, artless but picturesque, concerning the sorrows of the Countess of Forli who saw her father and two husbands killed before her eyes ; who was threatened with the massacre of her children before her face ; who twice defended her castle, once with success and once with failure, against her enemies ; who alone dared to defy the might of the Borgias. Each long stanza of this poem ends with the appeal to the audience :

> Ascolta questa sconsolata
> Caterina da Forlivo.

Such popular ballads have helped to keep the memory of Catherine green in the minds of the people of Italy. And the historian also can fairly state that though Caterina Sforza did not play a very *important* part in the political world of her day—she was but the countess of two small cities—yet she certainly appears as a remarkable and outstanding figure of her period.

VII

BENVENUTO CELLINI AND HIS *AUTOBIOGRAPHY*

(1500–1570)

IN the art of the Italian Renaissance we get many opportunities of knowing the portraits, the clothing, the banquets, the games, the architecture, and the customs of that brilliant age. But of necessity we cannot gather from art what manner of speech these people used to one another, or with what feelings of respect or disdain they regarded one another. We see in the frescoes and portraits of the period a rich and varied procession of men women, and children, but they are dumb and silent. It is left to the chronicler to explain to us the more human attitude of these people in their daily life, whether of the home, the street, the church, or the official reception. For this purpose the *Autobiography* of Benvenuto Cellini, jeweller and sculptor of Florence, helps to fill the void. His *Autobiography* is in fact a human document of the highest importance. In the letters of Isabella d'Este, Marchioness of Mantua, we certainly do possess some valuable insight into the inner life of courts and princes; and perhaps we may extract a good deal of information of an aristocratic sort from the *Cortegiano* of Castiglione. But we want something more than this: we want to know how all classes of life comported themselves. And this want of ours is largely met by Cellini's racy memoirs. For their author, although he gets to be in time on more or less intimate terms with popes and princes, was by birth and breeding a man of the people, a plain Florentine citizen, and it is from the standpoint of a plain citizen that he invariably observes and describes.

In his artless narrative, packed with incident from first page to last, we are made acquainted, from his blunt democratic point of view, with all sorts and conditions of men and women of the later Italian Renaissance. We are shown the Popes Clement VII and Paul III, the reigning Italian despots at Florence, Mantua, and Ferrara, the great King Francis I of France, and a host of lesser luminaries in the high society of the time. Great names, like swallows, flit across Cellini's vision ; we are shown the famous bibliophile, Grolier of Paris (in most uncomplimentary terms), the arch-artist Michelangelo, the patrons and *cognoscenti* of the Renaissance. But this is not the whole range of Cellini's recollections. He lifts the veil from the life lived by the artists of the day, with their rivalries, their junketings, and their violence ; we learn the ways of doctors, of soldiers, of courtesans, of bullies, of innkeepers, of jailers ; and, in short, the whole fabric of later Renaissance society from top to bottom is explained to us from these pages. We learn the ordinary discomforts and incidents of travel both outside and inside Italy ; we are brought to realize the pleasures and the perils of that fascinating but treacherous period, the middle of the sixteenth century. And Cellini, a true Florentine democrat in spite of his unswerving devotion to the Medici, treats high and low with equal impartiality. He spends as many words on a pope or emperor as on some rascal who has cheated him or sought to put poison in his soup. In short, the whole book is a mirror wherein we have only to look and see for ourselves the intimate life of the Italian Renaissance. Nor is our interest confined to our vision, for we can hear these people converse and scheme and shout, cry or make merry, according to the circumstances of the case. To sum up, as I have already said, the *Autobiography* of Cellini is a human document of his age, as varied in its contents as a newspaper and as amusing as many a picaresque novel. Moreover, one great blessing in this work must be recorded ; there is an almost ostentatious avoidance of all politics. The decisive battle of Pavia, for example, is barely mentioned ; and Cellini writes as little as the sense of his chronicle permits of current wars and diplomacy and palace intrigue. Again and again he states it is no concern of his, this warfare and diplomacy of princes ; and thus the reader is spared a succession of those wearisome details and opinions which fill the pages of all contemporary historians. We can read the book solely for pleasure and not for politics, which Cellini abhorred and avoided.

I shall now give a short sketch of the life and career of this remarkable Italian of the *Cinquecento*, first of jewellers, expert in mechanics, engraver of medals and plate, and finally sculptor—to say nothing of author, for besides the *Autobiography*, or *Vita da Lui Stesso*, Cellini wrote also one or two important treatises on his art and its methods, as well as some poems. Benvenuto (Welcome !) Cellini was born on the night of All Saints in 1500, the opening year of the sixteenth century, the Italian *Cinquecento*. His father, Giovanni Cellini, despite the imposing pedigree that his son concocted in maturer years, belonged to a humble burgher family in Florence. This Giovanni was an *ebanista*, or inlayer of choice woods and ivory, by profession, and he also played the flute as a young man in the private band of the great Lorenzo dei Medici, an occupation he lost through the revolution of 1494, when the Medici were expelled from Florence. Giovanni continued always a strong adherent of the Medici, a true *pallesco*, and he was prominent in his manifestations of sincere joy at the return of the exiled family in 1512, when Cardinal dei Medici (shortly to become Pope Leo X), his brother Giuliano, his nephew Lorenzo, and his cousin Giulio (destined later on to be elected Pope Clement VII) entered Florence once more in triumph. Benvenuto was then a boy in his twelfth year, and he must have cheered the returning princes, and watched his loyal

parent painting the Medicean coat of arms with the six
pellets over his doorway for the occasion. At an early age
Benvenuto began to learn the craft of goldsmith and jeweller,
to which art his natural wishes inclined, although his father
did all in his power to compel his son to become a musician
in the service of the Medici. As a youth, it is pretty evident
that the young Cellini was what is termed ' a broth of a
boy ', always in scrapes and street brawls ; and even more
wilful and violent was his younger brother, Cecchino, who
enlisted in the famous ' Black Bands ' of Giovanni dei
Medici, the father of Cosimo, the future first Grand Duke of
Tuscany. One of the first of the leading artists of the day
to discern the talents of this noisy young Benvenuto was
Piero Torrigiani, the rival of Michelangelo, who had lately
been employed on the fine tomb of Henry VII in West-
minster Abbey. Cellini, however, disliked Torrigiani,
because the latter abused the divine Michelangelo, who from
his earliest years to his dying day Cellini never ceased to
worship and applaud : ' From him,' he writes, ' and from
nobody else have I learned all that I know.'

  Cellini was still in his teens when he paid his first visit to
Rome. He had been annoyed by his father's constant
worrying and advice to abandon the goldsmith's art for
music, so one day in a huff he started for Rome in company
with the wood-carver, ' Il Tasso '. Here he remained for
two years, easily supporting himself by doing work for the
Roman goldsmiths, who appreciated his skill, and then at
his father's entreaty he returned to Florence. But here
again in his native city Cellini fell once more foul of the
police, and after a more than usually violent brawl he deemed
it expedient to retire to Rome. Here he practised drawing
Michelangelo's work in the Sistine Chapel, also Raphael's
frescoes in the Villa Farnesina, then the fine palace of the
Sienese banker, Agostino Chigi. In Rome too he led a jolly
noisy devil-may-care existence, and it is from this part of

the *Vita* that we can conjure up for ourselves the true life of the artistic fraternity then rejoicing in the lavish patronage of Clement VII and his cardinals.

Of Clement VII (Giulio dei Medici) we get what is perhaps the most valuable sidelight in all these pages. Cellini, a true Medicean, always speaks of this unfortunate Pope with respect, and often with praise. ' He was an excellent connoisseur,' he relates in one place, and no doubt from an artistic standpoint Clement was as proficient and judicious as he was ill-judged and indiscreet in political affairs. Curiously enough, it was his flute-playing and not his art that first brought Cellini to the notice of the Pope. One day at table Clement inquired who played the flute so exquisitely (this is Cellini's own account), and on being told the name, ' Benvenuto Cellini of Florence ', he remarked : ' So then this is the son of Maestro Giovanni ? ' whom he recalled as an ardent supporter of the Medici. This was the beginning of a long series of interviews and conversations with Pope Clement, some happy and others held under stress of grave misfortune. Discovering that the young flute-player was also a highly-skilled jeweller, the Pope gave him money and commissions. Vases, clasps, cups, and other objects were ordered from Cellini in rapid succession, and in particular the Pope was charmed with Cellini's design for the great brooch, or fibula, for the papal cope. Into this ornament Cellini introduced the finest diamond in the papal treasury, making of this gem a seat for the Almighty upheld by three cherubs. This jewel, which triumphed over many rival suggestions, is minutely described by Cellini, and was finished by him, but none seems to know if this masterpiece of the goldsmith's art still exists.

Cellini working and amusing himself in Rome was thus a witness of and a participator in the final phase of the brilliant Leonine Age, which is counted as beginning with the election of the first Medici Pope, Leo X, in 1512, and

ending ignominiously with the siege and sack of Rome in
the reign of his cousin, the second Medici Pope, Clement VII,
in the spring of 1527. For after the battle of Pavia, the
dissolute, cultivated court of Rome and its many satellites
were living from day to day in a false paradise. Retribution
overhung the city and the Vatican, and it came with the
advance of the ragged disreputable army of the Constable
of Bourbon in May 1527. This force, composed of Spanish
Imperialist soldiers, of German Lutheran mercenaries, and
some renegade Italian tenants of the Colonna family, laid
siege to the city and carried it by storm, with the exception
of the strong fortress of the castle of Sant' Angelo. Within
these walls was shut up the unhappy Pope with many of
his cardinals, and the place was ably defended. Not least
amongst these defenders must be reckoned our friend
Cellini, who showed his marked skill as a bombardier. He
even declared that it was he who killed the Constable of
Bourbon with his artillery, and wounded the Prince of
Orange. Be that as it may, it is certain that Benvenuto
played a prominent and indeed an honourable part in the
defence of the castle during the month of May 1527. During
these anxious weeks in Sant' Angelo two incidents befell
Cellini which later on were destined to do him great dis-
service. In the first place, he had the ill-luck in the
performance of his duty to upset the dignity of the irascible
old Cardinal Alessandro Farnese, afterwards Pope Paul III ;
and secondly, he carried out, at Clement's special request,
a commission which in later days he had often to rue. This
was the unsetting of the papal crown jewels, which Clement
concealed on his person, and the melting down of certain
gold plate. It is curious to observe how very cautious and
discreet Cellini is in his stirring account of the siege and sack
of Rome, although writing more than thirty years after the
event. He says nothing as to the causes and consequences
of the siege ; and as to the infamous treachery of the Duke

of Urbino with the papal army in not coming to the rescue of his suzerain, the Pope, he merely observes, ' On this matter, as it is not my business, I shall make no comment.'

After the abject capitulation of Pope Clement to the Emperor Charles V, Cellini left Rome and returned to his father and family in Florence. Here he found the plague raging, no unusual phenomenon in those days. To add to his other difficulties he was now called on to play a definite political part, and he hated politics. After the fall of Rome, Florence had thrown off the yoke of the Medici in that city, then represented by the two young Medici bastards, Ippolito and Alessandro ; the citizens had proclaimed the Republic, and were already preparing to put their city in a state of defence. Now, although his divine master, Michelangelo, had eagerly offered his services to the new Republic, Cellini positively declined to take up arms against Pope Clement and the Medici, whose bread both he and his father before him had eaten ; and I think this refusal on his part redounds greatly to his credit, though most modern critics blame him for his lack of ' patriotism ', as though they were better judges of his own views and circumstances than was Cellini himself. Although no politician, as I have said, and indeed a hater of politics, Cellini was throughout his career a firm *pallesco*, or partisan of the Medici, and he describes later on how the truculent Florentine republican exiles, of whom he speaks in terms of contempt, used to try to pick gratuitous quarrels with him at Venice and elsewhere. Accordingly, Cellini left Florence on•the eve of the great siege, which ended three years later in the surrender of the city to Pope Clement and the installation of that Pope's favourite, Alessandro dei Medici, as first Duke of Florence. There was also another and a domestic reason for his quitting Florence at this time. The plague of 1527 had swept off his father and nearly the whole Cellini family, leaving only his sister Liperata and his soldier brother Cecchino. On returning from a short visit to Mantua, Benvenuto found his sister in deep distress with Cecchino vainly trying to comfort her. Benvenuto joined for a while in the tears and lamentations of Liperata, and then the three decided, with true Renaissance philosophy, to prepare supper and to cease talking of their dead. So they made merry over wine and meat, referred no more to their losses, but discoursed gaily about weddings.

On the return of Clement and the papal court to Rome, a very altered and chastened Rome since its siege and sack, Cellini also returned and spent the next five years or so in the service of Clement. He undertook many commissions for the Pope and had several intimate conversations with him. Cellini, in fact, is almost the only chronicler of his day who has a good word for the hated and despised Clement, and for his fidelity to his patron I have always liked Cellini, despite his many faults and misdeeds. To the last he used to attend upon Clement, then sinking to the grave with a slow, consuming fever. During the last months of the Pope's life he was engaged on striking medals for his patron. ' On the 22nd September,' he writes, ' of the year 1534, I waited on the Pope, whom I found very ill in bed. Yet he gave me the most kindly reception, telling me of his wish to inspect both the medals and the instruments wherewith I had stamped them. He ordered his spectacles and a candle to be brought, but nevertheless he could discern nothing of my workmanship. So he set to examine the medals by the touch of his fingers, but after feeling thus for some length of time he fetched a deep sigh, and told one of the courtiers he was sorry for me, but if it pleased God to restore his health, he would make me a satisfactory payment. Three days later he died, and I had only my labour for my pains. . . .' Cellini adds that some days later, whilst all Rome was execrating the memory of the dead Pope, ' he put on his sword and repaired to St. Peter's, where he kissed the feet of the late Pontiff (who was then lying in state), nor could he refrain from tears.'

Some little time before the death of Pope Clement, Cellini lost his brother Cecchino, who was then serving under Duke Alessandro of Florence. The hot-headed young soldier was killed in a street quarrel, such as occurred nightly in the dark, narrow streets of Rome. The account of Cecchino's death forms one of the most striking passages in the *Autobiography*, and there can be no doubt that Benvenuto owned a full share of family affection, though in this case it took the characteristic form of seeking out and finally stabbing to death his brother's assassin, all of which is related with *naïveté* and full details. He had his brother's body buried, with a fine marble monument in the national church of the Florentines in Rome (San Giovanni dei Fiorentini), and above it he placed the alleged coat of arms of the Cellini family—a golden lion rampant upon an azure field with a label of four points and three lilies gules in chief.

After Clement's death Cellini returned to Florence, where he was cordially received by Duke Alessandro dei Medici, who set him to work on some fine medals. Cellini describes the duke and his cousin Lorenzino dei Medici, who was then always in his company, and he mentions his suspicions of Lorenzino's intended plot, which came to a head in January 1537, when Lorenzino murdered his kinsman the duke in the old Medici palace. It would have been better for Cellini had he remained in Florence ; but he always seems to have found a special attraction in Rome, and thither he now made his way. Cardinal Alessandro Farnese had meantime been elected Pope as Paul III, and to him Cellini now applied for patronage, which he soon obtained. Paul III was the last and probably the worst of the line of the secular or worldly popes, and Cellini draws a lurid portrait of him, and a still blacker one of his bastard son, Pier-Luigi Farnese, afterwards first Duke of Parma. That Cellini's account of

Paul III is highly coloured is quite possible ; yet any one
who has seen Titian's famous portrait of that suspicious
cruel old fox and his abominable heir can easily credit
anything evil concerning both father and son. Paul was
old, both in years and in iniquity, and Cellini, knowing that
he bore him a grudge ever since the days of the siege of the
castle of Sant' Angelo, was doubtless rash in placing himself
in the power of this pope. Yet at first Paul seemed well
disposed towards Cellini, whose artistic talents he was well
able to appreciate. What exactly caused the Pope to
wreak his vengeance on Cellini is not very easy to discover.
Possibly the insult of years ago still rankled, for Paul was
as unforgiving as he was treacherous ; also, Cellini held at
that time a lucrative post in the Roman mint, through the
gift of the late Clement VII, which Pier-Luigi coveted for
some minion of his own. Another reason, that on which
Paul and his son based their infamous treatment of Cellini,
was the charge that he had secreted and stolen some of the
papal crown jewels, which, as already stated, Cellini had
unset or melted down at the urgent command of the late
Pope. Clement during the siege of Rome. This was the
definite accusation whether really believed or feigned, and it
was on this plea that Cellini was one day arrested by the
papal police and conveyed to the state prison in the castle
of Sant' Angelo, where he remained a captive of the Farnese
Pope for over two years.

At first he was treated with distinction, and was allowed
to carry on his various works in the castle, and the Pope
from time to time continued to send him friendly messages
—so characteristic of Italian cunning to ensure a victim's
ultimate destruction. But after a time the unhappy man
was relegated to the dungeons below the level of the Tiber,
where he hardly saw a ray of daylight, where the floor lay
inches deep in foul water, and where he was fed on mouldy
bread, and precious little even of that. Combined with all

these miseries was the almost certain feeling that he would either be assassinated in his dark cell or else be brought out for summary execution. For this vile treatment on a charge of which he was wholly innocent, Cellini lays the blame partly on the Pope, but chiefly on Pier-Luigi. Once he escaped from his prison, breaking his leg in the attempt, but he was recaptured, and guarded more severely than before. The marvel is that Cellini ever emerged alive from that awful dungeon, or that he did not go mad under these fearful inflictions. As it was, he contracted a low fever, his hair and teeth began to fall out and he constantly prayed for death. It was during the long months of this terrible trial that Cellini was supported by his strong natural belief in God and by a strange spirit of resignation in misfortune, which constantly appears throughout his career. He had visions too to comfort him in his distress. In the gloom and stink of his dungeon he saw brilliant sunlight and savoured sweet scents ; he conversed with the Blessed Virgin and St. Peter ; he came into close touch with those mystical beauties that make the things of earth, whether good or bad, seem of small consequence. His description of his adventures in Sant' Angelo provides most fascinating reading, and the manifest sincerity wherewith he relates his subconscious experiences adds to their value. Amongst other things he declares with evident sincerity that ever since his colloquy with the Blessed Virgin a faint halo of light has always surrounded his head, and that in after years many of his acquaintances have often noticed this luminous aureole.

It was undoubtedly due to the persistent efforts of Cardinal Ippolito d'Este and the frequent appeals to the Pope on his behalf by King Francis of France that Cellini owed his life, and ultimately his release, which took place in 1540. He was now removed to the palace of the Cardinal d'Este in Rome, and here in course of time his iron

constitution enabled him to recover from the effects of his
late imprisonment.   Gladly now he joined the train of the
Cardinal d'Este, who was about to leave· for France on a
diplomatic mission to King Francis.   Under this safe escort
Cellini crossed the Mont Cenis passes in comfort and finally
reached Fontainebleau.   It was Cellini's second visit to
France, for a few years before he had travelled thither by
way of Switzerland, and he gives us a racy account of the
dangers and difficulties he encountered on this first journey.
On this second occasion he was pledged to enter the service
of the Most Christian King Francis, whose acquaintance he
now made.   Next to Pope Clement, the French King was
undoubtedly his favourite amongst Cellini's many royal
patrons.   In his narrative he rarely mentions Francis's
name without some epithet of affection or regard, and the
picture he draws of that monarch certainly serves to endear
Francis's memory to us.   He was warmly welcomed at the
French court, and the King promptly gave as a dwelling
and workshop for himself and his two apprentices, Pagolo
and Ascanio, the ancient Petit Tour de Nesle on the bank
of the Seine, almost opposite the royal palace of the Louvre.
Francis proved both generous and genial towards his
Florentine guest, and commissions began to pour in on
Cellini.   Many of the works he undertook in Paris have
been lost or destroyed, but there survives the ' Diana of
Fontainebleau ' in bronze, now preserved in the Louvre.
It shows a nymph beside a brook, surrounded by stags,
boars, and other animals of the chase, being intended for an
allegorical group of the château and forest of Fontainebleau.
For this Diana there posed as model Cellini's mistress of the
time being, the girl Caterina, whom he treated with a
brutality which even he admits with shame in the *Autobiography*.   Another elaborate piece which he executed for
King Francis still exists, and is, or was, in the Imperial
museum at Vienna.   This was a salt-cellar representing the

union of Earth and Sea, a Neptune and a Cybele with entwined limbs amid a host of minor accessories. It was wrought in solid gold with much translucent enamelling, and though overloaded and confused, like all Cellini's smaller objects, it owns a special interest for us owing to the artist's minute description of the design, difficulties, and completion of this table ornament. Again, the poor ill-treated Caterina was utilized for the nude figure of Mother Earth.

One point is curious and worth mentioning in this French sojourn, so carefully described. The wife of the Dauphin, afterwards King Henry II, was Catherine de Médicis, heiress of the Medici of Florence of the senior line, and though Cellini mentions her by name once or twice, he does not speak of her as having helped him or patronized him in any way, although, as a Florentine and a warm partisan of the Medici, Cellini certainly deserved her good offices.

The years spent in Paris were probably the busiest and most fruitful in Cellini's career. He was continually improving his art and extending its scope ; from mere minute goldsmith's work he was now producing figures on a larger and more ambitious scale. For the rest of his life Cellini never ceased to lament his unwisdom in deserting the congenial court of France, with its high pay and constant marks of royal favour and privilege. Probably he never would have returned to Italy but for the constant malevolence shown him by Madame d'Etampes, the royal mistress, whom he had mortally offended and had not the necessary tact to placate ; and, by the way, Cellini seems to have had a positive genius for provoking the great ladies of his day into hostility ; for the same annoyance was destined to arise later when he resided at Florence working for Duke Cosimo, whose consort, Eleonora of Toledo, he also contrived to turn into a personal enemy.

After a five years' residence in France, Cellini in 1545

returned to Italy, not a little to the chagrin of King Francis, who wished to retain him at his court. On his way back to Florence he had a curious adventure as he passed through Piacenza. Here in the street he suddenly found himself face to face with Pier-Luigi Farnese, now on the point of being created Duke of Parma and Piacenza by his father, Paul III. ' The sight of him made my blood boil,' records Cellini, and one is not surprised thereat. But, all the same, we read how the Farnese duke affected to welcome him and invited him to dinner at his palace, where the two men spent their time in covering one another with compliments and good wishes. Pier-Luigi threw all the blame of his guest's imprisonment in Rome on his father, declaring he had done all that was possible to obtain Cellini's release. Of course this was a lie, and both Pier-Luigi and his guest knew it to be so, but villainy and compliments often go hand in hand, and here was a case in point. Cellini adds complacently that Pier-Luigi was murdered two years later, and, to put it mildly, he hints that he got no more than his deserts.

In August 1545 Cellini reached Florence, where he found his sister Liperata a widow with six daughters and in the depth of poverty. Much to his credit he immediately took Liperata and his nieces into a house he bought in Via della Pergola and provided for them so long as he lived. After settling his domestic affairs he next went to pay his court to the reigning duke, Cosimo dei Medici, afterwards first Grand Duke of Tuscany. He was cordially received, and after some confabulation the commission was given him for a large bronze statue of Perseus with the head of the Gorgon that the duke wished to erect in the great square of Florence. From this date onward the pages of the *Autobiography* are largely occupied with the story of this remarkable statue, which to-day dominates the Piazza della Signoria from its prominent position in the Loggia dei Lanzi. It was the most ambitious work Cellini had yet attempted, and his account of his troubles and trials over the design, the casting, and the completion of his Perseus must be read in his own words. The eyes of every visitor to Florence to-day are irresistibly attracted to the Perseus of Cellini. Poised aloft above the corpse of the Gorgon, and proudly displaying her bleeding head, Cellini's beautiful if somewhat theatrical hero seems the embodiment of the art of the later Italian Renaissance, and we recognize in such a work what has been gained in strict technique and lost in antique simplicity. The statue surmounts a richly sculptured base of marble enriched with four small figures in bronze, and with a bronze bas-relief below of the Rescue of Andromeda.

This Perseus is of course Cellini's masterpiece, and he knew it. It exhibits at once his best and his worst qualities. It is essentially the true child of his versatile genius. A few paces off, in the arcade of the Uffizi, the statue of Cellini himself amongst the illustrious sons of Florence surveys his *chef d'œuvre* with complacency.

> I need no dusty garland at the feet
> Of mine own counterfeit in yon arcade,
> Whose cramping niches form a last retreat
> For such of us have this Florence made ;
> The father's happiness is all complete,
> If in the Loggia Perseus be displayed.

And, of a truth, if not the best in a strictly artistic sense, the Perseus of Benvenuto Cellini is the most effective and forcible of all the Florentine statues.

Two other works only I shall mention as belonging to the lengthy final phase of Cellini's career in Florence, which lasted from 1545 till his death in 1570, at the age of seventy. These are the fine but not very pleasing bust of the Grand Duke Cosimo, now in the Florentine museum of the Bargello ; and the large white marble crucifix on a black marble cross, which was presented after the artist's death by the Grand Duke Francis I to King Philip II of Spain, and now constitutes one of the chief treasures of the chapel of the Escorial near Madrid. Both these works and their vicissitudes are carefully described in detail by Cellini in his *Autobiography*.

These last twenty-five years of his busy, restless life were all passed in his native Florence in the service of Duke Cosimo, and not over-happily. The later pages of the *Autobiography* are filled with petty or unedifying quarrels between himself and the sculptors Bandinelli and Ammanati, who likewise enjoyed the patrongae of Cosimo and the Medici. Cosimo in Cellini's esteem fell far below his former patron, King Francis, both in sympathy and in generosity. ' I tried to deal with the Duke as with a Prince,' he comments querulously, ' but I found him only a merchant '—a trait that seems natural enough in the scion of a family of bankers. Besides this, Cellini had to endure the spiteful enmity of the Duchess Eleonora, whom, with his usual want of tact towards great ladies, he had somehow contrived to offend. But these latter years of anxiety and disappointment did produce one outstanding work, though not a work of the chisel or graver, but of the pen. In 1558 Cellini, in a moment of happy inspiration, decided to write his memoirs, and posterity is truly thankful for this decision. The *Autobiography*, or *Vita da Lui Stesso*, was first dictated to a scribe, but the concluding sixty-eight chapters are written in autograph. The whole book was laid aside in the autumn of 1562, and ends abruptly with the sentence, ' Then I betook myself to Pisa ' ('*Da poi me ne andai a Pisa*'), namely, to join the ducal court.

The original manuscript of the work can be seen in the beautiful Laurentian Library at Florence, a structure reared by his adored master, Michelangelo. It consists of two parts divided into numerous chapters. At the end of the first part is inserted the strange poem composed during his occult experience in the dungeons of the castle of Sant'

Angelo. There are no literary tricks or graces to be found in the *Autobiography*, which is apt to become obscure and rambling, though never tedious, in its long narration. Cellini cannot distinguish the trivial from the important events of his career. Yet, on the whole, it reads pleasantly and smoothly, as we pass from one incident to another in all places and in every grade of society without any sense of weariness. It has deservedly always been popular, and it has often been translated. Of the various English translations I need only mention the admirable one of John Addington Symonds, with its valuable introduction and foot-notes.

Benvenuto Cellini died on February 13th, 1570–71, and was buried in the Servite Church of the Annunziata, not far from the tomb of his detested rival, Baccio Bandinelli. He had in 1554 been admitted to membership of the new Florentine nobility, and had, about 1564, married a certain Piera Parigi, who bore him a son and a daughter, but his legitimate descendants seem to have become extinct in the third generation. Cellini himself at various times mentions no fewer than six bastard children, whose existence sat lightly on his conscience.

I have said that from Cellini's book we obtain some vivid sidelights on many of the important persons of his age. Yet one figure emerges somewhat blurred and uncertain from its pages, and that is none other than the author himself. We are left with a rather vague and hazy notion of the personality and character of Benvenuto Cellini, and yet it is on that very personality that the value of the *Autobiography* largely rests. One cannot help agreeing with a modern American critic, who declares that ' one always feels in reading the memoirs of Benvenuto Cellini, that the man who is telling the story is quite distinct from the man about whom it is being told. The fellow indeed was too noble an artist to do a mere portrait with fidelity ; he could not resist the temptation to repair a cauliflower ear here, to paint out a tell-tale scar there, to shine up the eyes a bit, to straighten the legs down '. That is only to say, a portrait of self must always err on the side of flattery ; and this much we are all ready to grant and admit. Nevertheless, two things stand out clearly to me in this narrative. First of all, Cellini was an honest man ; and secondly, he was truthful, despite some of his extravagance and bombast. His statements as to his fees and the offers made him by his patrons at various times have in many cases been amply confirmed by documents discovered in the archives, and this plain circumstance should of itself incline us to give credit to statements of his on other matters.

The extravagance lies on the surface ; it does not permeate the substance of the book. Here and there Cellini is clearly carried away by hate or prejudice, and we must make the necessary allowance for him. But where hate or prejudice does not arise, he shows himself a shrewd and fair judge of the persons with whom he came in contact. And more important to us than the light he throws on individual personages of his day, is the general light he throws on the manners and common philosophy of the whole of Renaissance society. We note too in his pages the gradual transformation of society from the older traditions and ideas of the Early Renaissance to the more modern views that succeeded the sack of Rome and the final establishment of the dynasty of the Medici in Florence. Cellini lived in a time of vast political and social changes. The political issues he always ignores, but the social changes, perhaps quite unconsciously, he records and expounds for us admirably. He perceived a great change from the Italy of his youth in the Italy of his old age. Law and order were asserting themselves. Life had become easier and less dangerous. The fast and furious days of the Leonine Age had given place to more settled and more civilized conditions. This development is

clearly reflected in his pages. His latter years spent in
Florence under the iron rule of Duke Cosimo must have
appeared indeed humdrum when compared with the merry
mad times he had enjoyed and braved in the Rome of
Clement VII. What a game life had been then for the
young artist and soldier and scholar in the Leonine Age !
He pictures for us the dare-devil, fatalistic attitude of
himself and his comrades who worked for Pope Clement.
How they drank and feasted and laboured and lusted
together. How one moment they hung round each other's
necks vowing eternal affection, and how the next moment
they were striving to dig their long, sharp knives into each
other's ribs. Cellini's account of it all rings true, and I have
no doubt it was true. He has presented us with a lively
picture of talented youth in his own young days, and we
must feel sincerely grateful for such a picture.

Again, Cellini is frequently described as a braggart and a
boaster. This, however, is only superficially correct. His
boundless confidence in his own powers certainly tempted
him to boast ; but what would be absurd in most people is,
after all, not so absurd in a Benvenuto Cellini, who proved
his versatile ability over and over again. True, he was
violent, but so was his age ; he did many mean things, so
did his betters ; he committed murders, so did his comrades
—doubtless under stress of a quarrel it was a case of your
life or my life, and your life in preference to my own. That
was not only Cellini's philosophy, but the philosophy of all.

He has been called bigoted and superstitious. In reality
he was neither. He was, in his way, sincerely religious,
though with a form and ideal of religion that repel our
colder northern nature. Shelley in one of his letters comments that the Italian wears his religion like a cloak that
he doffs or dons according to convenience. But it is always
ready to hand. And Cellini wrapped himself in his religious
cloak to good purpose during his awful trial in the dungeons

of Sant' Angelo. As to superstition, man always is superstitious ; it is really rather a question of concealment or of open display. I do not think we moderns, with our mascots and our wizards and our fortune-tellers and our crystal-gazing, have any right to twit the people of the Renaissance with undue credulity. On the whole, I think we may regard Cellini in his youth as a very fair example of the average young blood and artist of the Renaissance, neither better nor worse than his fellows in his morals, and superior to many of them in his transparent honesty. Cellini, moreover, possesses what is rare in an Italian—no small sense of humour. This crops up throughout his book, and gives it an additional attraction. He can even laugh at his own foibles and excesses. I quite agree that some of his acts are inexcusable—notably, for example, his truly horrible treatment of his poor model, Caterina, in Paris, whom he used to beat black and blue, and drag by her hair over his studio. Yet even here, it is worthy of record, Cellini does actually admit he was in the wrong to behave so brutally, and almost expresses his sorrow. One must take the *Autobiography* as a whole, and judge it as a whole, and not piecemeal so as to pick out stray specimens of its author's violence, or braggadocio, or exaggeration, or thirst for revenge.

I have quoted very little from the *Autobiography* itself, though it contains a succession of interesting or amusing events that might easily arouse in turn a laugh, or a sigh, or a blush. It should be read in its entirety both as a human and as an historical document of that period of transition from the Middle to the Modern Age which we sometimes call the Later Renaissance. If we seek history therein, we find a description of the siege and sack of Rome from an eye-witness ; we have glimpses, amongst others, of Popes Clement VII and Paul III, and of King Francis of France, Duke Cosimo of Tuscany and of the Duke of

Ferrara. We have sketched for us in sharp outline, some-times with sympathy and sometimes with bitterness, a number of the illustrious personages of the period in Italy and France. I have spoken of his appreciation of Pope Clement, to whom Cellini showed his loyalty and gratitude, both of which qualities, by the way, he certainly possessed. And what could be more sinister than his account of Paul III, the evil Farnese Pontiff, or more natural than the touch of posthumous malice in relating his love of wine, which he indulged in once a week till he was tipsy, and then took a vomit ? I believe it to be true ; indeed, I could believe anything evil of this odious, ambitious, violent old wretch who lived to be eighty-three, an almost unprecedented age in that period. How amusing is Cellini's account of Francis's thraldom to the whims and whinings of his mistress, Madame d'Etampes ! Into the home-life of Duke Cosimo and his duchess, Eleonora of Toledo, he admits us with singular freedom, and we are shown both the pleasant and the seamy sides of that upstart Medici court in Florence. We get glimpses of other famous men, such as the bibliophile Grolier (no friend to Cellini) ; the tyrant Pier-Luigi Farnese, Cellini's most dangerous foe ; the Cardinal Ippolito d'Este, son of the famous Isabella, Marchioness of Mantua, whose *Letters*, lately published, form, after Cellini's book, one of our most important sources of social information on the Renaissance.

But it is in dealing with the artists of every description of his age that Cellini most arouses our interest and curiosity. Above them all (and Cellini knew them all intimately) towers the majestic figure of Michelangelo Buonaroti, whom Cellini always worshipped as his special master. Yet, however they may have agreed on artistic matters, Michel-angelo and Benvenuto became widely separated by politics. Cellini was, as I have said, all his life a silent but faithful partisan of the Medici ; Michelangelo hated them as tyrants and had actually commanded the party of defence at the siege of Florence against Pope Clement in 1529. In later years Cellini was charged with a commission by Duke Cosimo to persuade the great Florentine exile to return and to enter his service. Cellini relates how he carried the duke's message to Michelangelo in Rome, and in reading between the lines it is pretty evident that the divine master on this occasion must have snubbed his devoted pupil for daring to bring any message from a Medici to him.

An altogether delightful, if not very edifying account, is Cellini's picture of the young artistic society of Rome in the days of Pope Clement. What jolly times those were, compact of congenial work, pleasure, and danger. What feastings and fun they had, a merry mad crew, living from day to day, now draped in silks and satins, and now in rags. Now in buoyant, almost insolent, health, and now stricken with some filthy pestilence or contagion and left to the mercy of their chance comrades' or mistresses' nursing, or to the still more incompetent attentions of the quacks of the day ; and there were naught but arrant quacks in medical practice at that period, as we may easily learn from Cellini's accounts of the nostrums and treatment supplied by these greedy impostors. Cellini relates as a memory of his apprentice days in Rome, a certain supper-party whereat each one of the guests was bidden to bring a model or a mistress by way of female element to the feast. But Cellini, with the Florentine's love of a practical joke, must needs dress up his young journeyman, a Spanish boy called Diego, as a girl with rich jewels (and Cellini's jewels were worth wearing, we may be sure !). The ruse succeeded finely, and the blushing Diego became the toast of the evening without his sex being discovered. This is only one stray incident gathered from a hundred and more, for the whole book is one long succession of tales, jokes, adventures, conversations, and reflections.

In conclusion, I must refer, though briefly, to the art of Cellini. He was of course admittedly the greatest goldsmith of his day, and perhaps of all time. In his book he gives descriptions, often at great length, of the fine objects of *virtù* he has made for pope or prince, but of all the mass of his productions very few *really genuine* specimens survive. One can count these undoubted pieces of his workmanship almost on one hand. They include the Cellini ewer, recently sold from the Beresford-Hope collection; the Neptune salt-cellar made for King Francis, which I have already mentioned; a gold cup in Florence; three small medallions preserved at the Vatican; a pair of richly-chased candelabra in a church, and a gold and tortoiseshell casket in a palace at Genoa. Many pieces are *ascribed* to Cellini, and in many places, but their authenticity is doubtful. Of his larger, later and more ambitious statues we have the Perseus, the bust of Duke Cosimo, and a restored antique Ganymede, all in Florence; the nymph of Fontainebleau at the Louvre; and his crucifix, on which he expended much time and trouble in his last years, now at the palace of the Escorial. It is not a long list for so active and enthusiastic an artist. Perhaps, after all, Cellini reared for himself a monument more lasting than his figures of marble and bronze in his *Autobiography*.

VIII

THE CONNEXION BETWEEN ART AND HISTORY
DURING THE ITALIAN RENAISSANCE

IT will be generally conceded that in certain aspects
Art is closely allied to History. Temples, churches,
castles, paintings, furniture, coins, and medals all
help us to evoke a true picture of past times and persons.
It is admittedly a vast subject, and I can only deal briefly
with one small section of it here, namely, the epoch of the
Italian Renaissance, and indeed only with a portion of that.
History as a whole, it has sometimes occurred to me, may
be likened to the human body. Its anatomy or framework
is Constitutional history ; its organs of action, such as the
heart, the brain, the liver, may be compared with Political
history. Yet there still remains a third component part
to complete the whole. Art, or Aesthetic history, I deem
to be that which in the body historical gives a sparkle to
the eyes, a sheen to the hair, colour to the lips, and grace
to the limbs. Hitherto this third element, this Cinderella
of the historical trinity, has been neglected, even despised.
Art has been left severely to the so-called artistic person,
who in his or her turn is often as ignorant of true history as
many a so-called historian is ignorant of art. But the
time has come for the modern historian to recognize the
claims of Art in his studies, and learn to blend its teaching
and significance with those constitutional and political
events and developments that up to now have engrossed
his sole attention.

In dealing thus with the Italian Renaissance we must ever
bear one important circumstance in mind—that the new
learning and the new culture from the East were permeating

Europe through the cities of Italy. In the history of human progress Italy ranks as by far the most ancient country in Europe, and its inhabitants have enjoyed a far longer stretch of civilization than any other part of our continent. We usually, but quite erroneously, think of Italy as starting into prominence with the rise of Rome ; whereas, in reality, long before Rome itself was founded there was the previous existence of the cities of Magna Graecia with their marked influence on the native population. And again, behind this background of early Greek colonial influence we have to reckon with the dim mysterious Etruscan civilization with its wonderful tombs, its sculpture, its jewellery, its evident if restricted knowledge of science and agriculture. Cumae was a flourishing port before Rome was a mud village ; and Etruscan Volterra was probably an artistic and highly-developed community before Cumae was founded. I mention this to show that the learning and light from the East only penetrated later to the raw young nations of the West through a well-prepared antique medium, which in its passing must have left Italian marks and tendencies upon it. So thoughtful and original a writer as the late Samuel Butler recognized this peculiar and innate quality in the Italian race, and he has descanted upon it with all his whimsical charm and acumen in his medley of travel and philosophy, *Alps and Sanctuaries*. In the days with which I am now concerned, namely, the Renaissance, the centre of Italian influence and culture had shifted from Rome to Florence, and in a less degree to Venice, Milan, Mantua, and Ferrara. Thus when we discuss problems and personages of the Italian Renaissance we are dealing with a people whose march of progress had been continuous for ages past, and not with youthful nations such as Britain, or France, or Spain, that owe their rescue from primitive barbarism to the expansion of the Roman Empire ; nor again with still younger nations, such as Germany and Scandinavia, that had later to work out their social salvation in the twilight of the Middle Ages. My point is, that in speaking of Machiavelli, of the Medici, of Raphael, of Michelangelo, of Leonardo da Vinci and a hundred other great names of the Italian Renaissance, we must remember that all these master-minds were not merely pioneers in their respective fields of learning, or art, or politics, or science, but were themselves the actual inheritors of the most ancient culture and tradition that Western Europe had yet known.

Now, in the Italy of the Renaissance we recognize the fount and origin of that marvellous flood of culture and learning that swept over Western Europe between the fourteenth and the seventeenth centuries. The popes, the clergy, the despots, the nobles, the burghers, the scholars, the artisans of Italy were all infected with this new spirit, which they in turn managed to infuse into more remote nations—France, Spain, Germany, England, Scotland. In the art of this period it is interesting to note two diverse tendencies—the Gothic or medieval, and the classical revival. Gothic art had never really taken firm root in Italy, so tenaciously did the tradition of Roman culture survive ; it was not dead, but only sleeping. True, there are many magnificent specimens of Gothic architecture to be found in Italy, but they impress and please us rather through their richness of exquisite detail than by their proportion and effect. Italy was in fact always ripe for the re-birth of its own vanished culture. Yet the early Italian pioneers of the revival of art belonged of necessity to the existing Gothic school—take, for instance, the case of the saintly painter Fra Angelico, whose medieval influence in the world of art may fitly be compared with that of Savonarola in the religious and political spheres. But the natural genius of the Italian people once aroused, it soon began to modify this Gothic spirit, and in time to replace it by forms and canons of art, which may be described as

Neo-classical or Renaissance. And this rapid change was so strong, so popular in the true sense, that during the fifteenth and sixteenth centuries Art was able for a period to win and hold its due place in the historical progress of the Italian people. Princes and peoples alike were possessed of this new aesthetic enthusiasm to such purpose that all the cities and petty states north of Rome were found vying with each other in their devotion to the arts. Civic prosperity and worth indeed came to be measured in terms of artistic possession rather than in terms of political power or mercantile wealth. ' We will build,' declared the guilds and the citizens of Florence, ' a cathedral as large and splendid as the brain of man can conceive and the hand of man can execute.' . And forthwith the present cathedral of Florence was begun. Thereupon, in jealous emulation, the neighbouring people of Siena decreed the rebuilding of their own church on a scale that was to eclipse the grandiose conception of the Florentines. Nor were Venice, Bologna, Milan, Lucca, and other cities slow in following suit. Such was the spirit of the age, and a study of this spirit will help the student of history in his task, and will sweeten his labours in disentangling its political questions.

It is possible in Italy still to observe and appreciate this close connexion of History with Art. Even to-day, in some of the smaller towns, we find ourselves amid the unspoiled settings of great men and of great events of the past. That old Tuscan free city, Siena, for example, remains a living museum, wherein its citizens on festal days still don the picturesque dress of their ancestors and for a few hours fall back easily and naturally into the stirring times of their own St. Catherine of Siena and of their famous fellow-citizen Aeneas Silvius Piccolomini, Pope Pius II. But this aspect of the case may perhaps be regarded as sentimental rather than historical, and it is therefore to the larger cities of Italy, and to Rome and Florence in particular, that I wish to draw your attention. For here in these two places you will be brought face to face with artistic treasures that own a distinct bearing not only on local history, but on the history of Europe—indeed, of the whole civilized world.

Now the history of Europe, whether political, constitutional or religious, from the Council of Constance in 1415 to the middle of the succeeding century, centres round the papacy with its seat at Rome. And it was the popes from Nicholas V onward who were the leading patrons of contemporary Art, then in the full flush of its strength and development. The popes were patrons, not necessarily by reason of their aesthetic sympathy or tastes, but as often as not for purely political or personal ends. Art actually predominates, I make bold to declare, during the critical reigns of Alexander VI (Borgia) ; Julius II (della Rovere), Leo X, and Clement VII (the two Medici pontiffs), and Paul III (Farnese).

In architecture, take St. Peter's alone. Why, that basilica is a veritable sermon in stone and marble of the Reformation and the counter-Reformation. To wander in St. Peter's, ' the world's cathedral ', as Nathaniel Hawthorne has happily termed it, offers to the historian and the philosopher an endless feast of meditation and criticism. There lurks ever a subtle intellectual atmosphere in St. Peter's which always brings to my mind the shrewd comment of poor old Pius IX, last temporal sovereign of Rome : ' In St. Peter's Man *thinks*.' Yes, and think what was the guiding force that raised this gorgeous modern temple, a building so vast that it would even be visible from the moon with a terrestrial telescope. It was the soaring ambition of Pope Julius II, the true founder of the temporal power of the papacy, and the genius of Michelangelo in unison that planned this enterprise. ' I mean to swing the dome of the Roman Pantheon five hundred feet in mid-air ! ' boasted the artist. ' And I mean to erect a throne beneath that dome where kings and emperors shall kneel at my footstool,' was Julius's hope and intention. Both pope and artist failed to attain their ambitious aims ; but I have seen a plan of the reconstruction of St. Peter's as originally arranged by this pair. It was to be designed in the form of a Greek cross, that is, with broad, shortened arms of equal length, crowned with a cupola, and having its interior largely filled with an erection that was to be partly tomb of Julius himself and adorned with Michelangelo's statuary, partly altar, and partly throne, whence the spiritual Caesars of Rome were to judge and administer the Christian world.

The Apostolic Palace, the Vatican, adjoins St. Peter's. Let us imagine ourselves as standing at its great Gates of Bronze, and with our heads well stored with the collected knowledge and researches of Ranke, Gregorovius, Creighton, Burckhardt, Roscoe, Pastor, Villari, and a score of other erudite writers on the Italian Renaissance. We enter, and as we proceed we note the blond Swiss halberdiers in gay parti-coloured uniform. Yes, it is the identical livery designed by Michelangelo for the bodyguard of the warrior-Pope, Julius II. We ascend the Scala Regia, the grand staircase, and thence proceed to the Sistine Chapel. Here, verily, we find art closely combined with history. Overhead in the vaulting, we strain our eyes and necks to inspect Michelangelo's frescoes, so severe and sombre that Julius had angrily asked why he had not used more gold in his composition. 'Sire,' replied the intrepid artist, 'the predecessors of Your Holiness were only poor Jewish fishermen with no gold to spare. Silver and gold had they none, but such as they had they gave.' If it happen to be a feast day of the Church, we should find the walls of the Sixtine Chapel hung with the famous tapestries of Raphael, those very tapestries of which we jealously guard the original sketches, the so-called Raphael cartoons, in our museum at South Kensington. The scenes woven on the arras represent the Acts of the Apostles, and they ought to be fairly familiar to all of us from engravings and photographs. But if we examine the borders and the *socles*, or lower portion of these tapestries, we find a whole series of smaller scenes which represent episodes in the early life of Giovanni dei Medici, afterwards Pope Leo X. These additional designs were no doubt suggested by Leo himself to Raphael, and they form a most interesting but very little-known series of illustrations of the stormy career of the young Medici, who was cardinal at sixteen and pope at thirty-seven. Every incident in his early life is portrayed—his flight from Florence in the disguise of a friar, his capture at the battle of Ravenna, and so on. It was Leo's intention as Pope to present an even more magnificent set of tapestries, showing events in the life of Our Lord with appropriate scenes beneath to commemorate the events of the reign of His Vicar on earth, namely, Giovanni dei Medici, Pope Leo X.

Above the altar is that truly pagan fresco, ' The Last Judgement,' also by Michelangelo. A mass of nude figures rises and falls to or from the avenging Christ above, whilst Charon of the classical barge lurks below for the sinners tumbling headlong to the Styx. *O tempora! O mores!* Yet how characteristic of the times and taste of that dissolute scholar, Alessandro Farnese, Pope Paul III, for whom it was painted. Farnese was a reformed rake and one of the most astute of the political popes. The sight of this famous fresco should rouse us to inspect the Farnese Pope's portrait by Titian, now in the gallery of Naples. Here we may see him, lean, bearded, suspicious, looking like a cunning old dog-fox, arguing with his detestable bastard son and heir, Pier-Luigi Farnese, founder of the ducal House of Parma. A study of these two portraits by Titian is worth a volume on the papal nepotism of the period.

From the gloomy grandeur of the Sistine Chapel let us

ascend yet higher till we reach the rooms of Raphael. Here we enter a new world of historical allegory, a world of light and gladness. Thanks to the genius of Michelangelo the Sistine Chapel recalls the ambitious heart and martial courage of the rugged Julius. The rooms of Raphael on the contrary, are all eloquent of the liberal, easygoing, ostentatious, extravagant Medici Pope who (in his own words) was determined to ' enjoy the papacy '. In these halls, still gay with glowing colours and rich in carving and fantastic heraldry, are mingled the divinities of Olympus and the Saints of Paradise, the philosophers of the antique world and the confessors of Christendom, the sages of Greece and Rome and the poets of medieval Italy. All are shown conversing together in happy concord, and in this cheerful medley of diverse faiths and persons we cannot but perceive the very essence of the spirit of the Italian Renaissance, that almost cynical humanism which did not hesitate to put the virtuous counsel of Plato and Seneca on an equal footing with the stern theology of Dominic and Thomas Aquinas. Again, every one of these subjects from the brush of Raphael or his pupils represents in allegorical form some personal triumph of Julius II, of Leo X, of Clement VII. Calmly do these three pontiffs watch the celestial emissaries scatter the evil forces of barbarism ; we are shown the invading Frenchman and Spaniard driven forth from the sacred soil of Italy by Peter and Paul and all the heavenly host. ' In the rooms of Raphael,' comments Lord Bryce, ' the triumphs of the popedom over all its foes are set forth with matchless art and with matchless unveracity.' So be it. Of the quality of that art there can be no two opinions ; in the veracity or the unveracity of the papal point of view the historian of to-day can still find a fruitful field of study and speculation. For here around us is a whole portrait gallery of the illustrious personages of the Renaissance who themselves watched and applauded the progress of Raphael's work. ' The rooms painted by Raphael,' so writes the learned Bembo, Leo's secretary, ' are quite beautiful, not only on account of the skill shown in their execution, but also on account of the great number of portraits he has introduced.' What a mental page of history can we not conjure up as we linger in these chambers, and realize they were the official head-quarters of the papacy during those years when it was the pivot of European statecraft and intrigue ! How entrancing must have been the aspect of these bare apartments when they were peopled with a constant come-and-go of prelates, courtiers, ambassadors, poets, scholars, and statesmen, whose faces still gaze spectre-like at us from the painted walls !

One more instance of historical art at the Vatican. In the Borgia Apartments, which have only recently been opened to the public, is a suite of rooms adorned by Pinturicchio for Pope Alexander VI. Here is to be seen one of the best portraits of that pontiff, with a sensual, heavy, but far from unpleasant face. Here too appears his celebrated daughter, Lucretia Borgia, afterwards Duchess of Ferrara. Winning, golden-haired, dainty as a fairy, she is shown to us in these frescoes dressed as St. Catherine and engaged in expounding the truths of the Christian faith to her pontifical father's Moslem hostage, Prince Djem. Last of all there is an authentic likeness of the ever-famous Caesar Borgia. Here that elusive historical figure appears before us as a handsome stripling in tight hose and with a mass of yellow curls escaping from beneath his jaunty scarlet cap. He seems just any gay young spark of the Renaissance, caring only for jollity and adventure, quite a different type of person from the dark, sinister schemer of popular tradition. A sight of this painting ought of itself to sweep away a good deal of the original prejudice wherewith we all study his career. Possibly after this glimpse of the real Caesar Borgia we may begin to comprehend Machia-velli's admiration for this young prince, in whom he recognized, or thought he recognized, a possible saviour of Italy from the foreign invader, and even a model con-stitutional sovereign for a united Italy, a forerunner of King Victor-Emmanuel of Savoy. Bishop Creighton was perhaps the first historian to perceive that the Spanish Borgia Pope and his children were not in reality so black as they had been painted by Roman gossips and Venetian diarists. And I strongly believe Creighton owed his sound critical judgement to his familiarity with Renaissance art, which he always studied closely on the spot whilst preparing his standard work on the Secular Papacy.

After Rome, Florence. Florence has suffered less from the changes of time and progress than has the Eternal City. In the main, it still keeps for us the features it presented in the far-off days of its powerful Guilds and of the early Medici of the *Quattrocento*, as the Italians name our fifteenth century. Now, the whole story of the Medici of Florence should be approached in a liberal spirit and with an unbiased mind ; for it shows us an unique example of artistic taste and patronage being handed down from generation to generation in a single reigning family for over three hundred years—in fact, till the extinction of the Medici line itself in the eighteenth century. In spite of reams of abuse, from the embittered Florentine republican annalists in exile down to the ignorant diatribes of Mark Twain in our day, it is a mere matter of plain fact that the doings and records of the much-abused Medici show up neither better nor worse than those of any contemporary dynasty in Europe. More-over, unlike any other royal dynasty, the maligned Medici have bequeathed to us people of to-day a heritage of art so rich and varied that the extent of our debt can only be gauged by a prolonged visit to Florence itself. In very truth, the history of Florence from 1434 for three centuries is the history of the Medici, and the history of the Medici forms one continuous chronicle of progressive art.

To deal with Art itself, especially of painting. Many persons who visit Italy, and particularly Florence, are apt to complain that nearly all the pictures they see in the galleries and churches are purely sacred in character. They deplore the lack of human interest in the endless Madonnas and Nativities and Adorations and Miracles and Last Suppers. Yet in reality a large proportion of these so-called religious paintings teem with secular interest and contemporary portraiture. To give a single example to show what I mean. In the vast Uffizi Gallery of Florence is a celebrated ' Adoration of the Magi ', a masterpiece of that very great master, Sandro Botticelli, who has here assembled the leading members of the House of Medici in the guise of the Magi and their followers. Old Cosimo is shown kneeling at the Virgin's feet, with his two sons Piero and Giovanni also in the act of worshipping, whilst Lorenzo il Magnifico, stands close by his handsome younger brother, ' Il Bel Giulio '—Giuliano dei Medici, the father of Pope Clement VII. A striking figure wrapped in a yellow mantle at the side of the picture has by tradition always been accounted a portrait of Botticelli himself. Knowing these interior details of this work, what a wealth of historical portraiture is offered in the ' Adoration of the Magi '.

Take another instance, almost at random. In the private rooms of the Pitti Palace hangs another remarkable work by Botticelli—his ' Pallas Athene and the Centaur '. It represents Athene, or Minerva, crowned with olive, in the act of taming a shaggy monster, half man and half horse, who cringes to the goddess. For years the theme or intention of this painting was a puzzle to all. Finally it was left to an English scholar, who was not a professional artist or critic, to point out that the long, flowing robe of Athene was thickly ornamented with a pattern of triple diamond

rings. Now the triple diamond rings formed the special
badge of the famous Lorenzo dei Medici, Il Magnifico, third
Prince of Florence and father of Pope Leo X. Once this
fact was realized, the historian came to the rescue with the
explanation that this picture was undoubtedly the long-lost
allegorical painting executed in 1480 to commemorate
Lorenzo's important diplomatic victory at Naples over
King Ferdinand. At great personal risk Lorenzo dei
Medici had travelled to Naples in order to persuade the
truculent and treacherous Ferdinand not to embark on a
disastrous policy of aggression, and by his arguments the
Medici succeeded in his mission. It was a signal triumph
of shrewd, farseeing Medicean statecraft over blind, selfish
ambition, which Botticelli has happily typified by showing
Athene, the Goddess of Wisdom, in the act of subduing the
Centaur of brute force. Lorenzo's action saved Italy from
internal warfare and external invasion for fourteen years.
Surely this superb work of art, specially painted by Botticelli at the request of his patron, Lorenzo dei Medici, offers
us a clear instance of Art in very close relation to historical
fact ?

In this connexion between art and history I should like
to draw attention to a beautiful picture by Carlo Crivelli in
our National Gallery of London. Its subject is 'The
Annunciation of the Virgin Mary,' but its whole setting is
that of a Milanese palace and street of the fifteenth century.
We are here presented with a number of architectural and
domestic features of Milanese life. The Virgin's bed-
chamber, illuminated by a single golden ray of celestial
light, shows us just the sleeping apartment of a young girl
of noble birth of the period. We note the bed, the chairs,
the books, the vases of flowers, the necessary furniture.
Outside in the street citizens and a quaint child, all clad in
the costume of the day, watch with interest the two attendant angels, who in their turn are habited in the gorgeous

canonicals and mitres of bishops. It is, in fact, a glimpse
of the splendours of Milan in the spacious days of Duke
Ludovico Sforza.

Again, let us in imagination enter the tiny Medicean
chapel or oratory in their ancient Florentine palace. It is
only a small, dingy room, originally without a window, but
on its walls has been depicted by Benozzo Gozzoli, the pupil
of Fra Angelico, with rare skill a whole cavalcade of historical
personages in the guise of the Three Wise Men of the East
and their train on the road to Bethlehem. But the road
to Bethlehem in this case is not the Arabian desert but the
rich Tuscan country-side with its towered cities and fruitful
orchards.

> With squire and burgher at their side,
>   In majesty these walls along
> The chivalry of Florence rides,
>   An ever-circling, shining throng.
>
> A Prince, an Emperor, a Priest,
>   Amble along with anxious eyes
> Fixed on the meteor of the East,
>   That hovers where the Saviour lies.

In short, the three Magi, who are on horseback, are none
other than Cosimo dei Medici the Elder, first Prince of
Florence ; John Palaeologus, Emperor of Byzantium ;
and the Priest, his Patriarch of Constantinople. Their
retinue also contains portraits of those who attended the
famous Council of Florence in 1439, shortly before the fall
of the Eastern Empire. So here we find an invaluable
representation of East and West, for the whole suite of the
Emperor and his Patriarch is included by the artist ; even
the Imperial huntsmen, with their trained leopards, are not
omitted in his scheme. What budding historian could find
the doings of the Council of Florence difficult or dull after
a visit to this Medici chapel ? Why, here are the very

members of the Council introduced to him in all their characteristic finery ! The frescoes of Gozzoli are simply a painted chronicle of an historical event in the dress of a sacred incident.

Indeed, it is true to state that in a large number of Renaissance pictures, though the subjects are ostensibly religious, the inner meaning and spirit are purely historical. Moreover, apart from the matter of portraiture, their backgrounds usually, if not always, present us with most valuable settings of contemporary architecture, manners, costume, furniture and all the details of Renaissance domestic life. To such a pitch, in fact, was this secular treatment of sacred subjects carried by the artists of the *Cinquecento*, that not a little scandal was caused to the devout and alarm to the priesthood. On one occasion even the Venetian painter Paul Veronese was threatened with penalties by the Inquisition on account of his picture, ' The Feast of Cana ', which he had treated as a typical Venetian banquet of his day, introducing all the luxury of dress, viands, and amusement of Renaissance Venice. ' He has shown Our Lord,' declared the shocked Inquisitor, ' seated at table with courtesans, dwarfs, buffoons, apes, Germans, and other indecencies ! '

To proceed. There is a special branch of art that is peculiar to Florence during the century of its palmiest days, to wit, from the accession to power of Cosimo dei Medici in 1434 to the siege of Florence in 1530. This was the manufacture of the Della Robbia ware, which consisted of figures and designs in terra-cotta that was afterwards covered with a high glaze in various tints, chiefly in blue and white. This artistic industry survived three generations of its inventors, Luca, Andrea and Giovanni della Robbia. You will find some good specimens of this beautiful Florentine ware amongst the Salting Bequest in our museum at South Kensington. You will ask, What possible connexion can

Della Robbia ware own with Florentine history ? Well, this family executed important orders for the Guilds of Florence and for the Medici, as well as for private citizens, and on many of these objects exist coats of arms of real historical interest : of such interest, in short, that recently there was published by the American professor, Dr. Marquand, a monumental volume dealing *only* with Della Robbia ware heraldry.

And at this point I should like to refer to *Heraldry* itself, that which of all artistic forms enters most closely and directly into Political History. I recommend young students of history to acquire a knowledge of heraldry. I can assure them from personal experience it is not a difficult subject to attain ; and its attainment I can only compare with that of learning a new historical language. With a backing of heraldry, the pleasure and profit gained by every visit to a church or castle or museum will be intensified— nay, doubled. I was deeply gratified a few years ago when I persuaded one of our most brilliant young professors to make a study of heraldry, whose historical value I was able to explain to him. Now, in the time of the Italian Renaissance, heraldry was the common property of all, and not of a mere handful of antiquaries, as it is to-day. In proof of my statement, I could quote innumerable allusions from the literature of this period which require an acquaintance with Italian heraldry for their clear understanding. Thus,'*Vivanno le Palle !* ' (' Long live the Pellets ! ') was the popular cry on behalf of the Medici, who bore red *palle*, or pellets, on their family shield. Indeed, their adherents are constantly termed ' *Palleschi* '. Alexander VI, the Borgia Pope, was frequently greeted by the populace of Rome with shouts of ' *Vive diu, Bos* ! ' (' Long live the Ox ! '), an expression clearly drawn from the ox which figures on the Borgia coat of arms. Still more remarkable is the famous dictum of Savonarola concerning the ill-starred alliance, for which he

himself was mainly responsible, between the revived Florentine republic and King Charles VIII of France—' *Gigli con
gigli sempre devono fiorire* ' (' Lilies must ever flourish with
lilies '). And this phrase remains absolutely meaningless,
unless we own the requisite heraldic knowledge of the
armorial bearings of the French Valois kings, which were
golden lilies on a blue field, and those of the city of Florence,
which are a red lily on a white field. In truth, the populace
itself in those days largely expressed its politics in terms of
heraldry.

Lastly, I come to the very important questions : Who
were these artists and sculptors and architects of the Italian
Renaissance ? What was the social atmosphere of their
birth and breeding ? What was their influence with the
government of their day ? Did they rise to wealth and
honour with ease or with difficulty ? Were they encouraged
or were they slighted by the great patrons and princes of
the time ? Now, these artists, as you will gather from the
pages of their biographer, Giorgio Vasari, were with very
few exceptions produced by the Italian populace. Art and
learning were intermingled with the very air they breathed.
So long ago as the thirteenth century, in the days of Dante,
the Florentine people were on familiar terms with art and
all that art connoted or implied. The first successful
picture of the revived art of painting, a Madonna and
Saints by Cimabue, had been carried in joyful procession
through the streets of Florence in 1280, and from that hour
the keenest interest and the most intelligent understanding
in the progress of all the arts were displayed by the whole
community of Florence. Thus the great artists of the
Renaissance were reared in humble but sympathetic sur-
roundings. Their early efforts were watched with interest
and approval. They rose to affluence and favour on their
own merits. No doubt, many aspirants failed, but many
succeeded. Sprung, as I said, from the people and received

on account of their talents into the intimacy of popes and princes, they formed a very important link between the rulers of the day and the general mass of the ruled. A goodly fraction of them rose to posts of real power. Thus, Leonardo da Vinci, the greatest thinker as well as the greatest painter of his age, was long the leading figure at the court of Milan. The architect Bramante was made *plumbator*, or keeper of the papal seals, at Rome. Raphael's wealth and influence were undisputed during the reigns of Julius and Leo. Michelangelo's genius was thoroughly appreciated by the unlettered Julius, to whom the artist often spoke out his mind with uncompromising frankness. Of a truth Michelangelo was too outspoken for the fastidious Leo ; but Clement VII, the second Medici Pope, always held him in high esteem. Not only did Clement employ him on many noble works which we can all see and admire to-day, but he even forgave the Master overt acts of rebellion. For it was Michelangelo who skilfully defended republican Florence for nearly a twelvemonth against the combined armies of Clement and Charles V in 1530. Clement has, and with justice, been held up to execration by all historians, but he owned one saving grace, namely, a true and discerning love of art. This sole virtue of the Pope's saved Michelangelo from a rebel's fate. On his artistic merits he was pardoned and set to work once more on the famous mausoleum of the Medici at San Lorenzo. Michelangelo, half defiant, half fearful, sulked at his task ; but his friend, Sebastiano del Piombo, the painter, wrote to him at this crisis, imploring him to lay aside both resentment and alarm ;—' for His Holiness speaks of you in such honourable and affectionate terms, no parent could praise a son more highly. True, he has been annoyed by whisperings as to your conduct during the late siege of Florence, but he shrugs his shoulders and only remarks : " *Michelangelo is mistaken, for I never did him any wrong* ".' In plain words, Clement deliberately ignored the late act of treason, to say nothing of ingratitude. Artists were indeed privileged individuals in those days !

Moreover, all this artistic patronage and enthusiasm were not confined to the great cities, such as Florence and Rome and Venice and Milan. Ferrara, Urbino, Lucca, Siena, Bologna, Perugia were equally centres of local artistic enterprise and owned their local schools of painting and architecture. Never before and never since has popular sympathy been in such close touch with art ; the people provided the artists, and in their turn the artists unofficially represented the people at the various Italian courts. Even to-day the fame of the sculptor Donatello survives amongst the populace of Florence. ' Ouida ', the novelist, writing only a generation ago, relates how the Florentine cabmen used to salute his masterpiece, the statue of St. George on the walls of Or San Michele, by cracking their whips as they passed, and how they used to inform the astonished tourist : ' Yes, it was *our* Donatello who carved that ! ' In our own annals we have no such connexion between royal patronage and popular genius to record. Not one of our monarchs, with the exception of Charles I, has ever shown any real appreciation of art, or treated artists and rewarded art in the practical spirit of the Italian Renaissance. I think of our George II, who openly expressed his contempt for ' boetry and bainting ' ; and of his successor on the throne, who was once persuaded by Fuseli to inspect some of William Blake's gorgeous fancies. ' Take 'em away, take 'em away, take 'em away ! ' was the sole Royal comment, after looking at a few of Blake's designs.

This official encouragement and recognition of art are of real historical interest and importance, for Italy is by far the longest civilized country in Europe, and Tuscany can boast the longest record of civilization in Italy. The Italian peasants and artisans own charming, graceful manners, and they are all true democrats at heart (as the visitor in Italy will soon realize, if he cares to investigate). Now, these artists, who were representative of the flower of the people, brought with them a bracing democratic influence straight into the Vatican and into the courts of the Medici, the Sforza, the Montefeltre, the Este, the Gonzaga, and other reigning families. I think you will appreciate this point, and will agree with my theory, when you come to read the *Autobiography* of Benvenuto Cellini. Believe me, that though here and there some of Cellini's accounts of his own doughty deeds may be taken with a grain of salt, his book is a human document of peculiar interest. In its pages we are made to live a while once more in the political and artistic world of the *Cinquecento*. In this volume we can satisfy ourselves as to the very real personal ties that then existed between the popes and Italian sovereigns and the artists (chiefly Tuscan) whom they protected. Cellini was born in 1500, and he died in 1570. As a boy he saw the triumphant restoration of the Medici in Florence after eighteen years of exile, and he describes the joy of the Florentine populace thereat and the discomfiture of the *bourgeoisie*. As the leading goldsmith of his day, Cellini had frequent conversations with Pope Clement, Francis I of France, the Emperor Charles V, and nearly all the Italian potentates. He was present at the siege and sack of Rome in 1527, and as an eye-witness of its horrors he has left us a vivid account of that tragedy. In later years he was arrested, tortured, and imprisoned by the savage Farnese Pope, Paul III—a very rare misfortune to befall any artist, but one which goes to prove that Paul rightly or wrongly credited him with personal influence. He worked finally for Cosimo dei Medici, first Grand Duke of Tuscany, of whom he was not over-fond and whose mercantile traits he contrasts acidly with the liberal attitude of his late master, King Francis. Cellini's whole career was, in fact, spent in the fierce light of Renaissance courts, and truly illuminating is the account he gives us of that brilliant society in his racy memoirs. But the most important point is that Cellini describes all these grandees of his official acquaintance from the standpoint of a plain Florentine citizen, who was never ashamed of his lowly origin. Like every true-born Tuscan, he was well-bred and wholly at his ease in whatsoever company he might find himself. And as with Cellini, with whose career we are intimate through his memoirs, so doubtless with many another of the leading artists of his day. They occupied a definite place, a very high place, in the social life and public movements of the Renaissance.

To conclude—in the wondrous and progressive art of the Italian Renaissance, in its painting, its architecture, and its sculpture, you will find a clue to its political problems. Art in those spacious days was something more than a mere whim of the wealthy and the pushful. It was part and parcel of the life of the whole community ; and, as I have stated before, it formed a very real bond of union between the rulers and the ruled. In other lands, both in the past and the present, we find the courts of sovereigns frequented only by nobles, politicians, financiers, and sycophants ; there is no place for the artist, especially for the rising young artist, in the modern court. But art was a pervading element and a vital force in the whole society of the Italian Renaissance. To-day, a painter *with a recognized reputation,* such as Perugino owned, might be permitted to penetrate so far as the royal antechamber, but his promising young disciple, one Raphael Sanzio of Urbino, would probably fail to get nearer to the royal presence than the back-yard of the palace. In our days art carries with it no political or historical significance ; it has sunk to the condition of a mere exotic, raised with gold and nourished by the caprice of fashion. But, as I have tried to explain, it was a very different story in the era of the secular popes and of the Medici, when its charm and influence leavened the whole mass of citizens from the top to the bottom ; when the successful artist was not only the privileged favourite of the Prince, but was at the same time acclaimed the darling of the People whence he had sprung.

IX

LEONARDO DA VINCI

(1452–1519)

THREE names stand out pre-eminent amongst the artists of the later stages of the Italian Renaissance —Leonardo da Vinci, Michelangelo Buonaroti, and Raffaelo Santi of Urbino. Of this trio, Leonardo is the earliest in date, and in the opinion of many critics is still held as the most gifted, the most versatile, and even the most influential of the three. Born about the year 1452 at the little walled town of Vinci in the valley of the Arno, a few miles west of Florence, it will be observed that Leonardo was some twenty-three years older than Michelangelo, who himself was eight years senior to Raphael. Leonardo was one of the many sons of Ser Piero, a Florentine lawyer. He was apparently of base birth, though afterwards legitimized by his father, who was devoted to the boy. From his childhood the young Leonardo showed marked signs of his innate genius, and was of a curiously inquisitive and original turn of mind. Yet his perpetual thirst for information and his dissatisfaction with the current rules and explanations of his elders do not seem to have affected a peculiarly sweet and winning nature. The boy was, moreover, remarkable for beauty of face and form. He owned immense physical strength, and, like some of the medieval heroes of romance, it was said he could bend a horseshoe in his fingers as though it were made of lead.

Vasari's *Life of Leonardo da Vinci* is one of the best of those biographical and critical studies which form the basis of nearly all our knowledge of the great Italian artists and sculptors, as well as the stock-in-trade of all critics, however

superior. Yet the monograph on Leonardo is both unsatis-
factory and inaccurate, as indeed are all Vasari's biographies,
wherein countless errors and misstatements have been
detected and exposed by modern writers. Yet Vasari's
account of Leonardo, with all its faults, gives us the clue to
the master's career with its immense and far-spreading
influence. He was the forerunner, and in many ways the
superior, of Michelangelo. Again, the few sacred pictures
of Leonardo that have come down to us surpass the highest
flights of Raphael. Nevertheless, the fact remains that
Leonardo is to-day represented amongst us by a very small
—one may almost say an insignificant—residue of the
fruits of his unique genius. Broadly speaking, the high
reputation of Leonardo is built largely on the evident esteem
of his contemporaries ; for a strangely perverse fate seems
to have pursued almost every work accomplished by the
master during his lifetime. His *opus magnum*, for example,
the ' Last Supper ', at Milan, was a wreck within fifty years
of its execution. Yet its fame remains world-wide, and the
Christian visualization of Our Lord's last supper will always
be that held and depicted by Leonardo. I shall discuss this
great work later.

The whole life of Leonardo da Vinci is a mystery—a
mystery that deepens with time. His movements to and
from Florence at various dates, his long residence at Milan,
his visits to Rome, and his final journey to France can be
easily traced and verified ; but all these actual events are
punctuated with anecdotes long accepted for facts but now
under the keen eye of modern research relegated to the sad
realm of fable. Some of these stories, it is true, appear
improbable on their face ; others, however, we grieve to
dismiss, so venerable have they grown. Thus, it is a fact
that the young Leonardo, still in his teens, was taken by
his father (who was proud of his son's powers) to study
under the great sculptor Andrea Verocchio in Florence.

Unfortunately it may not be a fact also that Leonardo startled his eminent master (who was far more sculptor than painter) by introducing the figure of an angel into Verocchio's famous picture of ' The Baptism of Christ ', once in the Academy of Florence. Vasari relates how Verocchio, returning to his studio one day, found this graceful angel added to his unfinished picture, and was so impressed by the obvious superiority of his pupil's work to his own that there and then he resolved never to attempt painting again. Certainly, the figure of the angel in question is by another hand than Verocchio's ; certain, it surpasses the remainder of the picture ; certain, the tradition is old and has often formed a theme for poetry. It seems a thousand pities to discredit so charming and really not so improbable an anecdote. Let us leave it at that. Vasari gives us the story in all good faith, and it has been accepted by generations of writers. Vasari may have been misled, or he may not.

It is enough to state that the remarkable gifts of Leonardo, as exhibited in a multitude of ways, were very quickly perceived and appreciated by the artists and patrons of the day. As in the case of Michelangelo, these powers extended to almost every branch of art and science. His genius was both aesthetic and scientific. The longer he lived and studied and experimented, the more Leonardo came to regard all nature, the whole cosmic world around him, as of equal interest and value in all its parts. His insatiable curiosity was ever seeking the true causes of things, wholly unfettered by the opinions of his age. He is probably the first geologist of the modern school, for he has left observations on record of the shell deposits in mountains, from which circumstance he came to certain conclusions as to the antiquity of the earth, correct conclusions which only began to be formulated seriously in the nineteenth century. He was likewise fully as much engineer as artist. Even as a boy at Vinci he planned the clever scheme for a canal to improve the commerce on the Arno between Pisa and Florence. He was deeply interested in natural history, in anatomy, and in botany. Some of his drawings of plants that survive show a marvellous delicacy of touch and an intimate knowledge of structure. He was for ever experimenting on and with everything. He was a poet too, though only one sonnet of his has survived. This is (as one might expect) more curious than lovely, and deals in somewhat obscure language with the limits of the human will and human performance :

> If what thou would'st thou can'st not, then content thee
> To will as thou may'st act. It is but folly
> To will what cannot be. Soon learns the wise
> To wrest his will from bootless wishes free.
> Our bliss and woe depend alike on knowledge
> Of what we should do, and that known, to do it.

He was likewise devoted to music, for which he loved to compose his own verses and sing them to the accompaniment of the lute. Vasari tells us that Leonardo made a sensation on his first appearance at the court of Milan by playing on a musical instrument of his own invention, wrought in silver and fashioned like a horse's head. There are also some rather absurd tales of Leonardo's fixing artificial wings to lizards and indulging in practical jokes with these sham monsters among his friends. In fact, the bizarre, and even the hideous and repulsive, seem to have owned a special attraction for him, and this eccentric taste is clearly shown in many of his extant sketches of dragons and devils and fantastic creatures.

Leonardo was mentally a solitary, ever seeking a solution of the secrets around him in nature, yet never satisfied with his investigations. On the other hand, he was socially a most agreeable, courteous, and witty companion. He was caressed by the princes and patrons of his age, and was popular with all his friends and acquaintances. No doubt it is the greatest tribute to the reality of his genius and the spell that it cast on all around that his fame has remained undimmed, although, as time proceeds, the number of his admittedly authentic works grows ever smaller. Works that had been confidently attributed to him for centuries have been, one by one, assigned, presumably with good reason, to his pupils. Indeed, one may say that Leonardo's artistic importance survives largely through his pupils. And yet, as painter, critic, designer, musician, botanist, engineer, and especially as farseeing thinker, Leonardo still stands out pre-eminent. Perhaps his constant attitude of a rare mental modesty may be rated not the least of his great qualities. Like Socrates of old, he knew that he knew nothing, and was therefore the wisest of all his peers, who were content to accept the current views and theories of their own day without question. For he admitted that all he did and thought was but human speculation, not real achievement. 'He first laid down,' says Hallam, 'the grand principle, that experiment and observation must be guides to just theory in the investigation of Nature.' Perhaps his main fault, that spoiled so many shining gifts of heart and brain, was his lack of perseverance. He was too erratic, too fertile in schemes. He ever sought the Infinite and neglected the Finite. As the Medici Pope, Leo X, sadly observed when he watched Leonardo's preparations for some commission he had given him at Rome : ' Alas, this man will never accomplish my work for me, since he is thinking of the end before he has even made a beginning of his task ! ' Thus it has come about that, while we possess enough examples of Michelangelo's life-work to prove to us his genius beyond the shadow of a doubt, in Leonardo's case the whole artistic legacy he has bequeathed to mankind is limited to a few—a very few—pictures, and even those defaced or faded : a treatise on painting, a mass of nondescript note-books, and a quantity of drawings or sketches of every conceivable subject.

Undoubtedly the most important epoch in Leonardo's whole career was his lengthy residence of nearly twenty years at the court of Ludovico Sforza, Duke of Milan, generally called ' Ludovico il Moro '. Sforza was one of the most cultured and enlightened tyrants of the Renaissance, and his court one of the most brilliant of that brilliant period. The master was invited by Ludovico to Milan about the year 1480, or perhaps a little later, when he was some thirty years of age and at the zenith of his powers. Here he appears as one of the most prominent and favoured members of the court, the duke treating his Florentine guest more as an equal than a subject, as a beloved brother rather than a salaried servant. Leonardo was well paid, well housed, and allowed to do as much or as little as he pleased, in his own way and in his own time. The Sforza seems in fact to have proved himself the ideal patron. Not that Leonardo was idle—far from it ; his whole life was one of feverish activity, but it was, alas, in the main misspent energy. Yet this Milanese period was the most fruitful and influential in his career. The name and reputation of Leonardo attracted to Milan all the rising young artists of Lombardy, who hung on his words and advice and followed his methods with eagerness. Thus the later Lombard or North Italian school of painting was the direct result, and a very noble result, of Leonardo's lectures and influence. Of his adoring pupils the most celebrated is Bernardino Luini, many of whose paintings have long passed current as genuine works by Leonardo, for Luini has faithfully imitated the style and spirit of his incomparable master. In particular, the sweet though rather sad expression of the eyes and mouth, which is so characteristic of Leonardo's work, has been admirably reproduced in the creations of Luini.

But the special task undertaken at Milan, which has made Leonardo's name resound throughout the whole Christian world, is his ' Last Supper ', painted on the wall of the refectory in the Dominican convent of Santa Maria delle Grazie. With this most famous composition the master was occupied at irregular intervals for several years. Sometimes he would be furiously painting from sunrise to sunset ; then he would leave the painting alone for weeks ; then again he would stand and meditate before it for hours, but without using a brush ; sometimes he would come and add a few hasty touches. It was apparently finished in 1498, and was at once hailed as a masterpiece. And so it was, but unfortunately Leonardo, never happy unless experimenting, must needs paint in oils on the damp stone wall, with the result that in its freshness of completion this superb ' Last Supper ' quickly began to deteriorate. Even in 1515, when King Francis I of France entered Milan as conqueror, the great painting had begun to show distinct signs of decay. The French king, anxious to preserve and possess this priceless work of art, made an attempt to cut away the whole wall, but in vain. The famous picture was left to perish gradually. Within fifty years the ' Last Supper ' was ruined, and at the present day it is but a ghost.

But though the original is but a ghost, its scheme of treatment has been handed down to posterity by a long succession of copyists, so that Leonardo's conception of the Last Supper has definitely implanted itself on the Christian mind throughout the world. It is everywhere conceded to be at once the most virile and most reverent representation of that event at the crucial moment of Our Lord's allusion to His betrayer at the supper-table.

' Leonardo,' says that fine critic, the late John Addington Symonds, ' undertook to paint a moment, to delineate the effect of a single sentence upon twelve men seated at a table, and to do this without sacrificing the tranquillity demanded by ideal art, and without impairing the divine majesty of Him from whose lips that sentence has fallen. . . . : The life breathed into each part of the composition, the variety of the types chosen to express varieties of character, and the scientific distribution of the twelve apostles in four groups of three around the central Christ, mark the appearance of a new spirit of power and freedom in the arts. What had hitherto been treated with religious timidity, with conventional stiffness, or with realistic want of grandeur, was now humanized and transported into a higher intellectual region. . . . We know not whether to admire most the perfection of the painter's art or his insight into spiritual things.'

Even in its deplorable state Leonardo's ' Last Supper ' fascinated the great poet Goethe, who wrote a description of the painting, ' the first masterpiece of the perfected Renaissance '.

' The artist represents the peaceful little band round the sacred table as thunderstruck by the Master's words, " One of you shall betray Me." They have been pronounced. The whole company is in dismay, whilst He Himself bows His head with downcast eyes. His whole attitude, the motion of His arms and hands, all seem to repeat with heavenly resignation, and His silence to confirm the mournful words, " It cannot be otherwise ; one of you shall betray Me " ! '

Although the painting is irretrievably ruined, the Milanese gallery of the Brera contains the original sketch for the head of Christ, which is of extreme beauty. Of the many coloured copies of this work, some of them executed not very many years after its completion, perhaps the most precious and satisfactory is the copy, in oils and of equal size to the original, by one of Leonardo's own pupils, Marco da Oggione, which is now in the Diploma Gallery of the Royal Academy in London. Of the hundreds of engravings, that of the celebrated engraver, Raphael Morghen, is the best. Morghen undertook his task with minute care and loving patience, studying for his purpose not only the faded original at Milan, but the many copies and engravings of this ' Last Supper ' that were scattered throughout Europe.

The invasion of Italy by the French at the close of the century, and the downfall of his friend and patron, Ludovico Sforza, rendered Milan neither an agreeable nor even a safe residence for Leonardo. The Sforza duke had been carried off a prisoner to France ; the French soldiery was occupying Milan, where amongst other acts of vandalism they amused themselves by turning Leonardo's vast model of an equestrian statue for the Milanese duke into a target. On this object Leonardo had spent—I think one may fairly call it *wasted*—an infinity of time and labour, repeatedly altering and enlarging his enormous model of plaster or terra-cotta, with the ultimate intention of having the statue cast in bronze. He had lived all too lavishly during his sojourn in Milan, and it was with a lean purse that he now returned to Florence, seeking employment. At this date, 1500, Florence was once more a republic and the Medici family in exile. Piero Soderini, the *Gonfaloniere*, or elected doge, of the Florentine Republic, gave him a warm welcome, and, what was more substantial, the commission to execute a large historical fresco in the great hall of the Public Palace, or Palazzo della Signoria. Michelangelo, then aged about twenty-five, was already engaged on the decoration of this immense chamber, for which he had prepared a celebrated cartoon of soldiers bathing in the Arno and suddenly called to arms. For the same purpose Leonardo now set to work on the cartoon of a large historical composition of a former Florentine victory at Anghiari, generally known as ' the Battle of the Standard '. There was no love lost between the young Michelangelo and the rather elderly Leonardo. Both masters began to paint upon the walls of the saloon in the Public Palace of Florence, but made little progress. It is interesting to note, however, that whilst so engaged both Michelangelo and Leonardo were being eagerly watched and studied by a rising young painter, a youth from Urbino of the name of Raffaello Santi. Thus for the first time were the three great artists of the Renaissance brought into close proximity.

As to the two frescoes themselves, they were never finished, and in the next generation such traces of them as survived were obliterated to make room for a new series of paintings by Vasari and his pupils. Michelangelo's cartoon is well known from engravings, but of Leonardo's battle-piece only a few fragments have come down to us, the best known of these being the group of soldiers contending for a banner, commonly called 'The Battle of the Standard'. It is a vigorous conception, six soldiers afoot and mounted struggling with almost bestial ferocity, whilst the very horses are likewise shown fighting with their teeth and hoofs. But here again the original sketch is lost, and what we see to-day is only a copy made a century later by Rubens, who has evidently touched up the cartoon not a little to suit his own taste. I confess I have always found it rather difficult to understand the enormous praise that has been lavished on either of these works of Leonardo and Michelangelo, and echoed down from generation to generation.

With the collapse of the Florentine Republic in 1512 and the return to power of the exiled Medici, Leonardo, who took little interest in politics (which were probably beneath his notice), remained on in Florence. But after the election of Cardinal dei Medici as Pope Leo X in 1513 he was attracted, like so many artists and scholars and philosophers, to Rome, which had now become the intellectual centre of Europe. Here he was at once welcomed by Leo and entrusted with certain commissions. But the master's dreamy, speculative nature and wayward independence did not commend themselves to the impatient Pope, who expected both speed and implicit obedience in the artists he employed. At this juncture King Francis I of France, who had lately entered Italy as a conqueror, applied for the services of Leonardo, of whose genius he was an enthusiastic admirer. Leonardo gladly complied with the French king's offer, which was both cordial and generous. In Leonardo's eyes the young monarch appeared another Ludovico of Milan, and though he was now well past sixty, the master gladly followed his new patron back to France. This was in 1516. Here Francis gave Leonardo a salary of 700 golden crowns a year and assigned to him for residence a pleasant little villa, the Maison de Clou, at Amboise, whither the French court often resorted. But Leonardo's mysterious life was drawing to its close. Infirm now as well as elderly, he fell ill at Amboise, where for some months he lay on a sick-bed. On May 2nd, 1519, Francis went in person to visit the ailing artist, and, if we can trust Vasari's account, Leonardo da Vinci, now aged sixty-seven, died in the King's arms.

' The King, who was wont frequently and affectionately to visit him, came to his room. . . . He was then seized with a violent paroxysm, the forerunner of death, when the King, rising and supporting his head to give him such assistance and do him such favour as he could, in the hope of alleviating his sufferings, the spirit of Leonardo, which was most divine, conscious that he could attain to no greater honour, departed in the arms of the monarch.'

It is a picturesque story, nor is it improbable. Yet later writers have dismissed it as fabulous, though it is given with detail by Vasari, writing at no great distance of time. Again, we must leave it at that. It is only certain that Leonardo expired at Amboise as the honoured guest of King Francis. No trace remains of his tomb or coffin at Amboise, where he was buried. It is all in keeping with what one may call the Legend of Leonardo da Vinci which tends to exhibit the great Italian artist and thinker as almost as mythical a personage as King Arthur or Prester John. Apart from some slight sketches of himself by himself, we have but one likeness of him—that which hangs in the Hall of Artists' Portraits in the Uffizi Gallery of Florence. This shows him as a singularly beautiful old man, with long, flowing silky hair and beard. Alas, even this portrait, precious as it is, is only a copy of the original by Leonardo himself, which has long been lost !

As I am only dealing here with Leonardo as an artist, and not as an intellectual luminary far in advance of his age, I shall confine my remarks to a short account of some of his extant pictures, which may be seen and studied, if not in the originals, at least in engravings or photographs. I have already spoken of his masterpiece, the famous ' Last Supper ', or *Cenacolo*, on the refectory wall of the convent of Santa Maria delle Grazie in Milan, and of the undoubted influence this work has wielded over Christian art and Christian thought for four centuries and more.

There are in truth not many works of the master to describe, and what exist are scattered widely over the various galleries and collections of Europe. I shall take first a little fresco-painting of Leonardo's in the convent of Sant' Onofrio on the Janiculan Hill in Rome. This work, if genuine, is the only extant specimen of Leonardo's art in the proper medium of fresco. It fills the lunette, or semi-circular arch over a doorway, and shows against a gold ground the Madonna in a green robe with the Holy Child on her lap. In the corner appears the donor of the picture in a dark dress. It is a charming little composition, simple and sweet, but much injured by time and bad restoration. It is usually attributed to the period of Leonardo's visit to Rome under Pope Leo, about 1515, when he was over sixty, although it has all the appearance of a youthful work, and may have been executed on some unrecorded visit to Rome in his early days. It has been admirably reproduced by the Arundel Society. Alas, I see now it is ascribed definitely to Boltraffio, a pupil of Leonardo's.

In Florence, the richest of all cities in artistic treasures, there exists to-day only one *undoubted* and undisputed work by Leonardo. This is an 'Adoration of the Magi', on canvas, of course less than half-finished. Yet it has always been highly valued, and its immediate influence is clearly traceable in a celebrated picture by Raphael, ' The Madonna del Baldacchino ', and in his cartoons for the Sistine Chapel tapestry.

Of Milan, where Leonardo spent the most fruitful period of his career, there remain only the ' Last Supper ', already described, and some sketches in the public galleries.

In London we possess in our National Gallery the beautiful ' Virgin of the Rocks ', in which the exquisite faces of the Virgin, the attendant angel and the infant Christ and John the Baptist stand out clear against a sombre background of chiaroscuro, which was perhaps the actual invention of Leonardo himself, for he lays special stress on this quality of chiaroscuro in his *Treatise of Painting*, a tract composed out of his loose notes and published a century after his death. Yet even in ' The Virgin of the Rocks ' doubts have arisen as to the authenticity of the whole picture. Certainly, it is hard to associate its gloomy and impossible rocky landscape with what we know of Leonardo's intense love for and intimate study of natural scenery. These crags seem like those familiar rocky landscapes coarsely painted on an Oriental plate. Two other examples of this picture with certain variations exist in Paris and Naples, but our London example is usually regarded as the original, and the other two as inferior copies. London is likewise fortunate in possessing, in the Diploma Gallery, Marco da Oggione's valuable copy of the ' Last Supper ' (already described). Also the original cartoon for an altar-piece for the Servites of Florence that was to represent the Virgin and St. Anne with the infant Christ. As usual, the commission was never carried out, but this preliminary sketch is truly a work of divine grace and sweetness.

> The soul and skill of that dead Florentine
>   Have traced his vision on the parchment here ;
> Shown us the anguish that is all divine,
>   Shown us the rapture that begets the tear.

The Louvre is particularly fortunate in owning three works of Leonardo's that are still reputed authentic. First there is ' La Belle Ferronière ', a young woman wearing a long necklace. Secondly there is a picture—unfinished, of course—of the Virgin, St. Anne, and the Holy Child playing with a lamb, which is said to have been a favourite possession of King Francis I, who used vainly to implore the erratic artist to complete his task. The third and last picture in the Louvre is the world-famous ' Monna Lisa ', also called ' La Gioconda '. It is the portrait of a Florentine lady, by no means in the first flush of youth, Lisa, the wife of Messer Francesco del Giocondo of Florence. It was executed during Leonardo's residence in Florence after his unwilling departure from Milan—that is, after the year 1500, and is stated to have occupied the dilatory artist over four years, nor is it totally finished. Bought by King Francis for the very large sum of 4,000 golden florins, the ' Monna Lisa ' was placed by that art-loving monarch in his collection at Fontainebleau, whence it was later removed to the Louvre. Amongst its many vicissitudes, the ' Monna Lisa ' has had the recent experience of being stolen from the Louvre, and of being mysteriously returned after some years of disappearance. It is all in keeping with the eternal mystery of the Legend of Leonardo, one of the world's greatest artists with next to nothing tangible to prove the extent of his genius to posterity.

The portrait shows us a young to middle-aged woman, reported to be of exceptional beauty in her day, whose air in this likeness is one of mingled sadness and resignation, an impression that is increased by the beautiful hands crossed over the breast. There is a curious enigmatical look in the eyes. That Leonardo infused the unique excellence of his powers into this picture is undoubted. Says Vasari at the end of a long account of this picture : ' In this portrait of Leonardo's there is so pleasing an expression, and a smile so sweet, that while looking at it one thinks it rather divine than human, and it has ever been esteemed a marvellous work, since life itself could exhibit no other appearance.'

The portrait is to-day in fair preservation, but the rose-tints Leonardo gave to the flesh and the amazing carnation bloom to the cheeks on which Vasari dwells, have long faded, so that the general effect of the skin and complexion is pallid, even sallow. In our own times the ' Monna Lisa ' has become a favourite theme for rhapsody. Walter Pater, for example, can gush for some pages in this manner :

' Here is the head upon which all the ends of the world are come, and the eyelids are a little weary. It is beauty wrought out from within upon the flesh, the deposit, little cell by cell, of strange thoughts and fantastic reveries and exquisite passions. . . . She is older than the rocks among which she sits ; like the vampire, she has been dead many times, and learned the secrets of the grave ; and has been a diver in deep seas, and keeps their fallen day about her ; and traffics for strange webs with Eastern merchants ; and as Leda was the mother of Helen of Troy, and as Saint Anne, the mother of Mary ; and all this has been to her but as the sound of lyres and flutes, and lives only in the delicacy with which it has moulded the changing lineaments, and tinged the eyelids and the hands.' And so forth *ad libitum*.

I hope you like it ; I hope you understand it. I may be

mistaken, but it all sounds to me perilously like nonsense.
What is the excuse for all this sentimental rhapsodizing ?
On what basis is this fantastical structure of appreciation
reared ?

As the excellent and sympathetic likeness of a Florentine
gentlewoman, who has known both joy and sorrow, who
owns obviously an interesting and perhaps a subtle personality, Leonardo's portrait of Monna Lisa ranks amongst
the greatest portraits of the world. But to read into it
sphinx-like secrets, as so many writers attempt, is unneces-
sary, I may add, absurd. ' Women,' said a clever writer
of the late Victorian era, ' are sphinxes without secrets,'
and I don't believe Monna Lisa was more of a genuine
sphinx than her fellow-women. Why not regard it as a
superb and interesting portrait full of character and grace,
like some others of the very great masters ? And, verily,
this habit of reading into a picture what is not visible to
the eye is of itself a dangerous habit. Our literary luminaries of this class have more than once been badly bitten
at this game, and held up to laughter or scorn. And a
Leonardo picture is a particularly unsafe peg to hang rhap-
sodies upon. Witness the case of Shelley and his verses on
' The Head of Medusa ', an impudent forgery but long called
an authentic work by Leonardo, that hangs in the Uffizi
Gallery of Florence. It is known that Leonardo *did* once
paint the head of a Medusa, or the Gorgon, with livid lips
and bloodless face, and with the dying snakes that formed
her hair writhing and hissing in agony. But like almost
everything else painted by Leonardo his picture of Medusa
had long disappeared. So some ingenious wight filled up
the missing gap by inventing a Medusa of his own composition, and this hideous, clumsy forgery hung under
Leonardo's name for ages in the Florentine gallery, where
it became a famous target of the sentimentalist. So Shelley
can write thus :

Yet it is less the horror than the grace
Which turns the gazer's spirit into stone,
Whereon the lineaments of that dead face
Are graven till the character be grown
Into itself, and thought no more can trace ;
'Tis the melodious hues of beauty thrown,
Athwart the darkness and the glare of pain,
Which humanized and harmonize the strain.

This may be fine poetry, though it is based on a wrong assumption, namely, that the art and mind of Leonardo had presented the poet with a lofty conception of the severed head of Medusa worthy of his muse. But poets and writers are not the only persons who have had their fingers burnt over the Legend of Leonardo, that pre-eminent yet most elusive spirit of the Italian Renaissance. The very art critics, who have so narrowed down the circle of his genuine works, have also made egregious errors in their own special field of study. The Legend of Leonard can deceive even the elect themselves. Thus a score or so of years ago all the artistic world of Europe and America was laughing over an absurd controversy, in which the late Herr Bode, the arrogant and authoritative critic and Director of the Berlin Museum, cut a ludicrous figure.

It is admitted that during his lifetime Leonardo used to fashion wax models, though he was not a sculptor in the usual sense of the term. Vasari, for example, relates how the bronze figures by Rustici of the ' Decapitation of St. John the Baptist ', placed in 1516 over the north door of the Baptistery in Florence, were designed from models of wax given to him by Leonardo. Whether this was the actual case or not, Herr Bode came to the conclusion that some at least of Leonardo's many wax models must have survived, and therefore he was constantly seeking to obtain an original specimen from the hand of the master. At last he found what he, with his great artistic knowledge and experience, considered to be an undoubtedly genuine work of this class.

He found it in England, and bought it for a comparatively small sum at a sale. It was a bust of Venus. Armed with his prize, the Herr Direcktor of the Berlin Kaiser-Friedrichs Museum returned to Germany, and boasted of his wonderful discovery—a real work of Leonardo's, which the dull Englishmen had failed to recognize in their midst. There was a cry of triumph from Berlin, and every one congratulated Herr Bode. Unfortunately, it was conclusively shown later by means of a very interesting correspondence in *The Times* that the bust in question was the work of an obscure English artist in wax, a Mr. Lucas, who flourished in early Victorian days and made a livelihood by executing classical busts in wax to adorn the parlours and even summer-houses of London merchants. After much delay and recrimination the precious bust was examined and opened, when the core of the wax was found to be composed of old copies of *The Times* of about 1850, which Mr. Lucas was in the habit of using for the foundation of his busts, wax being an expensive commodity. Such is another aspect of the Legend of Leonardo da Vinci.

How, then, do we stand in regard to this incomparable master and his extant works ? There are still many such attributed to him in certain galleries and collections. Are these in truth the copies or forgeries that the art critic would have us believe ? What is the true value of all this negative criticism of art ? Thanks to these critics, doubts have now been thrown on every one of his important so-called works, with the two exceptions of the unfinished ' Adoration of the Magi ' in Florence and the ' Monna Lisa ' in the Louvre. With all their superior wisdom and artistic jargon, may they not be mistaken, so that in reality there may yet exist a sufficiency of Leonardo's art to uphold his fame, apart from the drawings and treatises of which I have spoken ? If experts like Herr Bode can blunder outrageously thus, what guarantee have we as to the spurious character of the many works in public galleries that have for generations been ascribed to his genius ? As William Blake says : ' Every man is a natural judge of painting who has not been connoisseured out of his senses.' Surely common sense is as good and accurate a criterion as all this twaddle and misconception on the part of the artistic expert ?

X

MICHELANGELO AND THE SISTINE CHAPEL

(1508–1512)

IT would require a whole library to do anything like justice to the careers of Michelangelo and Raphael, which stand out so prominent in the artistic and intellectual life of the Italian Renaissance. I have therefore chosen a definite portion of the work of each of them, namely, their share in the adornment of the chief papal palace, the Vatican, in Rome. Both Michelangelo and Raphael worked for a succession of popes : Michelangelo for Julius II, Clement VII, and Paul III ; Raphael for Julius II and Leo X. The whole of these papal commissions at the Vatican cover roughly the years 1508 to 1541, that is, the reign of our Henry VIII in England. What Michelangelo and Raphael completed at the Vatican in that space of time represents still for us one of the world's greatest artistic achievements ; and moreover, apart from its mere artistic value, it owns a marked significance in the intellectual and political progress of their age. This close connexion between art and history, then, this *human* aspect, so to speak, I shall endeavour to explain in the course of this study.

Both Michelangelo Buonaroti and Raphael Sanzio, or Santi, belong to what is broadly called the Florentine School. Michelangelo was a Tuscan by birth, and as a boy when apprenticed to Ghirlandajo he used to make drawings of the pictures in the Florentine churches and to copy the antique statues that had been collected by that great patron of the arts, Lorenzo dei Medici, Prince of Florence. Raphael, though a native of Urbino, that beautiful little city perched on the mountains of Umbria, likewise studied under the great Florentine master, Perugino, and his early pictures clearly exhibit Perugino's influence and methods. Of these two great artists, Michelangelo was the elder by eight years, having been born in 1475. He was, if we omit Leonardo da Vinci, the noblest figure of the Italian Renaissance, as he was also its most versatile genius, for besides being distinguished as sculptor and architect, he was in addition painter, poet, engineer, thinker, patriot, and even to some extent an ardent politician. He represents for us in its highest form the liberal and serious side of Renaissance culture, which is itself the connecting link between the medieval and the modern eras. Raphael, on the other hand, though he was antiquary, poet, and scholar as well as painter, owned a lighter and happier nature than Michelangelo's. The political dangers and fears of the day sat easily on his young shoulders ; he had a sunny, careless disposition, he was truly, as Vasari says, ' *la gentilezza stessa* '—good-nature itself ; he was full of the joy of life ; a lover of women, a gay companion, a welcome guest both at the tables of the great and at the merry suppers of his brother-artists. It is interesting to observe how nearly the two artists' respective characters coincide with those of their chief patrons. Thus Julius II was the special supporter of Michelangelo ; whilst Leo X found Raphael altogether an artist after his heart. Julius II (della Rovere), the true founder of the temporal power of the papacy, which only collapsed in 1870, was, like Michelangelo, arrogant, serious, frugal, a deep thinker. Both men, too, owned what the Italians of that age called *terribilità*, a word that has no English equivalent, but signifies a hot temper combined with a strong will. Although the temperaments of Michelangelo and of Julius therefore were much alike, yet they held very diverse views and ideals on most subjects of their day, and this diversity of opinion often brought these two strong spirits into conflict and quarrel. Their relations were of course more or less those of master and servant; yet Michelangelo, to use a homely phrase, was not afraid to stand up to his wrathful papal patron, and though Julius often raged and stormed and (I believe) swore at the obstinate artist, he always respected him, and the pair after a sharp encounter usually became reconciled. Certainly, the vast painting of the roof of the Sistine Chapel, to which I shall refer presently, is as much due to the indomitable will of Pope Julius as to the responsive genius of Michelangelo, for the scheme was carried to completion by desire of the Pope and not by the desire of the artist. Of Raphael and Leo X I shall write later, when I come to the story of Raphael's work at the Vatican. I mean now to deal only with the story of the Sistine Chapel.

The Sistine Chapel, one of the most famous shrines of art in the whole world, was built by Sisto Quarto, Pope Sixtus IV, uncle of Julius II, in 1473. It is not a beautiful structure, being merely a lofty rectangular hall, one hundred and thirty-three feet long and forty-five feet wide, with vaulted roof lit by fourteen rounded windows at a great height from the floor. One may compare the Sistine Chapel with a tall, oblong box with a slightly curved lid. Already, under Pope Sixtus IV, the huge interior wall-spaces had been largely covered with decoration by the Florentine and Umbrian artists of that day. There was a fine marble pavement, and a fine marble screen to divide the chapel into two unequal parts. Now Julius, obsessed with grandiose ideas, had already decided to make the adjoining basilica, or church of St. Peter's, the World's Cathedral, the seat of Western Christendom; he had planned to make the Vatican the central palace of the Pope, the spiritual Caesar of the Christian world; and he now intended to make of this large chapel built by his uncle Pope Sixtus an official chapel for the Pope and his cardinals. It was to be the special seat of the inner circle and court attached to the

Pope, and here papal elections and state receptions were to be held. It was, in short, intended to fill the office more of a throne-room than a chapel. At this time—the year 1508—the Sistine was adorned by a series of frescoes along its walls, midway between the windows and the floor, by Botticelli, Perugino, Luca Signorelli, Cosimo Rosselli, and other famous painters. These two sets of frescoes represent the Life of Moses and the Life of Our Lord, and happily they still remain intact to-day. On the west wall, above the altar, were frescoes by Perugino ; and opposite, on the east, or entrance, wall, were two other frescoes of the same date. Of these latter, only the pair on the east wall still exist, and even these have been absolutely repainted. Below the line of the pictures was a considerable space or dado running round the whole chapel, which Leo X some ten years later covered with the superb tapestries of Raphael, to be dealt with presently.

Now the roof and its vaulting remained blank. This displeased Julius, and he determined to have the whole of this vast space, said to cover more than ten thousand square feet of surface, painted over, so as to render the Sistine Chapel still more beautiful and imposing. It was a grand conception on the Pope's part, and he bethought him of the only artist worthy of and equal to the stupendous task. This, I need hardly say, was Michelangelo, who was then busily engaged upon the statuary for the immense altar tomb that Julius intended to place in St. Peter's for himself and his successors in the papacy. As usual, there ensued a battle-royal between the Pope and the artist. Michelangelo was most unwilling to be taken away from Julius's own commission, that of the papal tomb. He declared he was a sculptor, not a painter ; therefore the work proposed was not in his line of art. Julius would not listen to any of these reasons—one can hardly call them excuses. Michelangelo, and no other, must and shall decorate the roof of the Sistine.

Finally, with a bad grace, the reluctant artist had to bow to the superior will of the Pope, and Michelangelo, after making due preparations for his gigantic task, arrived in Rome. The first thing he found fault with was the scaffolding, which Bramante, the Pope's head architect of the works at St. Peter's, had already set up for the purpose of painting the roof. Michelangelo refused to make use of Bramante's inadequate scaffolding, and on this plea hoped to escape the unwelcome commission. He also declared his inability to work in fresco, which he had only practised in his youth when he was an apprentice under Ghirlandajo in Florence. But Julius imperiously overruled every objection. Bramante was snubbed by the Pope and sent to the right-about, whilst Michelangelo was given a free hand for the project. Resigning himself to the inevitable, the artist now erected his own scaffolding and began, with the aid of his chosen band of assistants, to work upon the roof. Yet one more attempt to escape from the task, this time on account of the dampness of the surface plaster (compounded of Roman lime and marble dust), which caused all his brushwork to become blurred as soon as it was laid on. He begged to be allowed to return to his congenial work as sculptor. But Julius's will recognized no obstacle that he did not mean to overcome. So he merely sent the Florentine architect San Gallo to the Sistine, where San Gallo quickly discovered the cause of the mischief, and rectified the dampness of the plaster. This was the last protest of the master, and from that time onward Michelangelo worked hard upon his immense task till it was completed in its entirety.

Michelangelo's friend and biographer, Ascanio Condivi, has told us that the master finished the whole of the roof of the Sistine Chapel unaided, with his own hands, in twenty months, and this statement for many years was accepted without demur. Subsequent research, however, has dissipated this myth ; indeed, on reflection it would appear that such an accomplishment must be a sheer impossibility. In the first place, Michelangelo had his chosen band of helpers of all kinds, and the inferior handiwork of his pupils is apparent in many places. It was at some date in the spring or summer of 1508 that Michelangelo started on his task, and Julius's great commission was fully completed a little before All Saints' Day, 1512.

Three years before that date the scaffolding had been temporarily removed, so that the first portion of the huge composition could be inspected, that is, the flat surface of the ceiling, which shows the story of the Creation and Downfall of Man. The effect was magical on the minds of the many artists who witnessed this first unveiling of Michelangelo's masterpiece in fresco. Says Vasari : ' It lighted up a lamp for our art which casts abroad lustre enough to illuminate the world, drowned for so many centuries in darkness.' All the artists of the day, from Raphael downward, were filled with envy and admiration, and at once sought to imitate, or at least to adopt, the style of the great master. Once more the scaffolding was replaced, and then just three years later, the whole of the roof, ceiling, cornices, spandrels, and lunettes were exhibited to an admiring crowd in their finished form. Julius was fairly satisfied with the result, but made complaint of the absence of gilding. To this criticism Michelangelo is said to have replied that Adam and Eve and the patriarchs did not wear gold. There was talk of some gilding being added subsequently, but in any case this suggestion was never carried out, perhaps owing to the death of Julius II early in the following year. Altogether, the painting of the Sistine roof had occupied Michelangelo over four years.

Now let us take a survey of this famous and colossal masterpiece. Remember, it is a roof, and on entering the Sistine Chapel we cannot inspect it long without acute physical fatigue, and even pain. It can only be studied properly with the aid of large hand-mirrors. In the first place, the painting is made to fit into an architectural design, which was partly supplied by Michelangelo, and was partly enforced by the structure of the chapel. This being the case, Michelangelo, who was architect as well as sculptor, has treated his subject from an architectural standpoint. The whole work is, in fact, a combination of painting, architecture, and sculpture. The figures, said to be three hundred and forty-three in number, all fit into their proper places, as in some great plastic design; only in the long, flat space of the actual ceiling has the master a clear field for his inventions. Everything else had to be subordinated to the structural details of the chapel itself.

In the spaces over each of the twelve side-windows are shown five prophets and five sibyls of gigantic size. All these figures are seated; if they had been painted standing they would have all been eighteen feet in height. The eastern end space over the altar is occupied by the prophet Jonah, a marvellous example of foreshortening, and the western end space by Zechariah. These colossal figures of seven prophets and five sibyls naturally stand out to the spectator with the greatest prominence from the elaborate composition, and give a peculiar air of majesty and mystery to the whole. They rank amongst the best known and most popular of the master's works, and with good reason. The Delphic and Cumaean and Persian sibyls are perhaps the grandest in conception of this superb group. Next in size and importance rank the lovely scenes depicted on the flat ceiling, the earliest-painted portion of the roof. These are, from west to east, that is, from the altar to the doorway, the Creation of the World, the Creation of Man, the Expulsion of Adam and Eve from Eden, and the Deluge. On either side of these four major scenes are five minor scenes from Genesis, of which the most beautiful is the Creation of Eve, occupying the exact centre of the whole composition.

Each one of these five smaller scenes is set, so to speak, in a sort of framework composed of four lovely nude figures, in pairs, holding large classical medallions of bronze colour. The ornamental spaces round the prophets and sibyls are likewise well filled with graceful figures or genii that form part and parcel of the architectural setting. Very beautiful indeed are the ten cherubs, or *amorini*, that uphold the ten tablets engraved with the names of each prophet and sibyl. This roughly describes the flat portion of the great fresco; there still remains a considerable space that is occupied by the roof-vaulting itself, which casts a shadow, according to the light. This is also covered with designs, aiding and completing the main portion already described. Over each window, fourteen in all, are shown groups of kings, priests, prophets, patriarchs, holy women, all drawn from the Old Testament, many of them of exceeding grace and charm. In the four spandrels, or triangular spaces left at the four corners of the roof, are painted four designs from Old Testament history—of the Israelites in the wilderness with the brazen serpent; Esther and Haman; David and Goliath; and Judith with the head of Holofernes. In the pointed arches of the window vaults appear the Jewish ancestors of the Virgin, seated and waiting in calm expectation for the coming of the Messiah. The whole composition, intricate yet orderly in its marshalling, might fitly be termed 'the Old Testament of Michelangelo'. At the eastern extremity of the roof should be noted, beneath the figure of the prophet Zechariah, the coat of arms of Julius II—the golden oak-tree (*rovere*) on an azure ground, surmounted by the papal keys and tiara.

The colouring of the Sistine roof has often been described as sombre, but its present dingy tone is due to the lapse of four centuries and the constant action of candle-smoke and incense. The complete absence of all gilding, which at the time so disturbed Julius II, was no doubt an intentional omission on Michelangelo's part. In fact, the colouring is warm, soft, and harmonious, all the colours used being made subservient to the flesh tints of the many nude figures that the whole work contains. To emphasize these flesh tints there is an absence of any strong shade of red, the predominating colours used being yellow, blue, and green, that blend admirably with the general effect of silver-grey, which marks the composition throughout. The bronze colouring of the many classical medallions and of the figures of the genii above the points of the vaulting adds to the general softness of the colour scheme.

Yet it would be easy to show the revolution in contemporary art that such treatment as Michelangelo's wrought. Hitherto, the great painter Luca Signorelli alone had exhibited the tendency to avoid bright colour, and it is probable that Signorelli's work in the past to some extent influenced even so vast and original a mind as Michelangelo's. But the chorus of applause that greeted the unveiling of the Sistine roof may be called the death-knell of the beautiful and charming art of the *Quattrocento*. All the graceful and gracious accessories which were used by Botticelli and Perugino and the Ghirlandajos and Lorenzo di Credi (to mention but a few great names from the near past) are conspicuous by their absence in Michelangelo's huge and elaborate fresco. The blue skies, the delicate trees, the flowery lawns, the birds, the beasts, the elegant if meaningless ornaments that had hitherto played so prominent a part in the pictures of the artists of the *Quattrocento*, are all missing in the Sistine roof. And far more than these adjuncts, there is lacking the true devotional spirit, which reached its zenith in Fra Angelico. All the fascinating waywardness of the earlier old masters of Italy has been scornfully rejected by the master-mind of Michelangelo. What is gained in correctness of setting and drawing is lost in the absence of human fancy and of human piety. The frescoes of the Sistine Chapel form the great divide between the Early and the Late Renaissance ; it might not be too much to say that they separate the medieval school from the modern. Art is progressive, and it had now run its race and reached its final goal in Michelangelo's master-piece. There was nothing further to attain. Painting, sculpture, and architecture are all comprehended in this work, and it set a standard (as Vasari proudly declares) to the whole world which was henceforth adopted in its entirety. Yet the standard itself was almost bound to lead in time to mannerism and formality. If the roof of the Sistine is the last word of the forward movement in art, it is likewise the first word in its spiritual declension.

Of the inner meaning or argument of this great fresco it will be enough to say that it was intended to supplement the story of the frescoes already existing in the Sistine. It presented the Creation of the World, the Creation of Man, and then of Woman ; it showed the crimes, follies, and misfortunes of mankind. It showed also the underlying hope of the birth of a Saviour who should redeem the erring human race. The stately sibyls and prophets calmly bear their testimony to this divine hope ; whilst the ancestors of the Virgin sit in pious patience awaiting the promised Saviour of mankind. All this has been translated, so to speak, by the brain and brush of Michelangelo in conformity with the Christian Faith as he understood it in the days of the Renaissance. The master has imparted a logical and virile treatment to his mighty subject. Times change, and theological views change with them. The inner meaning of these scenes may no longer make the direct and obvious appeal to modern minds, but the beauty and order of the whole conception remain. It is the story of the Old Testa-ment as comprehended by Michelangelo, and pictured by him according not only to his unique skill but also to his interpretation of Holy Writ. Let us leave it at that, and setting aside our own theological prejudices, let us regard this fresco of the Sistine roof as a complete, perfect, and sublime interpretation of the Old Testament as it appeared to Michelangelo.

There is one point for special satisfaction in this work. It is *absolutely finished* both in design, detail, and colouring. So much of Michelangelo's long life of energy was wasted by impatient or ignorant patrons on futile commissions that we can here congratulate ourselves on possessing a perfect example of his genius, which was carried out in ample time and without interference. For this happy result posterity really owes a deep debt of gratitude to the imperious Pope Julius, whose firm desire and determination it was that the Sistine roof should be painted, and painted by none other than by Michelangelo. There is a good deal of the personality of that fiery pontiff in this work. True, Julius was not a connoisseur, but he had a sound sense of real grandeur, and in this case at least his natural flair did not play him false. When we survey this titanic fresco, therefore, we ought to recall the patron as well as the artist ; and, above all, we must recall the history and movements of the epoch wherein it was designed and executed. Remember, too, the peculiar status of the building which contains it. The Sistine Chapel is not a church in the usual sense of that term. It was rather a magnificent chapter-house wherein the Pope and his counsellors, the rulers of the Catholic world, were to confer together, to elect popes, and to receive deputations from the secular princes of the earth.

Within four months of the removal of the scaffolding in the Sistine Chapel, Pope Julius expired. In March 1513 the young Cardinal Giovanni dei Medici was elected his successor under the title of Leo X. For the next twenty years and more Michelangelo's connexion with the Vatican ceases. The reign of Leo X was more or less of a blank in his career. But before describing the master's later work in the Sistine Chapel, this will be the proper place to refer to another famous addition to this building.

Whilst Michelangelo was working on the Sistine roof the youthful Raphael of Urbino was busily employed hard by in the Vatican palace. There was little love lost between the two men, of whose utter diversity of temperament I have already written. Michelangelo sneered at the handsome young artist of twenty-five, always surrounded as he was by a bevy of adoring pupils. ' You go about your business like a general with his staff ! ' was his ill-natured comment. ' And you,' laughingly retorted Raphael, ' keep solitary like the hangman ! ' With the election of the Medici Pope, Leo X, Raphael rose higher than ever in favour ; and whilst Michelangelo was kept at Florence wasting his time and skill on projects that came to naught, Raphael was carrying out a multitude of commissions in Rome for Leo. Amongst these was the designing of a series of tapestries intended to represent the Acts of the Apostles, the tapestries to be hung so as to cover the blank space between the pavement of the chapel and the lower line of the earlier frescoes already mentioned. Raphael accordingly executed the cartoons from which the tapestries were woven by Flemish artificers at Brussels. They cost a hundred and fifty thousand ducats, an enormous sum, but for expense the lavish Leo cared not a jot, provided he obtained his heart's desire. Finally the tapestries were hung and exhibited to the people on St. Stephen's Day, 1519. ' All in the chapel,' records Paris de Grassis, the Venetian envoy, ' were struck dumb by the sight of these hangings, for by universal consent there is nothing more beautiful in the world.' These glorious hangings, thus placed, may be said to have completed the decoration of the Sistine. Imagine, then, the appearance of the interior of this huge box-like structure. The roof painted by Michelangelo in all its pristine beauty ; the west wall over the altar covered with superb frescoes by Perugino, the east wall likewise adorned by Salviati and Ghirlandajo. Then below the great painted figures of Michelangelo's roof the series of beautiful paintings by Perugino, Luca Signorelli, Botticelli, and Cosimo Rosselli ; and below these the famous tapestries of Raphael. Thus every inch of those tall, forbidding walls was now covered with painting, except for the broad dado of arras woven with gorgeous silks and gold thread. The Sistine Chapel in its freshness and gaiety of colouring must truly have been a glimpse of paradise, as one admirer did not scruple so to describe it. And add to this the mass of colour in the splendid crowds that here assembled—the Pope in dazzling white with his fan-bearers and his bodyguard in brilliant uniforms, the cardinals in flowing robes of scarlet, the bishops in violet, and the whole papal court in rich garments of every hue. As a mere spectacle of colour and decoration the Sistine Chapel on a festal day must have been perfect.

The pity is anything was ever altered. Nothing could have improved on its appearance as a shrine of most precious art and a stately chamber for the august meetings of the papal court. But Clement VII, the cousin of Leo and the second Medici Pope, was not satisfied. He decided to destroy the three frescoes by Perugino over the altar. These three frescoes by the Florentine master represented the ' Finding of Moses ' and the ' Adoration of the Magi ', two subjects that were in harmony with the rest of the older frescoes surrounding the walls which depicted the story of Moses and the Life of Christ, showing the type and the typified. The third fresco, just over the altar, was of the ' Coronation of the Virgin ', wherein the original builder of the Sistine Chapel, Pope Sixtus IV, was portrayed offering his tiara to the Virgin. Now, Sixtus IV was held in peculiar odium by the Medici, for he had been privy to the assassination of Pope Clement's father, Giuliano dei Medici, so long ago as 1478. I sometimes think, though I may be mistaken, that it was this portrait of the hated Pope Sixtus, uncle of Julius II, which caused Clement's decision to have Perugino's beautiful frescoes destroyed.   Or it may in truth have been that he wished the west wall to appear more in harmony with the roof as painted by Michelangelo.   Be that as it may, Clement called Michelangelo to Rome shortly before his death in 1534.   The master was now nearly sixty, filled with bitterness at the fall of the Florentine Republic a few years before, and well knowing that Clement had only spared his own life on account of his genius.   Clement was, unlike his cousin Leo, a fervent admirer of Michelangelo ; he was, in fact, as Cellini avers, an excellent connoisseur of art.   Clement now requested Michelangelo to draw a cartoon of the ' Last Judgment ' suitable for the space above the altar still occupied by Perugino's frescoes.   It was characteristic of the master that, unlike his rival, the sweet and gentle Raphael, Michelangelo seems to have made no demur at the proposed destruction of a noble work of art.   For Raphael used to plead hard, sometimes with success, for the retention of the works of former painters that he was requested to replace. Not so Michelangelo, who owned no scruples or sentiment on this head.   He complied with Clement's demand, and forthwith began to compose the cartoon, or sketch, for the ' Last Judgment '.   The frescoes of Perugino were ruthlessly covered over with plaster and duly prepared for the new fresco-to-be.   It would seem that Michelangelo had made no progress with his task by the date of Clement's death in the autumn of 1534.   Knowing the artist's dislike of Clement, the new Pope, Paul III, the founder of the Farnese family, himself an old man of seventy, was most anxious for Michelangelo to carry out this commission.   Accompanied by ten cardinals, the Farnese Pope now proceeded in person to Michelangelo's house—' an honour ', says the critic Lanzi, ' unparalleled in the history of art '—and requested him to complete the ' Last Judgment ' at the Sistine.   The

Pope wished the painting to be in oils, but the master insisted on fresco, and in fresco accordingly it was undertaken. Seven years were occupied in the task, the fresco being unveiled in the year 1541, when the master was sixty-six.

To describe this famous painting. In the first place, we must remember its size, which is, roughly, sixty-four feet high by thirty-two feet wide. The whole composition, which includes many hundreds of nude figures, divides itself naturally into four strata or planes, which can be studied singly. At the top, which is double-arched, just below the great painting of the prophet Jonah between the spandrels of the roof, appears the Almighty borne aloft by three cherubim. On either side of Him are shown groups of flying angels, who bear the Cross, the scourging-post, the reed, sponge, and other implements of Our Lord's Passion. These form the first plane. Below is seen prominent the figure of Christ, not as Saviour but as judge, and a merciless judge at that. He is represented as a naked youth, and is wholly destitute of any of the symbols or characteristics usually associated with Our Lord. His right hand is raised in anger. Beside Him almost crouches the Virgin, originally the only fully-clad figure in the whole fresco. On the right of the spectator are shown the saints and martyrs, some bearing their special symbols or engines of torture, but all alike, male and female, unclothed. On the left side are massed numerous figures arisen from the tomb for judgement, and apparently righteous. This forms the second plane. In the third one sees souls ascending to the judgement seat on one side, and souls descending to hell and damnation on the other. Between these two groups is introduced a choir of angels blowing mighty trumpets to wake the dead that are still sleeping, whilst two of their number display the Books of Judgement. This makes the third plane. The fourth, at the bottom of all, exhibits on the left the grave with the awaking dead ; and on the right hell, a classical hell, with Charon ferrying the souls of the damned across the river Styx. Minas sits in the background. Such is the main scheme of this celebrated work.

We must now examine its details. In the second or chief plane the figure of Christ stands out grandly, and at once rivets the attention. But he is *Judex Ultor*—judge and avenger. To Him turn the more prominent of the saints and martyrs. It has been charitably suggested that they are pleading for mercy for the damned, but their attitude is decidedly that of revenge also, like the Christ. Most striking of all perhaps is the St. Bartholomew, apostle and martyr, an aged man holding the scalping-knife wherewith he was flayed alive in his right hand, whilst his left grasps the whole of his skin, a truly horrible conception of a Christian martyr's attitude at the Judgement Day. Other saints can be recognized by their various symbols, some of them quiescent, but not a few in obviously exultant mood. The whole composition, though strictly classical in form and sentiment, seems permeated with the spirit of that wonderful Latin hymn of the medieval Church, commonly attributed to Pope Innocent III, the *Dies Irae* (the Day of Wrath), for Michelangelo clearly shows us a 'day of wrath, a day of mourning, Heaven and earth in ashes burning, thus behold the prophet's warning'. And this idea is further intensified by the looming figures of the prophets and sibyls of his earlier frescoes in the roof above. All the figures are carefully rendered with the master's special skill in drawing the nude, which is commonly reputed the highest aspiration of the artist. The varied expressions of the many faces too, especially of the damned, are admirably treated. So far as the artist's ambition is attained, the result is eminently satisfactory ; but whether this mass of naked bodies, writhing, flying, floating, falling, rising, sinking, and gesticulating, can ever be reconciled to the principles or spirit of true Christian art is another question. Although the work on its completion called forth numberless eulogies, yet there was a strong undercurrent of adverse criticism. The Bishop of Cesena, a court prelate, openly protested against this flaunting display of nudity over a Christian altar, whereupon the angry master promptly added the bishop's portrait, with horns on head and a serpent twined round his loins, among the damned. The poor bishop complained to the Pope, who only answered with a jest : ' I can release you from purgatory, but I have no power over hell.' But though his lordship of Cesena was only snubbed for his pains, there were other critics who did not hesitate to denounce the ' Last Judgment '. Of these the famous satirist, Pietro Aretino, expresses himself most strongly in a letter to Michelangelo. Aretino was a man of evil life and of even worse reputation, but his stinging words on this occasion have the basis of truth in them.

' Here there comes a Christian,' writes Aretino, ' who, because he rates art higher than the faith, deems it a royal spectacle to depict martyrs and virgins in unseemly attitudes, to show men dragged down by their shame. Your art would be at home in some voluptuous bagnio, but certainly not in the highest chapel of the world. Less criminal were it if you were an infidel, than, being a believer, thus to sap the faith of others. . . . Our souls need the tranquil emotions of piety more than the lively impressions of plastic art.'

This seems to me sound criticism both from the artistic and the moral standpoints. And what Aretino wrote openly was privately the opinion of many others. The whole conception of a day of divine wrath and vengeance, without pity and without sorrow, scandalizes the thoughtful Christian, and though Michelangelo had the Pope and the artists on his side, it was clear that he had given serious cause of offence to many good Christians who were by no means prudish or insensible to art. On the other hand, we must remember that the master was now an old man, saddened by the political fate of Italy, careless of the feelings of others, solitary, disappointed, soured. No doubt the ' Last Judgment ' of the Sistine reflects the starved and embittered soul of the artist.

Far from decreasing as time went on, the agitation against this famous work grew in strength. Under the fierce Caraffà Pope, Paul IV, whilst Michelangelo was still living, there was even some talk of obliterating the whole fresco. After some debate, however, it was decided to paint additional drapery for certain of the figures of the saints, and for this purpose the painter Daniele da Volterra was requested by Paul IV to carry out the miserable project. Michelangelo himself was consulted in the matter by the Pope, whose messenger brought back the enigmatic and characteristic reply of the master : ' Tell His Holiness this is a small matter, and can easily be set straight. Let him look to setting the world in order ; to reform a picture costs no great trouble.' Poor Daniele da Volterra, who could not help himself, won the nickname of ' Il Braghettone ', or the breeches-maker, from his uncongenial task.

But Daniele was not the only breeches-maker ; there were others in later times called in on the same puritanical business. Naturally, this continuous ill-treatment has ruined the unity of Michelangelo's mighty conception. Nor was this all. The taper-smoke from the altar, the constant fumes of incense, the burning of voting-papers at papal elections, have all helped to injure and deface this unlucky picture. Its colouring has gone beyond retrieve ; the gaudy draperies added by later hands stand out ; the whole surface of the fresco is blurred and darkened to a dirty blue-grey. We have but a ghost, and a very disreputable ghost at that, of the ' Last Judgment '. To-day the actual fresco owns little more than the interest of a ruin.

And yet Michelangelo's ' Last Judgment ' occupies a very important place in the history and development of art. Engravings of the work soon followed upon its completion, and passed into every city and collection throughout Europe. Artists everywhere rejoiced in the superb fancies of this grand composition. Indeed, from an artistic point of view, the ' Last Judgment ' was as great a secular success as it was a religious failure. Its influence is to be observed in many of our own artists. For example, William Blake was undoubtedly stirred by the grandeur of the ' Last Judgment ', and its effect upon his art was obvious and lasting. It is not too much to say that no artist of eminence has ever omitted to study these masses of nude figures, and to learn a valuable lesson from the general treatment as well as the details of Michelangelo's ' Last Judgment '.

Before concluding this account of Michelangelo and his work in the Sistine Chapel, I must allude to two other frescoes of his, the last paintings he ever completed, which exist close by, indeed, within a stone's throw of the Sistine. These are two frescoes, the ' Crucifixion of St. Peter ' and the ' Conversion of St. Paul ', that the master executed for his patron, Pope Paul III, in his new chapel, commonly called the Cappella Paolina. They were undertaken after the completion of his ' Last Judgment '. Though defaced by time and neglect and so-called restoration, these two frescoes go to prove that the old man's hand had not lost its cunning. Badly lighted and existing in a seldom-visited chapel, these two works are little known or inspected. I merely mention them, since they complete the tale of Michelangelo's labours at the Vatican under the two Popes, Julius II and Paul III. They were apparently finished about the year 1550, when Michelangelo was seventy-five years old, and with still fourteen years of his long, busy life to endure before he entered into rest.

XI

RAPHAEL AT THE VATICAN

(1508–1520)

IT was very shortly after Michelangelo had started upon his work at the Sistine Chapel in 1508 that Raphael Sanzio of Urbino, then aged twenty-five, was selected to decorate the suite of rooms in the Vatican that have long been known as the ' *Stanze di Raffaello* ' or ' Rooms of Raphael '. The young artist was chosen for this task largely on the recommendation of Bramante, Pope Julius's master of the works at St. Peter's ; of the great scholar and diplomatist, Bernardo Dovizi of Bibbiena, afterwards cardinal ; and last, but far from least, of the young Cardinal Giovanni dei Medici, the future Pope Leo X. A better choice of artist for the purpose could not possibly have been made, though as yet Raphael had not risen to the full height of his genius. Julius himself had no real love or comprehension of art, but he did regard it very seriously as a useful medium for the perpetuation of his own fame and the glorification of the deeds of his ambitious and blood-stained reign. With Michelangelo, then, employed on the roof of the Sistine, and with Raphael painting in the palace itself, Pope Julius was being served by the two greatest artists of his own or indeed of any age.

The rooms that Raphael was now called on to adorn are situated in the second story of the papal palace. Already their wall-spaces were largely covered with the works of a previous generation of artists. But all this earlier ornament was to be swept away to make room for the new compositions of Raphael. With his kindly, sympathetic nature Raphael did not relish the idea of being made the executioner of his forerunners' work, all of which owned great merit and beauty. He pleaded for their retention, but in vain, though in a few instances portions of these earlier frescoes were allowed to continue and form part of the new scheme. It is also characteristic of Raphael's tender heart that in every case before these paintings were obliterated to make room for his own work the master himself made careful drawings of the doomed pictures, and many of these sketches by Raphael still remain in various collections, both public and private.

The Stanze di Raffaello consists of four large chambers opening into one another, all owning beautiful marble pavements, many of them filched from Roman ruins. Their lighting was, however, ill-adapted for mural decoration. The first room to be decorated was the third from the corridor, or loggia (to which I shall refer later). This is commonly known by the name of the *Camera della Segnatura*—the room intended for the signing of papal briefs and letters. Leaving intact most of the ceiling decoration of the painter Sodoma, Raphael added to them the four splendid medallions containing his allegorical figures of Theology, Philosophy, Poetry, and Jurisprudence, truly noble inventions. These give the key to the four great frescoes on the walls of the chamber, which were painted in the following order :

(1) For *Theology*, the ' Disputa ', so-called, owing to the central design of the altar surmounted by a monstrance with the Host. The fresco aims at giving a comprehensive synopsis of Christian theology. God the Father, surrounded by the angelic host and holding the globe, appears above Our Lord, the Virgin, and St. John the Baptist, who are supported by a line of patriarchs, prophets, and saints upborne by clouds. Below, in two groups on either side of the altar with the Sacrament, are shown saints, doctors, confessors, and writers of the Church, who are engaged in

animated discourse. These last contain many fine portraits both of dead and living leaders of the Church.

(2) *Philosophy*. This most beautiful fresco admirably balances the Theology opposite. Here, against a gorgeous antique background (said to have been designed by Bramante, the architect), appear the great philosophers of the past, some fifty in all, engaged in study or argument. The two outstanding figures here are undoubtedly those of Plato, a venerable sage pointing heavenward, who is disputing with the middle-aged Aristotle, who passionately urges the study of Nature and of things earthy. This painting is commonly styled ' The School of Athens ', but it includes many sages and writers of various ages and countries. As usual, a few contemporary personages have been introduced, notably a graceful youth in the foreground (still unidentified), and at the extreme right-hand corner appear Raphael himself and his early master, Perugino.

(3) *Poetry*. This, perhaps the most pleasing of all these lovely creations, sometimes called ' The Parnassus ', shows an assemblage of Greek, Roman, and Italian poets. Its most prominent figure, who gives the motive to the picture, is Apollo, seated beneath the Delphic laurel and (in a true Renaissance spirit of wayward anachronism) he is shown playing on the violin.

(4) *Jurisprudence*. The side of the room devoted to Jurisprudence is differently treated, being cut up into three distinct compositions. Of these I shall only mention one group—at the side of the window—which is very important from an historical standpoint. This depicts Pope Julius in tiara and gorgeous cope delivering the decretals of the Church to a lawyer of the day, who is unidentified. It is an admirable portrait of Julius II, and may be compared with Raphael's better-known portrait in oils of the same pontiff, of which we have a fine replica in our National Gallery. The Pope is supported by members of his court, among

whom may be recognized the three future popes, at that time cardinals, namely (Medici) Leo X.; (Farnese) Paul III ; and (Del Monte) Julius III.

The many subsidiary designs and vignettes and figures of this apartment I have no space to describe, except to say that here, as elsewhere, they exhibit the exuberant fancy, the glorious colouring, and the surpassing skill of the master-mind of Raphael.

Of all Raphael's frescoes in the Vatican these in the Camera della Segnatura are certainly the freshest and most beautiful, though they do not show the full maturity of his genius.   This will be seen clearly enough in the succeeding halls of this suite.   The temporary display of Michelangelo's great fresco on the roof of the Sistine in 1509 doubtless produced a stimulating effect on the mind of Raphael ; he wished to expand his treatment of his themes ; he longed to add the cold grandeur of Michelangelo's correct designs to his own incomparable sweetness.   In my opinion this ambition is to be deplored, for what he gained in technique and confidence in his developing powers he lost in brilliance and appealing charm.   In the next room then, commonly called the *Sala di Eliodoro*, or ' Hall of Heliodorus ', we note a distinct change.   Four very famous frescoes cover the side walls of this apartment.   Of these the ' Expulsion of the Pagan Leader, Heliodorus, from the Temple ' at Jerusalem occupies the chief place, and is earliest in point of date.   The fresco vividly tells the story, from the Book of Maccabees, of how Heliodorus, the Greek general, entered the holy temple to rob and defile, when suddenly a celestial horseman in golden armour and mounted on a snow-white horse appeared in the midst of the terror-stricken Jews, and trampled with his hoofs the sacrilegious intruder to earth. Two attendant youths likewise sprang to view armed with rods to punish the despoiler.   The whole poetry of motion is shown in this spirited fresco.   The two youths seem scarcely to touch the ground with their graceful naked feet. It is an admirable illustration (in its true sense) of the episode given in the Apocrypha. The incident is here, however, connected with contemporary politics by the introduction of Pope Julius borne aloft on his chair of state and accompanied by members of the papal court. In other words, the crime and punishment of the impious invader of the Jewish temple are adapted to typify the invasion of Italy and defeat of the French at Novara in this very year.

Opposite the 'Heliodorus' is the fresco of the 'Defeat of Attila and the Huns'. Apart from its artistic beauty, this work owns a high historical importance. Although the fresco ostensibly deals with the discomfiture of Attila, King of the Huns, before the walls of Rome, yet this far-off incident is clearly meant to glorify the late papal victory over the invading French. Originally, the triumphant Pope, St. Leo, was represented with the features of Julius II. But whilst the actual fresco was still in progress—that is, in February, 1513—Julius died and was succeeded by Leo X. Raphael, delighted at Leo's prompt extension of the papal patronage to himself, thereupon replaced the portrait of Julius by that of Leo X. We have, in short, in the left-hand group of this painting an excellent likeness of Leo X as he rode on his favourite white palfrey in his coronation procession of that same year. The portrait may be compared with the very famous oil-painting of the same Pope, now in the Pitti Gallery at Florence, which Raphael executed four years later. Behind the Medici Pope, on horseback, appears the figure of Raphael himself, also mounted and bearing the pontifical cross. It shows the sallow but poetical face and dark hair, the sweet expression, and the long, flexible neck that mark every likeness of the divine painter from Urbino. This great allegorical composition then marks the dividing line of papal patronage in Raphael's career; henceforward he becomes the all-too-willing slave of the magnificent and extravagant Leo X.

In the same hall are two other frescoes over the windows. Of these the ' Miracle of Bolsena ', the story of the bleeding of the Host in the hands of a sceptical priest, introduces Julius and his court and is therefore prior to that Pope's death; the other, the ' Deliverance of St. Peter from Prison ' is an obvious and rather servile compliment to the new Medici pontiff, who only a year before his election to the papacy had been a prisoner in the hands of the French, and had escaped at considerable risk from their clutches. Apart from their historical allusions and interest, these four frescoes own amazing grace of form and beauty of colouring. They are on the highest level ever attained in fresco. The flowing drapery and the expressive faces in the ' Miracle of Bolsena ', and the wonderful effects of nocturnal and celestial light in the ' Deliverance of Peter ' make appeal even to the most uneducated. In fact, it is just this rare power of universal appeal to child and adult, to ignorant and learned alike, that is one of the most subtle and fascinating qualities in all Raphael's work.

Adjoining the Hall of Heliodorus is the so-called *Sala del Incendio*, or ' Hall of the Fire '. This owes its name to the chief composition in its scheme of paintings, for it represents an early medieval miracle under Pope Leo IV, whose prayers managed to extinguish a fire that had broken out in the Borgo, or quarter of the city around St. Peter's. It is not a very promising subject for a masterpiece, yet Raphael's skill and ingenuity were fully equal to his rather unattractive theme. For Raphael shows us here not the destruction of a Roman suburb but the burning of ancient Troy, as described in the second book of Virgil's Aeneid. There is pious Aeneas, founder of the Roman race, escaping with his aged father Anchises on his back; there is the little Iulus, his son, following in his sire's footsteps and clasping the household gods in his tiny arms ; there stands the unhappy Cassandra mourning over her own fulfilled prophecy of impending disasters. It is a grand composition, but it has not the compelling charm of the master's previous works. It will be noted too for the first time how the influence of his great rival, Michelangelo, is beginning to affect Raphael. Naked figures are conspicuous in this fresco of the ' Incendio ', which bears other points of resemblance to the scenes in the Sistine roof. The other large frescoes in this hall are of more historical than artistic interest, for they recall in allegorical guise some of the leading events in the reign of Leo X and are remarkable for the number of contemporary portraits they contain, such as Leo X, Giulio dei Medici (afterwards Clement VII), Ippolito dei Medici (who is acting as a page), King Francis I, Cardinal Bibbiena and a host of other notables of the court of Leo X. Yet very little of these frescoes is due to the actual hand of Raphael, who was now working with feverish haste upon a host of commissions of every kind for his appreciative but inconsiderate patron Leo. They are chiefly the work of Raphael's pupils, and especially of his favourite pupil Giulio Romano. It is interesting to note that the ceiling of this hall still contains its original decorations by Perugino, for in this case Raphael had successfully pleaded for the preservation of the paintings of his old instructor.

Still less of Raphael's influence is to be observed in the largest hall of the whole suite, *The Hall of Constantine*. Of its paintings, which were executed mostly under Clement VII, only the great battle-piece of the ' Triumph of Constantine ' over Maxentius, the pagan emperor, is taken direct from the master's cartoon. It is a superb work, an elaborate but by no means fearsome conception of a battle, although Giulio Romano's coarse colouring greatly spoils its effect. The other frescoes, valuable and interesting as they are from an historical standpoint, owe nothing to the master-mind of Raphael, who was already dead before the decoration of the Hall of Constantine was even started.

Apart from their inestimable artistic value, the frescoes of Raphael in the three halls of the *Segnatura* the *Eliodoro* and the *Incendio* present us with a well-filled gallery of the great personages who thronged the successive courts of Julius II and Leo X. 'The rooms painted by Raphael', so writes the learned Bembo to the Cardinal Bibbiena, ' are quite beautiful, not only on account of the skill shown in the execution, but also on account of the great number of clergy whose portraits he has introduced.' We ourselves to-day, who can but behold all this splendour after it has become dulled by centuries of neglect or injured by injudicious restoration, of necessity find it difficult to realize the original appearance of this series of paintings in their pristine freshness of colouring. How entrancing must have been the aspect of these stately apartments when peopled with a constant come-and-go of splendidly-clad prelates and courtiers, who as they swept proudly through these rooms paused from time to time to admire, to criticize, to compare, or to examine with delight or envy the speaking likenesses of their friends or rivals, portrayed on these glowing walls by the brush of the Prince of Painters! Admitting the lack of a proper environment for these superb but faded paintings, we can the better enter into the feelings of that fastidious scholar, Bembo, who considered all this wealth of art merely as an adequate setting to the official court life of the Vatican in the golden days of the Leonine Age. ' The halls,' he writes, ' which Raphael has painted, are already lovely beyond compare, but their charm is enhanced not a little by the crowds of passing cardinals and prelates.'

From the gloomy grandeur of the Sistine Chapel, peopled with Michelangelo's stately but sinister prophets and sibyls and his nude, contorted forms, we turn to enter a new world of allegory, a world of light and gladness, when we ascend

to the Rooms of Raphael. Although his beautiful frescoes
are not without certain admitted defects, yet the general
impression produced on the beholder at entering the Stanze
is so elevating and joyous, so full of bewildering charm, that
hostile criticism is at once disarmed. The mind may grow
pensive and sobered amid the huge masterpieces of the
Sistine Chapel, but the human spirits are cheered and
warmed with Raphael's succession of semi-historical scenes
that present to us in alluring form only the gay and pleasant
side of the Italian Renaissance. The Sistine Chapel does
indeed truly reflect the fierce mind and unbending nature
of the rugged Pope Julius; but the Stanze of Raphael are
all eloquent of the liberal, ostentatious, easygoing, extravagant Medici Pope, who was determined to 'enjoy the
papacy'. In these halls we see the divinities of Paradise
and of Olympus, the philosophers of the Greek world, the
confessors and martyrs of Christendom, the sages of Greece
and Rome, and the poets of medieval Italy meet, converse,
and argue together in cool and reasonable debate. We are
shown the very essence of that spirit of humanism of the
Renaissance, which did not hesitate to put the virtuous
counsel of Plato or Seneca on an equal footing with the dour
theology of the Middle Ages. No note of gloom or sorrow
or pain or mistrust is allowed to intrude within these realms
of bliss and brightness. Everywhere the Church is shown
triumphant, but never does her triumph suggest war or
rapine in its train. Calmly do the great pontiffs Julius
and Leo watch the celestial emissaries scatter the evil
forces of darkness and idolatry on their behalf. The Rooms
of Raphael constitute, in short, an epic poem in painting
of the preservation of the arts, the learning, the religion, and
last, but far from least, of the secular papacy of Italy from
the impious hands of brutish barbarians. And this work
is shown as being accomplished by direct divine agency;
whilst her venerable pontiffs, the natural guardians of

threatened Italy, the seat of true religion and of real culture, merely stand aside to permit Peter and Paul and the heavenly host in a blaze of golden glory carry out the pious task of deliverance.

For seven years Raphael served under Leo X, carrying out for the Pope a multiplicity and variety of conceptions which at last caused the exhausted artist's premature death. He had succeeded Bramante as master of the works at St. Peter's; he was painting portraits and drawing plans; he was preparing a treatise on the ancient ruins of Rome (which, to his eternal credit, Leo was most anxious to preserve from the hands of the masons and contractors who were using these relics of antiquity as mere quarries). Leo was young for a pope, and he had a presentiment of an early death; therefore he hastened to urge Raphael to perform more and more tasks. And Raphael, who was good-nature itself, meekly yielded to his exacting patron in all things, although this fearful exertion was sapping his strength and vitality. And besides this, Raphael was one of those generous souls who could never say ' no ' to any request, whether such request came from the Supreme Pontiff or from the humblest of his pupils. During these seven years he poured forth such a multitude of designs, drawings, portraits, frescoes, sketches, suggestions on paper that we cannot wonder at the artist's final and sudden collapse under stress of so much work. Moreover, Raphael was not only the first artist of Leo's brilliant court; he was likewise one of its most prominent members. He could hold his own in debate with the scholars and antiquaries and poets whom Leo delighted to entertain. He was man of the world as well as artist. He had grown rich in the service of two popes; he owned a fine palace near St. Peter's; he was affianced to the niece and heiress of the great Cardinal da Bibbiena. He was beloved as much as he was admired on all sides.

Amongst the innumerable tasks which Raphael had in hand during this short but prolific period of his brief career, both for the Pope and for private patrons, was the decoration of the upper story of Bramante's façade of the papal palace. This upper story, now always known as the *Loggia di Raffaello*, or 'Corridor of Raphael', was on the same floor as the Stanze, or suite of rooms, that I have just mentioned. In fact, it is separated only by a doorway from the Hall of Constantine. At this period the long and lofty corridor stood open to the sky and afforded a superb view of Rome and the Tiber. It was Leo's intention to decorate this loggia, or open arcade, and for this purpose he fixed at once on Raphael. The Loggia itself consisted of fourteen open arches forming thirteen bays or sections, each one of which was crowned by a small dome or cupola. The whole of these lofty walls were to be completely covered with ornament, and the thirteen domed recesses were to be painted with Biblical scenes. Already the Florentine artist, Luca della Robbia, was covering the floor with a pavement of the beautiful glazed tiles, for the production of which both he and his father Andrea before him were famous. Raphael at once decided to treat the tall wall-spaces in the spirit of the ancient Roman style of fresco, commonly called *grottesche*. This word is derived straight from the *grotte*, or subterranean chambers excavated on the Palatine and elsewhere among the ruins of Rome, which were often found to be adorned with fanciful designs in colour, that showed all kinds of object, plant, figure, industry, scene, or incident that could lend themselves to artistic treatment. Taking this form of classical decoration for his guide, Raphael now prepared a number of 'grotesque' designs for this Loggia most of which were carried out by Giovanni da Udine, the best decorator of his day, though he does not rank in the first flight of its artists. In addition to these grotesques and arabesques in colour, there was

added richly wrought stucco-work, whose pure white sheen
served well to set-off the gay designs and bright gilding
employed in the whole scheme.

But all this gay and fanciful decoration of the walls and
pilasters of the Loggia was made subservient to the main
idea of the whole project. This was the painting of the
thirteen domes of the long, narrow ceiling of the tall
corridor. In these domed recesses overhead Raphael
painted, or at least caused to be painted from his own
designs, fifty-two scenes from Scripture, a series that is
generally known as the ' Bible of Raphael '. The ' Old
Testament of Raphael ' would be a more correct title for
this work, for of these fifty-two designs only four (those in
the last cupola) are drawn from the Gospels. The ' Bible
of Raphael ', then, in the ceiling of the Loggia may be
contrasted with the ' Bible of Michelangelo ' as displayed on
the roof of the Sistine Chapel hard by. One cannot, one
may not, compare them, for the notion of comparison does
not arise. I have referred already to Michelangelo's
creations in the Sistine, and I have explained how his
superb but complicated arrangement of his subject can
appeal only to the scholar and the artist. Even to this
day doubts exist as to the exact meaning or allusion or
argument the great master intended to convey. It is not
so with the ' Bible of Raphael '. Here we have a number
of scenes from the Old Testament, beginning with the story
of Adam and Eve, and carrying us through the principal
events as related in the various books of the Bible. All these
paintings are conceived and carried out with a directness
and simplicity that make their subjects easily recognizable
to all persons, whether learned or unlearned, who have
any knowledge of Bible history. Raphael has here, in fact,
aspired to reproduce what was known in the Middle Ages
as the ' Biblia Pauperum ', that is, a series of popular
illustrations of the Bible which should teach in easy, pleasant

and reverent manner the incidents of Holy Writ to all and sundry. It was to be a Bible ' comprehended of the people '. And it is in this radical difference of treatment that there lies the main contrast between the two great masters. Michelangelo's method or view of the story of the Old Testament is obscure and enigmatical ; Raphael's is simple and human. I have already spoken of this quality of universal appeal that underlies so much of Raphael's work in the frescoes of the Stanze. It is of course still more marked in his Bible of the Loggia, where cheerful colouring, simple grouping, and clear illustration present the whole Christian world with a popular series of pictures for the Book of Books. I may also add here that the designs worked on the tapestries of Raphael in the Sistine—his sole contribution to the decoration of that chapel—exhibit this identical quality of popular appeal. And to this day the graceful illustrations of Raphael retain their vogue alike in Catholic and Protestant communities, where children as well as men and women find no difficulty in understanding exactly what the great painter meant to convey. Raphael therefore must always rank as the first exponent of Biblical illustration ; in short, as the greatest of *Christian* painters. His works are full of dignity, simplicity, and purity of feeling. They are as free from the false and sickly sentimentality of the later Italian schools as they are devoid of that coarse secular treatment, almost pagan in its general effect, that Michelangelo introduced.

The Loggia of Raphael is but the shadow to-day of its beautiful self. Time and the weather have dealt hardly with it. As I have said, the Loggia was originally open to the air, and it was only in the last century that the enormous glass windows were fitted into the tall arcades so as to preserve what was left of the wall decoration. The lovely pavement of Luca della Robbia has long perished. We find it therefore very difficult to conjure up the appear-

ance of this great open corridor in the days of Raphael and
Pope Leo. So damaged indeed is this fine specimen of the
arts and architecture of the Renaissance that we can but
re-echo the lament of the critic Lanzi, when he says :
' The exposure of this gallery to the inclemency of the
weather has almost reduced it to the squalid appearance of
the ancient *grotesques*. But they who saw it after it was
first finished, when the lustre of the gilding, the snowy
whiteness of the stuccoes, the brilliance of the many tints,
and the freshness of the marbles made it resplendent with
beauty on every side, must have been struck with amaze-
ment as at a vision of Paradise.' And Vasari, in his *Life
of Raphael* records : ' It is impossible either to execute or
to imagine a more beautiful work.'

In any case, the Loggia of Raphael, though sadly defaced
and injured, still remains for us to admire and to exercise
our imagination upon. It has at least fared better than
another work of Raphael's at the Vatican, which was carried
out during this period, these seven years of his artistic
fertility. This was the Bathroom of Cardinal Bibbiena,
the special friend of the master, who gave him this commission. The witty and learned cardinal wished to have
a bathroom constructed and ornamented in the true fashion
and spirit of the antique. As a theme for painting Bibbiena
suggested the story of Venus and Cupid, which was, to put
it mildly, not a very suitable theme for the decoration of the
palace of the first celibate in Christendom. The idea
appealed strongly to Raphael, who soon covered this little
apartment with a charming series of frescoes in a pure
classical style. He made and adorned in fact what we
should describe to-day as ' a Pompeian chamber ' (although,
of course, the buried city of Pompeii was a sealed book to
the people of the Renaissance). The scheme and colour of
the decoration employed is wholly diverse from that of the
Loggia, for it follows closely the peculiar patterns and

arrangements found in the *grotte* of subterranean Rome. Most elegant and fanciful are the designs and medallions and arabesques on these walls, and for many generations artists were wont eagerly to study this little chamber in the Vatican. But a spirit of prudish reticence and a sense of the ' pagan ' character of this bathroom in the nineteenth century seem to have affected the authorities at the Vatican, and for many years now the Bathroom of Cardinal Bibbiena has been closed to the public. It is said to have been badly mutilated by some illiberal censor of morals ; in any case it has long been strictly kept under lock and key. Fortunately, artists of the past who studied here in less particular times have left published drawings of its graceful and varied ornamentation.

It is marvellous to think that all these works of Raphael at the Vatican during that short spell of seven years were carried out concurrently with a host of other commissions outside the palace. No wonder the artist's health, never very robust, began to flag under his severe but congenial burden. Leo seems to have owned no consideration for his favourite artist, though he dearly loved him in his selfish Medicean way. The end was very sudden and tragical. Raphael in the early spring of 1520 was engaged (among a score of other duties) upon the decoration of the palace (now the Villa Farnesina) of the rich banker, Agostino Chigi of Siena. Leo sent for him post-haste one morning, and the artist walked fast, or rather ran, to obey the papal summons. Arriving hot and fatigued at the Vatican, Leo kept the artist in conversation for some time beneath a draughty archway, with the result that Raphael caught a severe chill. With his powers already overtaxed, the painter soon sank under this attack. He retired to his bed, never to rise again. His room was thronged with friends and admirers, lamenting his illness ; all Rome was aghast at the thought of losing the divine Raphael of

Urbino ; Leo was sending continually to inquire after the stricken artist.

Into the dying man's room, at his own request, there was now brought his great unfinished picture of ' The Transfiguration ', which is to-day the gem of the Vatican picture gallery. The painting had been commissioned by the Cardinal Giulio dei Medici, afterwards Pope Clement VII, and so far Raphael had but completed the upper portion of his composition, which represents Our Lord ascending in glory to Heaven with Moses and Elijah floating in mid-air on either side of him. It is admittedly unique as a perfect conception of celestial splendour and grace. Long and sadly the artist gazed on this splendid but uncompleted canvas, and not long afterwards Raphael Santi of Urbino, the most delightful if not the greatest painter of the world, passed quietly away on the night of Good Friday, 1520. He had only just passed his thirty-seventh birthday. He was buried amid the universal mourning of the city of Rome in the Pantheon, where his tomb can be seen to-day. ' He has been interred in the Pantheon ', writes the Venetian ambassador, Michiel, ' whither he was borne with great honour. His soul has doubtless gone to contemplate the edifices of Heaven, which are not subject to corruption. His name and memory will live long in his works and in the remembrance of all honest men.'

I have written of Raphael's work at the Vatican as contained in the Stanze, the Loggia, and the little Bathroom of Cardinal Bibbiena. In addition to these I may add that the famous Picture Gallery of the Vatican likewise contains several of his most important canvases. There is amongst many the ' Madonna di Foligno ', painted for Sigismondo Conti, perhaps the most charming and graceful of all that group of Raphael's Madonnas. There are others too, but I shall only mention once again ' The Transfiguration ', which represents the climax, the zenith, of Raphael's fame, and owns a special pathetic interest owing to the story of the painter's last hours, when this work was carried to his sick-room and was afterwards borne in his funeral procession to the Pantheon. For nearly three centuries it was the chief treasure of the church of St. Pietro in Montorio in Rome. Thence in Napoleonic days it was carried off by the French to Paris, and after the fall of Napoleon it was returned to the Pope, Pius VII, who insisted on keeping this glorious painting in the Vatican, which seems to me its proper and natural resting-place.

XII

FRA ANGELICO

(1387-1455)

IN dealing with the story and the course of the Italian
Renaissance we are often inclined to regard it and
treat it solely as a progressive movement, or at least
as a continuing impulse, which leads us step by step to
modern aims, questions, and politics. Such a view is
partial only. There were other currents in the Italian
Renaissance besides that of the main stream. The Age of
Faith was not wholly swept away in the flood of the New
Learning; on the contrary, that age in Renaissance days
owned its exponents and its votaries, who, whilst using for
their purpose the new arts and discoveries, still urged men
to preserve intact the lofty spiritual ideals of the past.
Such persons did their best to stem the main current of
fashionable scepticism and to denounce the new classical
influences that were disturbing the medieval theories of
human life and morality through the revived works of the
Greek and Latin philosophers. In this band of spiritual
reactionaries (if one may so describe them) two great names
stand out clearly before us as those of exponents and
upholders of past ideals, namely, Girolamo Savonarola,
Prior of St. Mark's, and Fra Giovanni da Fiesole, otherwise
the Blessed Fra Angelico, the friar-painter. Savonarola
was but a child at the date of Fra Giovanni's death in 1455,
but I am inclined to believe that Angelico's moral influence
reacted strongly on the great preacher, whose period of
energy and power was spent in the famous convent of St.
Mark in Florence, where he hourly saw the beautiful painted
lessons of the holy artist on the walls wherein he was destined

to rule as prior. Certainly, Fra Angelico stands to the world of art for what Savonarola stood to the theology and politics of his time, so that the influence of both was thrown heavily on to the side of the spiritual claims of humanity.

Fra Giovanni was born about 1387 at Vicchio, a hamlet in the valley of the Mugello below the ancient cathedral city of Fiesole, the classical Faesulae, a few miles to the north-east of Florence. He seems to have come of sturdy Tuscan peasant stock, and his baptismal name was Guido. This name he later exchanged for Giovanni (no doubt in compliment to St. John the Baptist, the patron saint of Florence) on his reception as a novice into the Dominican convent of San Domenico, which stands on the plateau below the steep crest of Fiesole. His life therefore was spent largely near or in Florence, for San Domenico is only about three miles distant from the vast Florentine cathedral, whose dome was brought to completion by Brunelleschi during Angelico's lifetime. His works, then, are chiefly associated with Florence, so that Fra Giovanni belongs of right to that noble group of Florentine citizens whose eminence in art, learning, science, and literature has shed a peculiar lustre on their native city. Vasari tells us, and we can well believe it, that the young friar's genius showed itself at a very early age, when he began to study as an apprentice under the painter Gherardo Starnina. But if his taste for painting was developed early, it is also equally certain that his vocation for the life of the cloister asserted itself in his boyhood. And in Fra Angelico these innate impulses of religion and of art were not only concurrent, but were so closely intertwined that their joint result becomes apparent in all his work. In short, Fra Angelico's career as a Dominican friar and his reputation as a painter cannot be treated separately; one is naught without the other, for he was perfect recluse and perfect artist, and, moreover, both in perfect unison.

Of his youth there is next to nothing to record. At nineteen he was admitted a novice of the Dominican Order, the Order of Predicants or Preachers. He became, together with his brother, Benedetto, a member of the newly-founded house at San Domenico, whose church and convent still stand in the small piazza of the village. ' Brother Johannes, son of Peter of Vicchio in Mugello, who excelled as a painter and adorned many tablets and walls in divers places, accepts the habit of a clerk in this convent . . . and in the following year professed (1408).' San Domenico is a charming spot, set amidst the rich fertile country-side of Val d'Arno, a sweet region of fig and vine and olive, sprinkled with ancient farm-houses or stately villas. To the south one notes the Arno flowing through the broad valley till it is lost within the walls of Florence ; and then once more, looking to westward, one can trace its course, like a silver snake, gliding towards the setting sun and the white marble mountains of Carrara. Eastward, facing the convent of San Domenico, uprise the spurs of the Apennines with the conspicuous bare hill topped by the walled monastery of the Incontro. Here it was, on yon bleak hill-crest, that the two great founders of the mendicant Orders, St. Francis and St. Dominic, had met and, as true servants of God, had embraced with holy tears of mutual thanksgiving. This meeting, or *incontro*, has been generally deemed a historical fact, and it has been treated as such from time to time in Italian art, notably in the fine Della Robbia lunette in the arcade of the Florentine piazza of Santa Maria Novella. No doubt the pious tradition of this encounter had been kept fresh in local memory, so that an additional sanctity rested on the fair Tuscan landscape which was spread before the windows of the little friary at San Domenico.

In 1414, owing to some domestic trouble, the friars of San Domenico migrated for four years to Cortona, one of the hill-set cities of Umbria, surrounded by Cyclopean walls.

And as a result of this temporary migration there are still to be seen at Cortona some fine specimens of Fra Angelico's early work, including an ' Annunciation ', which appears somewhat similar to his later and more famous ' Annunciation ' within the walls of San Marco in Florence. The wandering friars returned to their proper home at San Domenico in 1418.

The convent at San Domenico was itself only founded in 1406, so that the Blessed Angelico must have been one of the earliest of its inmates. Some of the original buildings remain, though the little tower and pretty portico that we see to-day belong really to a later date than Angelico's. The conventual church was once rich in the works of its distinguished artist-friar, but all his productions have one by one disappeared from the church, so that little now is left to remind the visitor of his long residence at this spot. As San Domenico itself stands within three miles of the centre of Florence, it is probable that Fra Giovanni frequently went for the day only into the city to his labours at San Marco, the Church of the Annunziata, and elsewhere, either walking on foot there and back, or else obtaining a lift in one of the many country-carts, rough wooden concerns drawn by oxen, that still ply their course daily to and fro, bringing the *contadini*, or peasants, with their wine and oil and fruit to the Florentine market.

The life of the cloister has been described and criticized over and over again, and little remains to be said on this score. Those who imagine the monastery, or nunnery, to represent a life of idleness relieved by elaborate services and congenial piety and gossip, are wholly mistaken ; the average religious house was and is a hard-working, self-supporting, self-denying community, in which every member must bear a part and take a share. No doubt Fra Giovanni did his share of the daily round, the common task, for many years in San Domenico, and it was only in later life, when his marvellous art had been recognized as unique by Cosimo dei

Medici, that all his energies were concentrated, by order of his Superior, on his painting and its attendant studies. Thus, in his early days Fra Giovanni had the calls of his chosen vocation as well as the calls of his chosen art to attend to ; there were many duties and tasks of a less attractive and romantic nature than that of painting to be performed daily. These were the teaching of the novices, the sweeping of the cells, the garden, the refectory, the guest chambers in all of which things Fra Giovanni had to perform his allotted measure in the daily life of the community. One can feel sure that those conventual duties and obligations were faithfully undertaken by the artist-friar with the same loving care and precision that he bestowed on his artistic work on wall, easel, and choral book, for he was illuminator as well as artist. His was the choice spirit described in later years by a famous English poet and mystic, who himself belongs to the same category of holy men in all ages and in all lands—I mean, George Herbert. No doubt Fra Giovanni carried out his domestic tasks in that true spirit of service which George Herbert has commended in the lines :

> Who sweeps a chamber by Thy law,
> Makes that and the action fine.

Of yet another duty that fell to Fra Angelico's lot we have unhappily no record. He had entered the great Dominican Order of Preachers, so presumably he had at times to occupy the pulpit. What sort of a sermon did this marvellous artist preach on such occasions ? Did he, I wonder, manage to impress his hearers with the full sense of the beauty of holiness such as pervades every picture that ever came from his brush ? Was he eloquent ? Probably not ; and yet it is impossible to doubt that the sermons of Fra Giovanni, however simple and halting their language, could not but influence his audience for good. It must have been an object lesson in sanctity and humility to have seen and heard this holy, humble man of genius in the pulpit. Fra Angelico has introduced his portrait in one or two of his larger compositions, very much in the background and usually diminutive, yet we study the earnest kindly face, with the rough-hewn features and dark complexion and eyes of the typical Tuscan son of the soil, with a deep interest, and we are not disappointed in our survey. His face somehow recalls to me the rather rugged countenance of the late Pope, Pius X, the Lombard peasant, Giuseppe Sarto, who rose through sheer benignity and uprightness from the humblest origin to become a bishop, a patriarch of Venice, a cardinal, and finally, in spite of his tears and protestations, Supreme Pontiff. And it is interesting to note that Fra Giovanni himself, had he not sternly declined every ecclesiastical honour, would have risen to be Arch-bishop of Florence, and no doubt a cardinal or prince of the Roman Church. For in his later years Pope Eugenius IV expressly wished him to accept this position. But Fra Giovanni made no use of this splendid offer (which brought him no temptation) other than to recommend for this post the one friar whom he thought suitable to be so honoured. And thus the holy and well-beloved St. Antonino was consecrated Archbishop of Florence at the earnest request of Fra Angelico.

The convent of St. Mark (San Marco) in Florence is to-day reckoned one of the most interesting buildings in all Italy, and each year brings thousands of reverent pilgrims to this spot as to a recognized shrine of art and history. Five great names are closely associated with this Dominican priory of St. Mark : Cosimo dei Medici, its founder ; the excellent St. Antonino, Archbishop of Florence ; Savonarola ; the painter Fra Bartolommeo ; and last but very far from least, Fra Angelico, whose matchless work can best be studied and appreciated within those walls. Founded

in 1436 by the wise Cosimo the Elder, first of the Medici
dynasty in Florence; built by his favourite architect,
Michelozzo; and consecrated by the great Pope Eugenius IV,
St. Mark's continued for over sixty years the principal focus
of Florentine religious, political, and artistic life. At first
glance the famous convent, with its low whitewashed walls,
its small, rounded windows, and its dull baroque church
façade, offers no striking appearance from the dusty square
wherein it stands. Yet its interior courts remain to-day in
much the same condition as they appeared in the far-off
times of the *Quattrecento*. Everywhere the historic Medicean
shield, with its six pellets, is conspicuous, and serves to
remind us of its foundation by the Medici. In its first
court, or cloister, still exists the little garden with the damask
roses, that are descendants of the very rose-trees that
Cosimo, and Fra Angelico and Savonarola loved. Above
the doorways we see the precious frescoes that Angelico
painted to symbolize the salient rules of the Dominican
Order—the rules of Silence, Discipline, Obedience, and
Hospitality (the last showing Our Lord as a pilgrim being
welcomed by two friars), all treated with the charm and
piety that Angelico's brush could alone bestow.

' The frescoes of the first cloister of San Marco exhibit
Angelico not as a mere painter of Madonnas and the joys of
Paradise, but as one who could delineate passion in various
forms and degrees; who could reveal in each action its
peculiar nature, and who fitly presents his meaning with
repose, propriety, grace, and truth.'

In the spacious and rather gloomy chapter-house leading
out of this cloister is to be seen the great doctrinal ' Crucifixion ', perhaps the finest and most moving representation
of this subject. Over this work Angelico wept and fasted
continuously, and the whole composition bears mute
witness not only to his skill but also to his mental attitude.
It discloses the scene on Calvary, with Our Lord crucified

between the two thieves, the penitent and the impenitent, whilst below are grouped the three Marys, with St. John the Divine. Beside them are introduced St. Mark, patron saint of the monastery ; the Baptist, as patron of the city of Florence ; St. Dominic, founder of the Order ; St. Lawrence, with Saints Cosmo and Damiano, as tutelar saints of the Medici family. Below is shown a galaxy of saints, popes, bishops, and doctors of the great Dominican Order. ' We may read it,' says Mrs. Anna Jameson, that admirable critic, ' like a sacred poem. Every separate figure is a study of character. I hardly know anything in painting finer than the pathetic beauty of the head of the penitent thief, or the mingled fervour and intellectual refinement in the head of St. Bernard.'

Unfortunately space will not allow me to describe, as I should like, the various masterpieces of Fra Angelico that are contained in St. Mark's. We ascend the steep stone staircase with its worn steps to the upper floor below the great open roof of rough Apennine chestnut beams. Here are the cells for monks and novices ; the official apartments of the prior, head of the community, ever-famous for their personal connexion with Savonarola ; the library ; the suite of rooms reserved for Cosimo dei Medici. And everywhere, on every wall, in each cell, we perceive exquisite pictures, the emanations of a genius that was in close communion with God Himself. Fra Angelico acts as interpreter, so to speak, between the friars of St. Mark's and the God whom they seek by their vows to serve. He must in very truth be a scoffer, a dullard, or a philistine who could fail to be moved in such an atmosphere of antique piety and celestial beauty. The very spirit of heavenly things breathes through all. As we open the door from the stairway we look straight at Angelico's conception of the Annunciation, with its glorious kneeling angel before the humble Virgin, half-terrified, half-overcome with joy at his message.

In the adjoining little stone cells, so meagre and so bare, each inmate had for guide and ornament a fresco by Angelico to fix his thoughts. All are of exceptional beauty. We inspect them only in our passing for a few moments, but what must have been the effect of these pictures upon those who lived constantly with them ? No wonder the friars of St. Mark's were a unique monastic race, with such perpetual aids to faith and to the devout life they had chosen for themselves. In our age these glorious pictures of the Life and Passion of Christ, of the story of the Virgin and of St. Dominic, have been copied and reproduced all the world over, and many thousands have been strengthened and helped in their struggle for moral improvement by these works of the Blessed Angelico painted nearly five hundred years ago. Surely such a task as his has borne fruit abundant, not only in the noble history of St. Mark's but over a far wider audience than that of Florence ? Hearts are uplifted to-day in this our twentieth century by a sight and study of these divine glimpses, which have been bestowed on humanity by their delineator. It is in this aspect that the true power and importance of Angelico lie. He can transport us to another sphere where the Way of Christ is shown to us in its perfection of beauty ; and even though we cannot attain to it, we are led to appreciate and to understand its true significance, so that we derive some benefit and assistance thereby.

Nor must I neglect to mention the lovely easel pictures that are included in some of those cells. The frescoes have faded and have become exquisite ghosts, but these little oil-paintings remain fresh and bright as when Angelico painted them amid prayers and tears of joy. The ' Madonna della Stella ', Our Lady with the star of St. Dominic above her brow, presents to us an ideal portrait of the Maid Mother smiling, Babe on arm. It is faultless in pose, colouring, sentiment, and form. No painter has ever blended with such happy sympathy the dual elements of human maternity and of divine dignity. The Virgins of Raphael and the great painters who succeeded Angelico seem earthly and insipid beside this perfect little gem of purest ray serene. Indeed, on reflection, it seems clear that none other than Fra Angelico could have produced such a masterpiece, which combines artistic genius with true celestial vision.

What peculiar quality is it, then, that from the view of moral teaching raises Fra Angelico's art above the art of his own era, or of any era which succeeded ? How comes it that his pictures make as strong an appeal to mankind to-day as ever they did to his own contemporaries ? Why are they ever fresh and young ? Why are they independent of the casual values of mere historical or artistic interest ? I think the true reason of this continuous appeal from generation to generation of men lies in the fact that the Blessed Angelico not only lifts us to the celestial plane of rapture, but he also insists on keeping us there. Never does he descend to the earthly level, and though his work from one point of view loses thereby in human interest, it gains immeasurably in another and a higher sense. True, we miss in his many pictures that delightful humanism which pervades the works of nearly all the Italian artists of the *Quattrocento*, who tempered, so to speak, the austerity of their scriptural themes with scenes and details of the daily life around them. In Italian art we are shown continually the contemporary life of Renaissance Italy ; we can inform ourselves of the manners, customs, dress, furniture, buildings, and domestic employments of the Italian people in the days of the Medici. And very charming and instructive those extraneous details are, for of a truth from them we can contrive to build up a lively and agreeable presentment of fifteenth-century Florence or Siena. But we find none of these accretions, none of these attractive irrelevancies, in Fra Angelico's work, wherein nothing of the world is admitted and the whole composition is permeated by the central and spiritual thought of a sacred subject. His appeal is made solely to the spirit, not to humane or historical interest and curiosity. Truly his art

> Dissolves the soul in ecstasies,
> And brings all Heaven before our eyes.

Yes, a Heaven absolutely disconnected from all earthly objects and interests, however innocent or picturesque such interests may be deemed by the spectator. All such flattering humanism, no matter how tempting, is sternly repressed in such lofty themes as his. He appeals to the soul, and to the soul alone, and the soul of man in every age can recognize and appreciate the beauty of holiness as it was conceived and painted by a true mystic. For Fra Angelico by his art has lifted the veil from the heavenly mysteries, and shown us the vision splendid that is only vouchsafed after deep meditation and earnest prayer to the rare, holy, self-sacrificing soul.

Perhaps I shall make my point clearer by offering two examples of what I have specially in my mind, but which I find it somewhat difficult to convey in words. In the Brancacci Chapel of the Carmine Church in Florence are to be seen some famous frescoes by Masaccio (who was a contemporary of Fra Angelico's) and by Filippino Lippi (who belongs to the next generation). These paintings, which represent the story of St. Peter's life and teaching, have always been very popular, and most deservedly so. The Brancacci Chapel attracted Perugino, the youthful Raphael, and even the boy Michelangelo, to study these works, so that they possess a peculiar value in the development of Italian art. But their value, their influence, their attraction are in no wise spiritual; on the contrary, it was the excellent grouping, the correct anatomy, the harmonious use of colouring that drew artists hither to

study and future travellers to admire. And apart from
their admitted artistic value, the costumes, scenes, architecture, and particularly the many portraits introduced,
have given an added interest in our eyes to those famous
frescoes. Beautiful as are these works, they never did, and
they never can, make any appeal to the soul. The celestial
atmosphere we find in all Angelico's work is here wholly
wanting. The frescoes of the Carmine attract and hold the
artist, the scholar, the historian, the dilettante ; but they
offer no heavenly interpretation, they stir no thought
of rapturous emotion in us ; despite their scriptural
subjects admirably treated, they can work no moral
miracle.

Again, in the tiny chapel of the ancient Medici Palace in
Florence, now called Palazzo Riccardi, one regards with
immense pleasure of the intellect Benozzo Gozzoli's composition of the ' Visit of the Magi ' to the stable at Bethlehem.
Now, Gozzoli was a pupil of the Blessed Angelico, and he
was a worthy follower of his master, in that he was a superb
painter. He also owned, though to a very limited extent,
the spiritual vision of his master. The group of angels
adoring the Holy Babe, as they kneel humbly in their
bright robes and with their peacock-hued pinions, certainly
recall Angelico's wondrous celestial creations. It is a truly
angelical glimpse of the painter's Paradise. But the bulk
of the wall-space of this little oratory is occupied with a
long procession of jovial horsemen and footmen moving
through Tuscan scenery. It offers a most interesting and
valuable record of Medicean Florence, with the wise old
Cosimo dei Medici and his clever young grandson, Lorenzo,
ambling beside him, and with their Imperial guests and
courtiers following. Of a truth, it is all very fascinating,
and all redolent with the spirit of history. But wherein
lies the appeal to the soul ? Of course there are the adoring
angels I have already mentioned, and there are the Holy

Family and the shepherds at the manger of Bethlehem. But the Medici princes and the Emperor of the East and his patriarch and their gay cavalcade apparently care little for these things ; they form no integral part of the sacred subject of the fresco. The artist's appeal is therefore made more to the intellect than to the soul. The spiritual interest is confined to one corner only of the whole composition, as is the case with nearly all other *Quattrocento* works of art save those of Fra Angelico.

I have already said that the secret, the key-note, of Angelico's work, that which makes an ever-fresh appeal to generation after generation, and remains unaffected by human progress and changing thought, is its intense spirituality. His pictures are sermons in terms of celestial eloquence. No artist, for example, has ever approached Angelico in sheer glory of colouring. His paintings positively dazzle with their divers tints. His figures either stand out against a background of pure gold, or else float in a sapphire sea of atmosphere. One is perpetually being reminded of a gorgeous sunset, which is the nearest approach we can conceive to the glories of Heaven as described by Dante and the mystics. The saints and angels and prophets of Angelico are all clothed in robes of brilliant hues, such as befit their luminous setting. Many of the great painters are praised for the splendour and boldness of their colouring ; perhaps of all Andrea del Sarto is most justly commended on this score. But the colouring of Andrea appears timid and dingy beside that of Fra Angelico. And yet this truly angelical riot of tints is quite natural ; it is perfectly blended. How is this effect attained with such apparent ease ? What is the secret of this harmony of brilliant reds and blues and pinks and yellows and greens ? Is it not to be found in this—that the painter looked up to God through Nature, and only made use of Nature's own tints for his celestial raiment ? His deep scarlet, for example, is just the scarlet of the wild Tuscan tulip which blooms in the orchards where (in the words of Robert Browning) :

It blows out its great red bell,
For the children to pick 'neath the olives and bring to the town to sell.

Again, that marvellous pink is the exact colour of the beautiful little anemones, or windflowers, that appear by thousands on every grassy bank in early spring. This vernal anemone is characteristic of the Italian spring, and Angelico deemed its exquisite hue as well suited for angelic robes. And that wonderful green! Is it not to be seen constantly in the masses of sun-illumined wheat that grow on every little Tuscan farm? This bold use of Nature at her best, her brightest, and her cheerfullest offers the true solution of Angelico's success as a colourist. Other painters with a higher reputation than Angelico's fall beneath him in this matter of colouring, for they lacked the divine understanding of Nature, which belonged to the holy artist who painted not for money or for fame, but simply and solely for the glory of God.

It has sometimes been objected to Angelico's art that it is merely the art of a superb illuminator, because most of his figures are on a small scale, and bear some resemblance to those beautiful illustrations we see in the fine old missals and choral service books of his era. This is not true. Certainly, Fra Angelico's paintings are in many instances on a small scale, but that he was perfectly competent to achieve the grand style is clearly shown by such a work as his great fresco in the cathedral of Orvieto. Here his conception of Christ as the Saviour of the world with the globe in His hands recalls in its majestic pose the great figures of Michelangelo that are so universally admired. I shall quote a passage from Lord Lindsay's *Christian Art* on this wonderful work at Orvieto, which is seldom visited by travellers in Italy :

' The two compartments coloured by Fra Angelico would
of themselves repay a visit to Orvieto.   Above the altar the
Saviour is seated in judgement, supporting the globe of the
universe, a most majestic figure.   The noble host of the
prophets of Israel, attended by angels blowing on trumpets,
rise in a pyramidal form till they culminate in the swarthy
John the Baptist ; the Moses is especially fine, a prophet
indeed. . . .   For majesty these are certainly Fra Angelico's
masterpiece ; they show how capable he was of expressing
the loftiest thoughts as well as the tenderest and softest ;
hell and sin were alone too difficult for him to delineate.'

This magnificent composition was painted in the
summer of 1447, and though one of the finest is perhaps,
popularly speaking, the least-known of all Angelico's many
works.

It has also been objected that Fra Angelico knew no
anatomy—not that this particular deficiency would in my
opinion detract from the characteristic value of his art.
But this charge also is not true.   Certainly his figures are
nearly all fully clothed in raiment of brilliant hues, but the
heads, the limbs, and the attitudes all appear easy and
natural.   There is no crudeness or angularity in his figures.
They are all what the humble artist in his prayers essayed
to make them, the true inhabitants of Heaven, of a refined
beauty clad in celestial garb.   Nude figures, as one may
suppose, occur rarely ; and when they do appear they do
not own the muscular or fleshy detail that one finds in the
later schools of painting.   But they are always found
correct and adequate to their setting.

That the unique genius of Fra Angelico was not deemed
contrary to the progressive and inquisitive spirit of the age
is plainly proved by the fact that amongst his special
patrons—and also his intimate friends—were two of the
great leaders of Humanism in Italy, namely, Cosimo dei
Medici—Cosimo ' il Vecchio ', or the Elder ; and the Pope

Nicholas V. I have already spoken of the Medici's whole-hearted recognition of Angelico, and how he invited him to decorate the walls of his newly-founded priory of St. Mark's in Florence. Of Cardinal Tommaso of Sarzana, who was elected pope with the title of Nicholas V in 1447, I must add a few words. Nicholas is generally reckoned as the first and one of the most fervent papal patrons of that band of scholars who were then giving to mankind translations and commentaries of the revived works of Greek and Latin authors. Nicholas was essentially a man of the world, and aimed at making Rome the centre of learning and art for Western Europe. Yet despite his enthusiastic devotion to the New Learning and all that it implied, Nicholas was likewise drawn with admiration to the simple monk and his art, and he treated him with friendly familiarity. A pretty story, recorded by Vasari, tells how on one occasion Angelico was dining at the Pope's table on a day of abstinence. The painter, apparently oblivious of the example of the Vicar of Christ, refused to touch meat, despite the fact that the Pope was openly indulging therein. But Nicholas, though domineering and irritable, was by no means offended by this tacit and wholly unintentional rebuke on Angelico's part, and he laughed off the awkward incident with a graceful jest.

These years spent in Rome were the last in Fra Angelico's life, and for some reasons they cannot have been very happy. There was a sense of disaster and of humiliation in the air owing to the recent capture of Constantinople by the Turks in 1453; the selfish disunion and indifference of Western Christendom were very apparent; the Roman court, with its quarrelsome self-seeking scholars and prelates, could hardly have proved a congenial atmosphere for so rare and spiritual a personality as Angelico. He must often have thought with longing of his quiet convent at San Domenico and the fair valley of the Arno. Yet he continued to labour

on the special task set him by Pope Nicholas.   This was the
Pope's private oratory within the Vatican, known as the
Cappella di Papa Niccolò.   The walls of this small but lofty
chamber Angelico covered with a series of frescoes to depict
scenes in the lives of St. Stephen and St. Lawrence, the first
deacons of the Christian Church.

'In the execution of this series Angelico, though now
nearly sixty, not only displayed a vigour equal but superior
to that of his youth. . . . The architecture especially is not
merely in harmony with the figures, but in good proportion
and of a fine style.'

By a fortunate chance these paintings remain almost
intact to-day, and very lovely they are, although the
visitor to the Vatican usually neglects to visit this obscure
shrine of early art, which is only shown to the public on
special application being made.   For some unexplained
reason this oratory in course of time fell not only into disuse,
but even into oblivion.   This neglect was fortunate ; had
the chapel continued in use, probably some successor of
Nicholas V would have commissioned a later artist to
obliterate the work of Fra Angelico and replace it by something more in accord with prevailing artistic fashion.   Its
doorway had been blocked up with masonry, and it was
only in the middle of the eighteenth century (so the great
Italian critic Bottari relates) that search was made for these
lost frescoes of Fra Angelico.   Bottari himself describes his
forcible entrance into the forgotten chapel by means of a
window, and how he was rewarded for his labour of love by
finding these long-lost paintings fresh and uninjured.
Another and an earlier work undertaken for Pope Eugenius
IV, his first papal patron, fared disastrously.   Angelico had
decorated the Chapel of the Sacrament for this Pope with
scenes from the life of Our Lord, but in the following century
Pope Paul III demolished this chapel to make a stairway,
and Angelico's beautiful paintings were all destroyed with

the exception of a few details, which the historian, Paolo Giovio, had the good taste to rescue and remove to his own residence.

It was in Rome, at his lodgings in the Dominican convent of Santa Maria sopra Minerva, near the Pantheon, in the early spring of 1455 that the long, busy, blameless, unselfish life of the famous painter drew to its close. There was real grief shown by the mourners at his burial in the choir of the Dominican church, where his effigy can be seen to-day. It was erected by order of Pope Nicholas, himself destined to die that very year, who is also credited with the Latin verses engraved above the effigy :

> Non mihi sit laudi, quod eram velut alter Apelles ;
> Sed quod lucra tuis omnia, Christe, dabam :
> Altera nam terris opera extant ; altera caelo ;
> Urbs me Johannem flos tulit Etruriae.

which I shall roughly render into English :

> Apelles' fame was mine ; 'twas nought to me
> Save that, O Christ, I gave all gain to thee :
> The Tuscan flower-city gave me birth ;
> My guerdon Heaven ; my art I leave to Earth.

At the feet of the figure appear the words, ' Here lies the venerable painter, Brother John from Fiesole, of the Order of Preachers, 1455 '. By a curious chance Fra Angelico's monument is situated close to the costly but unlovely tomb of Giovanni dei Medici, Pope Leo X, his brother-Florentine. What a strange contrast do the two monuments present ! The jovial child of fortune who openly declared he meant to enjoy the papacy, and the humble holy friar, whose emaciated form worn with prayer and fasting, meets our eyes with arms meekly folded on his breast. Yet that Italy could produce two such diverse types of churchman in the years of the Renaissance is not the least of the marvels

of that incongruous age.   Thus Leo X stands for the power,
the splendour, the paganism, the patronage, the learning,
and the intense worldliness of that period; the gifted
Dominican artist for the extreme piety and simplicity that
found their vent in the painting of sacred masterpieces,
such as succeeding ages have failed to rival in their naïve
but perfect loveliness.

Fra Angelico's works, which were originally confined, as
I have explained, chiefly to Florence and Rome, have been
widely scattered.   With the dissolution of the Tuscan
monastic houses in the last century many specimens came
into the open market.   The result is that most of the larger
public galleries in Europe possess examples of his art.
There are two or three Angelicos in our National Gallery.
In a picture gallery his work is not seen to advantage, when
divorced from its original setting, some dim Tuscan chapel
or Roman oratory, and appears overwhelmed by surrounding pictures on a larger scale.   Florence is, of course, still
the one place where Angelico can be properly studied and
enjoyed.   Within the convent (now museum) of St. Mark's,
which I have already described briefly, there are preserved
many of his best works that have in recent years been moved
hither from the Academy of the Fine Arts, the third in
importance of the Florentine galleries, which until lately
housed them.   Prominent amongst these new treasures at
St. Mark's, stands out the superb composition usually
called the 'Last Judgment'.   This is probably the finest
and most characteristic creation of the master, exhibiting
to us, as it does, both his holiness of life and his marvellous
artistic vision.   Above sits the Saviour in judgement in an
azure sky, with a semicircle of saints and prophets at his
feet.   Below is depicted the Last Judgment.   In the centre
we see the opened graves and the resurrection of the dead,
the virtuous going into life eternal and the evil into hell.
Hell is represented as grotesque rather than awful, and it is

probably the work of a pupil of the master. Its presence mars the amazing beauty of the whole picture, and should be mentally excluded by the spectator. But the groups and figures on the right hand that move or float on golden rays into the Holy City, or the Souls of the blessèd that dance on the flowery sward, or those that embrace in ecstasy, go to complete the loftiest imagination of the apocalyptic Heaven. It is a revelation to us of the saintly artist's conception of the beauty of holiness. It sets before us the Heaven of the New Testament, as it was regarded by the most spiritual genius that flourished during the Age of Faith. It forms a noble complement in painting to the picture in verse that was composed by Dante more than a century before. We cannot, alas ! rise to a full admiration and understanding either of Dante's *Paradiso* or of Fra Angelico's composition, but after reading Dante and studying the ' Last Judgment ' our minds are filled with wistful musings and indefinable longings. Both poem and picture make a profound appeal to the highest ambition of the human soul. We are momentarily exalted, and even to ' sit some moments on a throne of love ' must prove beneficial to us, though we cannot long endure the rarefied atmosphere of those mystic heights whereon Dante and Angelico learned to breathe naturally. As I said before, the secret of Angelico's art is that it leads us to these heights above, and gives us for a brief interval that Pisgah-vision of the Promised Land which our feeble and material natures will not allow us to contemplate for any length of time. Yet, even for these brief glimpses of Paradise, we ought to feel eternal gratitude to Fra Giovanni, the simple friar from Fiesole, who owned in his day the fame of Apelles, yet only sought to lay all earthly reputation, honours, and wealth at the bleeding feet of Christ crucified.

INDEX